KU-048-359

Contemporary women's fiction:
Narrative practice
and feminist theory

Contemporary women's fiction:
Narrative practice and feminist theory

Paulina Palmer

University Press of Mississippi

Jackson and London

Learning Resources
Cent

131 45 436

Copyright © 1989 by Paulina Palmer

First published in 1989 in the United States of
America by University Press of Mississippi
by special arrangement of Harvester Wheatsheaf.
All rights reserved. No part of this publication may
be reproduced, stored in a retrieval system, or
transmitted, in any form, or by any means, electronic,
mechanical, photocopying, recording or otherwise,
without the prior permission, in
writing, from the publisher.

1 2 3 4 5 93 92 91 90 89

Library of Congress and British Library
Cataloguing–in–Publication data are available

ISBN 0-87805-396-4

For C L L

Contents

Notes on the Author

Paulina Palmer works in the English Department at the University of Warwick where she teaches an undergraduate course in 'Feminist Approaches to Literature' (previously 'Literature and Sexual Politics') and an option for the Womens Studies MA. Her publications include a short story in Jan Bradshaw and Mary Hemming, (eds), *Girls Next Door* (Women's Press, 1985), an essay on the fiction of Angela Carter in Sue Roe, (ed.), *Women Reading Women's Writing* (Harvester, 1987), and an essay on lesbian fiction in Linda Anderson, (ed.), *Contemporary Women's Fiction* (Edward Arnold, forthcoming). She is at present working on *An Annotated Bibliography of Women's Fiction and Feminist Theory* for Harvester Wheatsheaf and a book on *Contemporary Lesbian Writing* for the Open University Press.

Preface and
Acknowledgements

This book, a study of the interrelation between contemporary women's fiction and feminist theory, is intended for a variety of different readers. Teachers and students in colleges and universities, whether engaged in exploring works of fiction in departments of English Literature or participating in Women's Studies courses of an inter-disciplinary kind, may find it useful in their work. So too may teachers of 'general studies' courses in sixth-form colleges and the upper sections of secondary schools. The general reader who enjoys novels and stories by contemporary women writers and seeks to learn more about their ideological context and the links they reveal with feminist theory and practice will also, I hope, find it interesting.

The circumstances that led me to write the book, and the different aspects of my life, academic and non-academic, which it brings together, are described in Chapter 1. My interest in analysing works of fiction in the light of feminist theory has also been stimulated by the undergraduate option in 'Literature and Sexual Politics' which I teach in the English Department at the University of Warwick. I am grateful to students taking the option in recent years for their lively discussion of texts. In choosing works of fiction for analysis, I have been forced to be rigorously selective, making reference to only a small proportion of the texts published in the past twenty years. Readers will no doubt be disappointed on occasion that I fail to refer to their favourite novels or that, in commenting on them, I do not mention those particular facets which they consider to be of primary importance. In discussing the works of fiction I have selected for review, I have made every effort, of course, to give a fair evaluation of their salient features, thematic and stylistic.

Here it is necessary to explain the procedural methods which I have adopted as regards the dating and editions of the novels to which I refer. Many of the novels were originally published in hardback and subsequently in paperback. On first mentioning a particular novel in the text, I cite the initial date of publication (frequently in hardback). In quoting from the novel, however, I use the paperback edition since this is usually more easily available to the reader, and give details of it in a note. Details of both hardback and paperback editions are to be found in the Bibliography.

In writing the book I have been fortunate to receive assistance and encouragement from many friends and colleagues. For helpful suggestions about topics and authors, assistance with the chore of proofreading, and critiques of the final draft, I wish to thank Linda Berry, Barbara Kirkby and two of my colleagues in the English Department at the University of Warwick, Pamela Dunbar and John Goode. And I am very grateful to Sue Roe of Harvester Wheatsheaf for recognizing the value of the project, lending me books from her own library, and being, in general, a source of encouragement and support. I also need to express a word of thanks to John Fletcher, another colleague in the English Department at Warwick. I initially taught the option in 'Literature and Sexual Politics' as a jointly presented course with him. As well as possessing a profound knowledge of psychoanalytic theory and theoretical approaches to literature, he is exceptionally generous in sharing his insights and ideas. Conversations I held with him and references to critical and theoretical works he has given me have proved to be of great value.

Chapter One

Introduction

The aim of this study is to explore the interaction between feminist theory and narrative practice in a selection of works of fiction by contemporary Anglo-American women writers. My investigation of the links which exist between the two different areas – the theory produced by the Women's Movement on the one hand, and the themes and narrative strategies of contemporary women's fiction, on the other – is motivated, to a degree, by my personal interests and situation. The study represents among other things an attempt to bring together, or at least relate in creative tension, two strands of my life which over the past fifteen years have frequently appeared disturbingly incompatible. As well as contributing to the kind of 'academic feminism' which is centred on the teaching of courses in Women's Studies and Feminist Criticism in a university department of English Studies, I also belong to a small radical feminist group. The perspectives of the two are, I have discovered, by no means easy to reconcile. Academic feminism exists in the male-dominated, hierarchical and predominantly middle-class context of the institution of higher education; it tends to privilege psychoanalytic and socialist feminist approaches. The radical feminist group to which I belong is totally different in character. Formed in the 1970s by myself and a number of friends, it focuses on running a phone-line providing information and support for women in the area who are interested in radical feminist experience and ideas. Members of the group meet on an informal basis and adopt a policy of separatism. We favour structures which are non-hierarchical and make decisions by collective discussion. Answering the phone and meeting callers bring us into contact with women from different classes and walks of life. My involvement in these two very different kinds of feminism has given rise to numerous problems and conflicts. On a positive note, however, it has also given me the opportunity to make connections and comparisons of a very valuable kind. In trying to clarify my own ideological position, I have studied many of the theoretical works produced by the Women's Movement, and have been impressed by their varied perspectives. In reading works of fiction while preparing for the academic courses I teach, I have become increasingly aware of the generative influence which feminist theory exerts on novels and short stories written by women. Writers utilize ideas and motifs taken from theory in a highly inventive manner. The interrelation between theory and narrative strategy is, in fact, remarkably strong and diverse.

Although critics frequently interpret works of fiction by women in the light of feminist critical theory and ideas about 'women and writing', it is less usual for them to read these works in terms of feminist theory in general, making reference to ideas about sexual politics, patriarchal relations, motherhood and the other topics to which I allude in this study. These ideas and theories do, however, as I hope to show, form an appropriate context for their analysis. Many contemporary novels and short stories can only be fully understood and appreciated in the light of the theoretical ideas which the writers appropriate and re-work. As well as illuminating the links with theory which these novels and short stories reveal, I also hope to promote an interest in the critical discussion of contemporary texts. Critical studies of fiction written by women over the past twenty years since the rebirth of feminism are, I am surprised to discover, relatively few. During this period feminist criticism has been active in a number of different areas.[1] Critics have engaged in the rediscovery and re-evaluation of novels written in earlier eras – the eighteenth and nineteenth centuries in particular. Making use of psychoanalytical and sociological approaches, they have carried out appraisals of popular genres of fiction such as the Mills and Boon and Harlequin romance and Ace Books Gothic.[2] Meanwhile French feminist theorists such as Julia Kristeva have promoted the analysis of 'avant-garde' literary texts. Many of these are by male writers, including Dostoevsky and Nerval. What feminist critics – somewhat ironically – have failed to do is investigate those very texts which relate most closely to the rebirth of feminism in the late 1960s – novels and short stories which re-work and popularize the concepts and theories which the Women's Movement has produced. Other critics besides myself have commented on this omission. Janet Batsleer and her co-authors point out that feminist criticism shows a marked 'lack of engagement with contemporary writing'. They express disappointment at the failure of critics to expand the interest in the area apparent in the early 1970s, 'so that feminists could really claim contemporary writing as a proper object of study and work, and so that feminist criticism could speak to contemporary readers about contemporary writing as well as about past traditions'.[3] The lack of interest shown by critics in contemporary women's writing has had, of course, unfortunate repercussions on higher education. In depart-

ments of Literary Studies in colleges and universities and even in
Women's Studies courses, fiction by contemporary women writers
often plays a minimal or non-existent role in the curriculum. It is
marginalized or erased in favour of works of fiction from earlier
periods.

The failure of critics to engage seriously with fiction by contemporary women writers is, in my view, something of a scandal. It results
in the neglect of a significant area of female creativity. It also encourages a disregard for a set of topics and areas of experience of vital
importance to women. These topics – ones which enjoy primacy in
women's fiction at the moment – are, on the whole, radical feminist
in emphasis. Elizabeth Wilson, commenting on the way radical and
cultural feminist attitudes have supplanted socialist feminist ones in
popularity in the 1980s, remarks: 'Radical feminist groups have determined contemporary feminist debates on male violence, lesbianism, pornography, and, indeed, on such issues as peace and race, to
which traditionally socialist women gave more emphasis.'[4] The
themes which Wilson cites, with the addition of a few others of a
similarly radical and cultural feminist kind such as women's community and motherhood, dominate women's fiction today. Topics
traditionally associated with socialist feminism, such as women's
position in the labour market and communal childcare shared between men and women are – it is interesting to observe – notable for
their absence. This is not to say, of course, that socialist feminist ideas
are totally absent from fiction. The role they play, however, is a
subordinate one.

The treatment by writers of the radical and cultural feminist
themes mentioned above differs considerably from novel to novel. It
does reveal, however, certain typical features. Writers deliberately
choose to prioritize those categories of women and aspects of female
experience which the representational practices of the dominant
phallocratic culture tend to marginalize or even erase. Black women,
women who identify as lesbian, 'spinsters', older and elderly women
are examples. Important themes include woman-identified relationships, lesbian motherhood and relations between mothers and
daughters. Two or more of these themes frequently come together
within the frame of a single text. For example, the novel Peeling (1986)
by the Australian Grace Bartram, in recounting the experiences of
fifty-four-year-old Ally, explores relations between mothers and
daughters, and also touches on the topic of lesbian motherhood.
Interesting affinities of theme occur between writers of different nationalities and cultural backgrounds. A Reckoning (1978) by the
American May Sarton, and Cactus (1980) by the British Anna Wilson,
differ considerably in style and structure. However, both novels

focus attention on the figure of 'the older woman' and explore, from very different viewpoints, lesbian relationships and ideas of woman-identification. Topics such as these are, in fact, international in scope in the English-speaking West. In the following chapters we shall examine some of the disparate ways in which writers of different nationalities treat them.

Several reasons help to explain the lack of critical attention which contemporary women's fiction has received up to now. The radical nature of the themes which many novels and short stories introduce along with their frequently separatist emphasis, no doubt acts as deterrent. Despite the efforts made by the reviewers in the popular magazine *Spare Rib* to counter this trend, literary criticism continues to be dominated by academia. The majority of academics are male – and male critics, whether expressing conservative or radical sympathies, are unlikely to show much interest in the fictional representation of these themes. Women academics (very much in the minority) are also unlikely to concern themselves with them. Academic feminism, as mentioned above, tends to privilege psychoanalytic and socialist feminist perspectives, while ignoring or disparaging theories and issues of a radical feminist kind.[5] One of the aims of this study is, in fact, to draw attention to the importance of radical feminist theory and to illustrate the influence which it has on women's fiction. Radical feminist concepts of patriarchy, lesbian continuum and analyses of male violence, seldom receive discussion in seminars held in the English Studies departments of colleges and universities. They play, however, an integral part in many novels written by women. In certain cases, in fact, it is impossible for the reader fully to comprehend and appreciate the novels without possessing a knowledge of them. As we shall see, works of fiction by Margaret Atwood, Marge Piercy, Fay Weldon and Anna Wilson either make creative use of these concepts or respond to a reading in the light of them.

Another factor which no doubt deters critics from interesting themselves in contemporary women's fiction is that, even in the field of feminist criticism, the topic is a contentious issue. This is especially true of fiction which appropriates ideas from feminist theory. The debate it has sparked off is very relevant to this study and is thus worth exploring here.

The controversy centring on contemporary women's fiction forms part of the current dispute about feminist publications in general. Literary publications (the term includes theoretical studies, journals and works of fiction) play an important function in the Women's Movement. There are signs that they compensate for the defects which it reveals in other areas. The sociologist Jo Freeman, commenting on the increasing fragmentation of the Movement and its failure to effect any major degree of improvement in women's material circumstances, describes it as constituting 'a diffuse social system rather than a political movement'. The one area in which she claims the Movement has been successful is *ideology* and *culture*. Describing it as 'innovative ideologically', she remarks on the variety of 'ideas, disputes and debates' and the amazing number of publications which the Movement has produced.[6] Rosalind Delmar comes to a similar conclusion. She points out that the fragmentation of the Movement in the 1980s into a number of divergent feminisms has been accompanied by an increasingly 'buoyant market for feminist publishing'.[7] The possibility that a connection exists between these two phenomena is mooted by the writer Fay Weldon. Giving playful advice to her imaginary cousin Cynthia on 'How to be feminist', Weldon instructs her to 'read feminist publications which currently hold the Movement together' and 'frequent the few feminist book-shops and read the books issued by the brilliant new publishing houses'.[8] Weldon's address to Cynthia is deliberately humorous, serving partly as an amusing puff for her own novels. Central to it, however, is the serious suggestion (a very feasible one, in my opinion) that in the present fragmented state of the Movement, literary publications acquire a new practical import. By disseminating ideas and informing readers of shifts in thought, they provide a unifying intellectual thread, thus giving a much-needed, if perhaps spurious, appearance of cohesion. Many of these publications, as critics observe sometimes disapprovingly,[9] are works of fiction.

Feminists generally agree that the market in women's fiction is experiencing a current boom.[10] They disagree strongly, however, about the political value and significance of this boom. Should the publishing of novels by women writers be regarded positively as helping to promulgate and popularize feminist attitudes? Or does it represent, on the contrary, an example of the publishing industry cashing in on feminism and, in certain cases, conning readers into accepting as 'feminist' novels which, in actual fact, are not? An essay by Rosalind Coward which interrogates the term' feminist novel' illustrates the latter view. Focusing attention on novels such as Marilyn French's *The Women's Room* which have been popularly hailed as 'feminist', Coward suggests that the message they promote is not really feminist at all. It perpetuates, on the contrary, traditional stereotypes of femininity, confirming women as 'bearers of sentiment, experience and romance (albeit disillusioned)'.[11]

Coward's comments, of course, represent only one point of view. Many feminists disagree with them. Taking the opposite line, they draw attention to the instructive and supportive function which women's fiction performs in the field of sexual politics. Alison

Hennegan, introducing the Women's Press collection of lesbian feminist short stories *Girls Next Door* (1985), writes:

> People learn from fiction. They look to it for information, reassurance, affirmation about the ways in which other (fictional) people feel, believe, act and - most important of all, it sometimes seems – love ...[12]

Similar claims are voiced by writers of fiction themselves. The experience of browsing in feminist bookshops and buying paperbacks published by the women's presses is a key motif in the novels of the 1970s and 1980s. Writers describe it as playing a formative part in the female protagonist's initiation into feminism. An episode in Ann Oosthuizen's *Loneliness and other Lovers* (1981), depicting the visit paid by the main character Jean to a real London bookshop, illustrates the kind of importance it can assume:

> At Compendium she bought books by Simone de Beauvoir and Marge Piercy. She looked at their shiny new covers, smelled the new pages and smiled to herself. Inside them was a world in which she would recognise bits of herself. There would be women in them who thought as she thought, or felt the same pain. And they would show her the way, make room for her.[13]

The passage is clearly a fascinating one – not least on account of the contradictions which it articulates. While confirming the reader's assumptions of the political value of women's fiction, it simultaneously alerts us to the problematic aspects of the feminist publishing industry. The self-reflexive element in the passage establishes a strong sense of community between reader and writer – between the fictitious Jean and the writers Piercy and de Beauvoir whose books she buys. This sense of community radiates outwards to encompass us, the actual readers of Oosthuizen's novel. At the same time, however, the sense of community is undercut and called into question. Oosthuizen's choice of the 'star names' Piercy and de Beauvoir has this effect. The two writers are internationally renowned. The success they have achieved separates them from the situation of most women readers – both the fictitious reader Jean and us, the readers of Oosthuizen's novel. The description of Jean admiring the shiny new covers and smelling the pages of the books is similarly ambiguous. While vividly evoking the sensuous pleasures of buying paperbacks, it also alerts us to the marketing strategies adopted by the publishing industry. It reminds us that, in order to be read, texts require publishers, packaging and promotion. These items remove the text from the control of the writer. They turn it into a commercial object to be 'consumed' by the public, like any other commodity.

The passage from Oosthuizen's novel also raises other issues relevant to the debate about contemporary women's fiction. Jean looks forward, Oosthuizen indicates, to enjoying a sense of identification with the 'world' of women's community represented by the characters in the books she buys. This pleasure is one chiefly associated with the realist text. As Ann Barr Snitow remarks, it helps to explain the sudden growth of a readership for feminist publications: 'Female community, a major social development of the decade [the 1970s] provides women writers with that audience, eager to recognize itself.'[14] Feminist publishing houses such as the Women's Press and Onlywomen Press have made, of course, a deliberate effort to promote this readership. The compilation of volumes of short stories, the setting up of book clubs and the organization of events around the Feminist Book Fortnight, are successful strategies which they employ. Feminists are, however, sharply divided over the value of concepts of 'community' and 'identification', as well as over the realist text itself. Again, a rift between 'academic' and 'popular' kinds of feminism is apparent. Academic critics, influenced by deconstructive and psychoanalytic theory, challenge the humanist notion of a unified subjectivity. They warn us against regarding the text as a transparent medium reflecting authentic experience. They urge us to reject realist fiction in favour of 'interrogative' and anti-realist narrative modes.[15] Other critics, however, question the current emphasis on the value of the disruption of the subject, one which in academic circles unfortunately threatens to become a new orthodoxy. Alison Light, bravely swimming against the stream, defends – though with an element of caution – the reader's capacity to identify with the unitary self in the text; she argues cogently:

> It is this sense of 'self', a coherent and powerful identity, which we must recognize both as an effect of language and as the fiction which keeps us sane and active. The problem then in teaching is how not to undermine the strategic importance of that pleasure in texts in creating real political solidarity – 'every-woman's history' – whilst remaining critical of its forms and of any final fixing of that 'identity' and 'experience'.[16]

The points which Light makes are important ones, and deserve more attention from critics. There is, in my view, a place in feminist culture for a variety of different modes of writing, both realist and anti-realist. Rather than mechanically dismissing the first and promoting the second, we need to discover, by analysing a selection of works of fiction, the attributes and capabilities each possesses. This study aims to make a contribution to this process.

In the following chapters I make reference to both kinds of text – realist and anti-realist. The reader will thus have ample opportunity to compare their relative merits and limitations. Many of the works

I discuss belong to the currently unfashionable category of so-called 'realism'. I say 'so-called' because, if we accept standard definitions of realism, the term appears totally inappropriate. It bears little if any relation to Marge Piercy's *The High Cost of Living* (1978), Nancy Toder's *Choices* (1980) and Anna Wilson's *Cactus* (1980), novels generally taken as examples of realism. All three works present a treatment of events and characters which is highly selective and condensed, frequently operating on a symbolic level. On reading them, one quickly perceives that the writers' chief interest lies not in the detailed delineation of individual character and personal relationships. The characters emerge in certain cases as mere briefly sketched profiles or stereotypes. It lies, on the contrary, in the field of *ideas* – in the author's creative representation of concepts of sexual politics, women's community and patriarchal power. These concepts are, of course, ones appropriated from feminist theory. Readers who engage with these texts thus do not merely enjoy identifying with the central characters – though the pleasures of identification certainly are available. They find themselves confronting and deciphering, sometimes rigorously, a set of feminist ideas and debates.[17] A more suitable term for fiction of this kind is, in fact, *fiction of ideas*. Novels and stories contributing to it often reveal limitations in describing internal psychological areas of experience such as sexual desire and conflicts of personal identity. They constitute, however – as we shall see in Chapters 3, 4 and 6 – a very effective vehicle indeed for the treatment of topics which are overtly social or political. These include incidents of feminist struggle and the challenges women level, either individually or in a group, at male-dominated structures and institutions. Fiction of this kind possesses the important asset of presenting women as active, self-determined agents. It shows them playing a positive role both in feminist work-projects and in society as a whole. And far from failing to respond fruitfully to critical analysis, as academics generally assume will be the case, it reveals a wealth of interest in the field of narrative strategy and design, as the writers seek to embody the ideas they treat in features of style and structure.

The word 'debate', which I introduced in the paragraph above, takes on a quite specific meaning in relation to women's fiction. The propensity for dispute which, as Freeman observes, is a feature of the contemporary Women's Movement, is also reflected in novels and short stories. With the fragmentation of the Movement in the 1980s into a variety of divergent feminisms, the practical and theoretical issues confronting women have become increasingly complex and controversial. In order to cope with this, a new genre of fiction has emerged which aims to problematize and debate feminist ideas and issues. Examples of the genre are Valerie Miner's *Blood Sisters* (1981) which discusses the contrary choices facing Irish feminists, and Nicky Edwards's *Mud* (1986). The latter debates the strengths and weaknesses of the Women's Peace Movement. This study also provides an opportunity to take a fresh look at 'modernist' or anti-realist fiction. This narrative mode, it is interesting to note, tends to be employed by women writers in relation to a particular set of topics. These include the construction of femininity and areas centring on the motifs, appropriated from feminist psychoanalytic discourse, of the pre-oedipal and semiotic. These motifs are to the fore in novels exploring topics of motherhood and relations between mothers and daughters. Texts written in this mode, as we should expect, are generally organized around the concept of the fractured self. They reveal – as we shall see in Chapters 2, 5 and 6 – both merits and limitations. While admirably suited to exploring complexities and conflicts of female subjectivity, the mode emerges as an unsuitable vehicle for treating themes which are overtly social and political. These include women's community and acts of feminist resistance to patriarchal power. It reproduces, in fact, many of the problems which continue to beset psychoanalytic approaches to feminism. The unresolved conflict which exists between 'psychoanalysis' and 'politics' is succinctly summed up by Elizabeth Wilson. Pointing to the disservice which certain of the contributors to the now defunct journal *m/f* have done to the social and economic aspects of feminist struggle by promoting a narrowly psychoanalytic concept of the sign woman, she writes:

> Nor, they argue, is there such a thing as a 'unitary' woman – we are all bundles of contradictory atoms and impulses. The idea of the unitary self is a fiction. Leading on from this there is no such thing as 'women's oppression' in any unitary sense. This may be logically correct in the perfect world of Mind: it is politically dubious, to put it mildly, when the Tory government is starting to argue that women should be in the home as a cloak for their spending cuts and unemployment.[18]

It is, of course, open to writers of fiction to use ideas of the fractured self and the pre-oedipal for purposes which are either conservative or radical. In a number of works – for example, Emma Tennant's *Alice Fell* (1980) and Emily Prager's 'Agoraphobia' (1983) – emphasis is placed on the entrenched and almost immutable nature of the structures of the family unit and the female psyche. Changes which do take place do little to destabilize the oppressive aspects of the status quo. Other works, in contrast, such as Michèle Roberts's *The Visitation* (1983) and Aileen La Tourette's *Nuns and Mothers* (1984), celebrate the occurrence of transformations in these structures. Both kinds of text, however, tend to present the female protagonist as a passive subject, as opposed to an active, self-determined agent. The reader often gains the depressing sense that, to quote Lynne Segal's critique of psychoanalytic approaches to feminism, 'women are merely "subjects" and subjects are denied autonomy, trapped within the operations of linguistic structures and laws'.[19]

To suggest that a total divorce exists between so-called realist and anti-realist modes of writing would be, of course, false. Many writers successfully combine in a single text elements associated with both modes. However, chiefly on account of the conflicting theoretical discourses they inherit, writers experience considerable difficulty in uniting a psychoanalytic focus on female subjectivity with the radical feminist themes of the political implications of patriarchal power and collective feminist struggle. One of the few writers to succeed in bringing the two together is the Canadian writer Margaret Atwood. Atwood's fiction emerges, indeed, as decidedly more experimental, multifaceted and accomplished than that of any other writer discussed in this study.

My decision to focus solely on an analysis of texts by women writers reflects my desire to draw attention to a number of novels and short stories which critics fail to take seriously and often ignore. As Nancy A. Miller concludes in her discussion of the issue, lists and courses which are based on the signature woman, despite the contradictions they reveal, serve an indispensable political function:

> Even though such lists and such courses may betray a naive faith in origins, humanism, and centrality, because they also make visible the marginality, eccentricity and vulnerability of women [in existing phallocratic culture], they concretely challenge the confidence of humanistic discourse as *universality*.[20]

Moreover, the interplay between feminist theory and narrative practice which is the topic of this study is, in fact, a distinctive feature of works of fiction written by women. It is these which understandably reveal especially strong ties with feminist theoretical discourse.

This study of the interaction between contemporary women's fiction and feminist theory is very much a pioneering work. A difficulty which I encountered in writing it was how to decide which topics to focus attention on and which to omit. Concepts such as femininity, patriarchy and sisterhood, which I take as the basis for the various chapters, have numerous facets and interpretations – and it is impossible in the space available to discuss them all. In selecting topics, I decided to give priority to those which are of particular contemporary interest and which have received little critical attention. For example, in considering femininity (Chapter 1) I include a section on the topics of 'anorexia' and 'body image' since critics have, on the whole, ignored the role they play in contemporary fiction.

However, I omit reference to the topics of 'madness' and 'hysteria' since the fictional treatment of these has received consideration in several critical studies.

It remains for me to remind the reader that the province of this study is to explore a selection of works of fiction by women in the context of feminist theory and to offer readings of them in the light of the ideas produced by the Women's Movement. I do not aim to track down particular theoretical sources to which writers are indebted nor to trace the influence of particular theoretical works on novels and stories.

Notes

1. For a discussion of contemporary feminist criticism see Janet Batsleer et al., *Rewriting English: cultural politics of gender and class* (Methuen, 1985), pp. 106-39; Sydney Janet Caplan, 'Varieties of Feminist Criticism', *Making a Difference: feminist literary criticism*, ed. Gayle Greene and Coppélia Kahn (Methuen, 1985), pp. 37-58; and Toril Moi, *Sexual/Texual Politics: feminist literary theory* (Methuen, 1985).
2. See Tania Modleski, *Loving with a Vengeance: mass-produced fantasies for women* (Methuen, 1984); Jean Radford (ed.), *The Progress of Romance: the politics of popular fiction* (Routledge & Kegan Paul, 1986); Janice A. Radway, *Reading the Romance: women, patriarchy and popular literature* (University of North Carolina Press, 1984); and Ann Barr Snitow, 'Mass Market Romance', *Desire: the politics of sexuality*, ed. Ann Snitow et al. (Virago, 1984), pp. 258-75.
3. Batsleer et al., op. cit., p. 113.
4. *Hidden Agendas: theory, politics and experience in the women's movement* (Tavistock, 1986), p. 117.
5. An example is Toril Moi, *Sexual/Textual Politics*, ed. cit.
6. *The Politics of Women's Liberation* (Longman, 1975), pp. 104, 145.
7. 'Broken Agenda', *New Statesman*, 112, no. 2887 (25 July 1986), p. 21.
8. *New Society*, 68, no. 1123 (31 May 1984), p. 354.
9. See Rosalind Coward, 'Are women's novels feminist novels?', *Feminist Review*, 5 (1980), pp. 53-64.
10. See Coward and Delmar, op. cit. See also features in *The Guardian*, 9 August 1983, p. 8; 31 March 1985, p. 43; 13 April 1988, p. 20.
11. Coward, op. cit., p. 60.
12. Jan Bradshaw and Mary Hemming (eds), *Girls Next Door* (Women's Press, 1980), p. 3.
13. *Loneliness and other Lovers* (Sheba, 1981), p. 158.
14. 'The front line: notes on sex in novels by women, 1969 – 1979', *Women: sex and sexuality*, ed. Catherine R. Stimpson and Ethel Spector Person (University of Chicago Press, 1980), p. 161.
15. See Catherine Belsey, *Critical Practice* (Methuen, 1980); and Moira Monteith (ed.), *Women's Writing: a challenge to theory* (Harvester Press, 1986), pp. 11-14. An important exponent of the supposedly 'revolutionary' potential of the anti-realist mode of writing is Julia Kristeva. Toril Moi gives an excellent critique of Kristeva's thesis, demonstrating its flaws, in *Sexual/Textual Politics*, pp. 163-73.

16. Light, Brighton LTP Group, 'Problems of the progressive text: *The Color Purple* by Alice Walker', *Literature Teaching Politics 6: Conference Papers, 1985*, p. 131.
17. Mary F. Robertson and Elaine Tuttle Hansen argue a similar case in *Contemporary American Women Writers: Narrative Strategies*, ed. Catherine Rainwater and William J. Scheick (University Press of Kentucky, 1985), pp. 119-42, 209-23.
18. *Hidden Agenda*s, ed. cit., p. 70.
19. *Is the Future Female? Troubled thoughts on contemporary feminism* (Virago, 1987), p. 131.
20. 'The text's heroine: a feminist critic and her fiction', *Diacritics*, 12 (Summer 1982), p. 52.

Chapter Two

Femininity
and its Construction

Women always experiment at certain moments in their life with the
view that 'femininity' is a pretence. This garment that they must don
often transforms itself into an unbearable shell.
Monique Plaza, '"Phallomorphic power" and the psychology of
"woman"', *Ideology and Consciousness*, 4 (1978), p. 27

Introduction: Sex, gender, femininity

A key concept in feminist theory, one which underpins the Women's
Movement's analysis of the subordinate status assigned to women in
phallocratic culture, is the distinction between biological sex on the
one hand, and socially constructed gender on the other. This concept
involves the recognition that, while the sex of the individual depends
on anatomy, gender is a culturally constructed artefact. Angela
Carter, whose novel *The Passion of New Eve* (1977) furnishes a delightfully witty example of the fictional representation of the concept,
expresses the distinction as follows:

> There is the unarguable fact of sexual differentiation; but separate from
> it and only partially derived from it, are the behavioural modes of
> masculine and feminine, which are culturally defined variables trans-
> lated in the language of common usage to the status of universals.[1]

The idea of the cultural construction of gender, as well as forming the
basis for feminist demands for sex equality and women's liberation,
has inspired a number of novels and short stories. As the examples
discussed in this chapter illustrate, they make frequent use of symbolic narrative and other anti-realist devices. It is femininity rather
than masculinity which writers of fiction choose to foreground.
However, the latter topic does receive some attention. Since femininity and its construction form the basis of contemporary feminist
thought, it makes the obvious starting-point for this study.

In treating in fictional form themes related to the topic of femininity and its construction, writers draw on two main strands of theoretical research. The first investigates, generally in sociological terms, the topic of gender-role stereotyping. Theorists such as Betty Friedan, Kate Millett, Elizabeth Janeway and Ann Oakley paved the way for this approach in the early 1970s. They drew attention to the oppressive effects of the stereotypical representation of women as sex object, wife and mother. These roles, they demonstrated, had the effect of relegating women to the private sphere of sexual relations and family life, while debarring their entry into the public one of professional work and political struggle. Social scientists and anthropologists have subsequently refined these early studies. They reveal the way expectations of femininity differ according to culture, class and historical era.[2]

The second strand of research which has influenced women's fiction is philosophical and psychoanalytical. It is associated chiefly with French feminists and their reinterpretation of Lacanian ideas and Derridean deconstructive theory. Hélène Cixous, Julia Kristeva and Luce Irigaray, building on Simone de Beauvoir's portrayal of women as the 'other' of man, have examined the part played by the set of binary opposites, produced by a phallocratic culture, in perpetuating women's subordinate position.[3] A familiar set of polarities is the identification: man: mind, culture/woman: body, nature. This, as we shall see later in this chapter, has received a number of poweful representations in works of fiction.

Also of relevance to the novels and short stories discussed here are certain important shifts of perspective which have taken place in the feminist approach to gender. Theorists such as Phyllis Chesler, writing in the early 1970s and seeking to emphasize women's oppressed circumstances, presented, on the whole, a negative view of the feminine identity and position. They identified femininity with a number of undesirable attributes, including passivity, dependence, indecisiveness and a propensity for excessive self-sacrifice. Treating masculinity as 'the norm', they tended – unwittingly perhaps – to regard femininity as a kind of 'disorder' or 'mental illness' from which women need curing. The goal for which feminists strove in that period was the elimination of gender difference. The model of androgyny, with men and women adopting a combination of 'masculine' and 'feminine' attributes, was then fashionable.[4] Angela Carter's *The Passion of New Eve*, as we shall see, reproduces this particular approach to gender.

In recent years, however, the problematic aspects of the androgyny model have been recognized. The acceptance of it has been found to result in women striving to adopt 'masculine' instrumental attributes, while masculine, phallocratic value-schemes continue to exist unchallenged. A re-evaluation and valorization of the feminine identity and traditional 'feminine' attributes is now starting to take place. With the advent of the cultural feminist movement, emphasis is placed on the positive value of 'feminine' qualities. These include sensitivity, gentleness, the ability to cooperate and to nurture. The re-evaluation of femininity is accompanied by a critique of masculinity and the attributes of aggression and competitiveness traditionally assigned to men. Femininity is increasingly seen as the behavioural norm, with masculinity regarded as an aberration or distortion. Verity Bargate's *No Mama No* (1978), with its celebration of the feminine, is a novel which reproduces this cultural feminist perspective.

Major shifts have likewise occurred in the explanation of the construction of gender and the means available to the individual to achieve liberation from its restrictive aspects. The sociological theory of a 'gender role' into which the subject is socially conditioned, adopted by many feminists in the early 1970s, now tends to be rejected as simplistic and essentialist. It implies, as critics point out, the existence of an unreal division between the individual and society. It also appears to posit some kind of essential 'self' underlying the gender construct.[5] A psychoanalytic account of gender, based on feminist reappropriation of the ideas of Freud and Lacan, is increasingly gaining currency. This has the advantage of acknowledging the part played by the unconscious and the fractured self in the production and transformation of the subject. On the debit side, however, it can make processes of self-transformation and social change appear insuperably difficult to achieve.

The different ideas and approaches to gender summarized above form the basis of the works of fiction reviewed in this chapter. It is necessary to recognize, of course, that novels and short stories published over the past twenty years are by no means the first to depict femininity as a cultural construct. Nineteenth-century writers such as Mary Wollstonecraft, Charlotte Brontë and Mrs Opie take as their theme 'the collision between the female hero's evolving self and society's imposed identity'.[6] Women writing in the first half of this century also analyse and deconstruct aspects of the feminine role (restrictive ones, generally).[7] However, on account of the range of discourses and theoretical approaches currently available, contemporary writers display in their treatment of the topic a variety and complexity of outlook and narrative design unprecedented in earlier periods.

The term 'femininity and its construction' in contemporary fiction possesses a multitude of different meanings. I have therefore been forced to limit my study of the topic to three of the most important. They are as follows: the fictional representation by writers of the social and psychological aspects of the construction and deconstruction of gender; the treatment in novels and short stories of the identification of woman with nature and the body; and the theme of the dominance of the male gaze and the circulation of images of woman which it promotes.

The interaction between theory and narrative practice in works of fiction takes place, it is interesting to note, not only in the realm of ideas but also in metaphor and imagery. Descriptions of femininity employed by theorists frequently have a fictional and specular ring to them. This is the case with Mary Daly's representations of femininity as a type of 'robotitude' in which woman acts out a part or script.[8] It is also apparent in Friedan's description of the male editors of popular beauty magazines for women as 'Frankensteins' who 'no longer have the power to stop the feminine monster they have created',[9] and in Irigaray's depiction of femininity as a type of masquerade with woman trapped in the role of mimic 'acting out man's contraphobic projects, projections and productions of her desire'.[10] These images understandably recur and receive elaboration in certain novels and short stories.

Femininity and its construction

The focus of interest in this section is three particular novels – Carter's *The Passion of New Eve* (1977), Bargate's *No Mama No* (1978) and *Gaining Ground* (1978) by the Canadian writer Joan Barfoot. Though published at a similar period, each adopts a radically different approach to femininity. Carter, accepting the feminist perspective on gender current in the early 1970s, identifies it with undesirable attributes such as dependence, passivity, masochism and a propensity for maternal 'smothering'. The female characters in her novel seek to liberate themselves from these qualities and achieve a mode of behaviour which is supposedly androgynous. In actual fact, it is not so. It is composed of attributes which are predominantly 'masculine' and instrumental. Bargate's *No Mama No* takes the opposite view of femininity. Adopting an approach which is in many ways cultural feminist, Bargate celebrates the attributes of gentleness, sensitivity and nurturance traditionally assigned to women. Femininity is presented as the behavioural norm, while masculinity is treated as an ugly distortion. It is men, not women, she suggests, who require liberating from the tyranny of gender roles.

Despite the ideological differences between Carter's and Bargate's novels, the two works do have certain features in common. Central to both is the feminist concept of the distinction between biological sex and culturally constructed gender. It is the importance of this idea that the two writers seek to convey to the reader. In order to do so, each adopts a set of strategies which is highly inventive. The two novels also contain interesting representations of male protagonists. Both writers contrast reconstructed forms of masculinity with ones which are traditionally oppressive.

Barfoot's *Gaining Ground* illustrates yet a third approach to the topic of gender – one which looks forward to the feminist appropriation of psychoanalytic theory current in the 1980s. Abra, the female hero, finds the roles of wife and mother increasingly burdensome and alienating. She achieves liberation, however, not by taking a professional job or by joining a feminist group or organization as would have been the case in the early 1970s. Leaving her family, she sets up home in a cabin in the forest, effectively isolating herself from other people. Retreating into herself, she undergoes a process of psychological and spiritual self-analysis. She rejects the humanist goal of maintaining a unified ego and, instead, accepts the existence of the 'fractured self' and the release of multiple identities which it involves.

An interesting feature of the three novels – especially Carter's and Bargate's – is the ideological problems and contradictions they reveal. Although the topic of the construction and deconstruction of femininity proves extremely attractive to writers of fiction, it is by no means easy to treat successfully for it presents numerous pitfalls. The contradictions and inconsistencies apparent in the novels reflect the flaws in the theories of gender the writers appropriate rather than their own naivety or lack of narrative skill.

Carter's *The Passion of New Eve* is, to quote her, an 'anti-mythic novel', illustrating her view that 'myths are products of the human mind and reflect only aspects of material human practice'. She further describes it as 'a feminist tract about the social creation of femininity'.[11] As the title suggests, the myth she chooses to deconstruct on this occasion and, in so doing, rewrites, is the biblical story of the creation of Eve. Allusions to Mary Shelley's *Frankenstein* are also discernible in the text.

The events Carter treats, recounted by the eponymous Evelyn/Eve, take place in an unspecified future when urban civilization is on the verge of collapse. The opening chapters serve to establish Evelyn's chauvinistic attitudes. He regards women as inferior, treating them as sex objects. While infatuated with the glamorous image of the film-star Tristessa, representing the unobtainable, he is involved in a torrid love affair with the black prostitute Leilah. His sexist perspectives are the butt of Carter's ironizing humour. The reader's suspicion that he is less in control of his life than he likes to believe is strengthened when, tiring of the involvement with Leilah, he leaves the city and gets lost in the surrounding desert. Here he is captured by a band of feminist guerrilla fighters who deliver him up to their leader Mother, a parodic portrait of a matriarchal super-woman. Mother uses him as material in her experiment to create the perfect women. Renamed Eve, he is forced to undergo a sex-change operation followed by a process of psychological conditioning which transforms him into a woman. Eve/Evelyn's subsequent adventures include a period of incarceration in the harem of the local tyrant Zero where she/he experiences at first hand the sexual and domestic exploitation women habitually suffer. Zero, to judge from his name, represents the impotence which Carter envisages as underlying a phallocratic culture.

The events summarized above are a vehicle for Carter to decon-struct the feminine role, enabling her to foreground the distinction between biological sex and culturally constructed gender. The novel offers three different examples of the construction of femininity. The first centres on the figure of Evelyn/Eve. His metamorphosis into a woman involves, as Carter emphasizes, two separate stages. The sex operation he undergoes serves merely to transform him *biologically*. It is the subsequent inculcation of the attributes of dependence, passivity, masochism and the desire to nurture which women are expected to possess, that makes him *feminine*.

Carter's second example of the construction of femininity relates to the film star Tristessa, the object of Evelyn's initial infatuation. In the course of the narrative, this alluring figure, adored by her male admirers as the epitome of romantic female suffering, is discovered to be not a woman after all but a male impersonator masquerading as one. Poking fun at the gullibility of the general public, Carter suggests that in certain cases anatomical surgery and psychological conditioning are unnecessary. The male actor's desire to appear *feminine*, combined with the expectations of the cinema audience, who are addicted to fantasy images anyway, are sufficient (with the help of make-up and dress) to effect the sex-change. Carter exploits the episodes focusing on Tristessa to celebrate mischievously the triumph of culture over nature, fantasy over reality.

The third example centres on Leilah, the black prostitute with whom Evelyn has an affair. Towards the end of the novel this exotic figure, a model of apparent narcissism and sexual allure, lays aside the role of sex object and vamp, revealing herself to be a feminist fighter, one of Mother's followers. In the latter role she possesses, it is interesting to note, the instrumental qualities of leadership – independence and a capacity for action and aggression – traditionally regarded as masculine. Carter's account of these three different methods by which femininity can be constructed is humorous and entertaining. The device of intertextuality, combined with episodes of deliberate narrative contrivance such as the baroquely ornate passages describing the erotic 'masquerades ' Tristessa and Leilah perform, advertise the fictionality of the text. They distance the reader from events, alerting us to the fact that the novel is first and foremost a vehicle for ideas. Carter's treatment of gender also raises certain interesting ideological issues. It foregrounds, as no doubt the reader will have perceived, the question, discussed by the French theorists Monique Plaza[12] and Julia Kristeva[13], *What is woman?* Does femininity reside in biology, gender attributes or, as Kristeva suggests, in the marginal position assigned to the female subject in the dominant culture? Carter rejects the first possibility, accepts the second, and toys, on occasion, with the third.

The strategies Carter employs to explore this topic give rise, however, to certain obvious contradictions. First, by focusing attention on the construction of the sign woman and ignoring that of the sign man, she may justly be accused of representing masculinity as the behavioural norm, thus unintentionally promoting the very essentialist attitudes to gender she seeks to challenge! The critique she offers to the macho attitudes of the tyrant Zero conflicts with this dominant perspective of the novel, drawing attention to the problematic aspects of masculinity. The episodes focusing on him, however, occupy a peripheral position in the text. They seem to me to run counter to its main ideological gist.

The novel also reveals a second, more serious contradiction. Carter's aim is to write 'a feminist tract about the creation of femininity'. However, by revealing the female characters to be either biologically male (as with Eve and Tristessa) or to possess instrumental 'masculine' attributes (as with Leilah) she does the very opposite. She effectively erases feminity from the text. The novel, in fact, contains no positive representation of the feminine. Mother, the leader of the feminist fighters, is a grotesque parody of the maternal, modelled on Freud's and Laing's chauvinistic paradigms, while the women she leads possess qualities which are stereotypically male. Carter's erasure of femininity becomes even more strikingly visible if we approach the text in the light of the theories of trans-sexualism produced by Daly and Janice Raymond. Carter presents the trans-sexual Evelyn/Eve to us as the ideal feminist, the perfect woman constructed according to an androgynous blueprint. Daly and Raymond, however, take a very different view of trans-sexualism. Adopting a radical feminist stance, they describe the male-to-female trans-sexual as a threat to women's liberation. She is, they point out, not a woman at all but an anomalous hybrid created by a patriarchal culture with the aim of usurping woman's place and power.[14]

Bargate's approach to gender in *No Mama No* is, as I pointed out earlier, the opposite to Carter's. She subjects masculine codes of conduct to a stringent critique and celebrates attributes traditionally seen as feminine, treating them as the behavioural norm. The following affirmation of the value of feminine qualities, articulated by a radical feminist, sums up the view of gender informing the novel:

> We are proud of the female culture of emotion, intuition, love, personal relationships. ... It is our male colonizers – it is the male culture – who have defined essential humanity out of their identity and who are 'culturally deprived'.[15]

In celebrating 'the female culture of emotion, intuition, love' and presenting men as lacking in 'essential humanity', Bargate adopts a perspective similar to that of Jean Baker Miller, Adrienne Rich and Daly. Baker Miller is notable for pointing out in the mid-1970s that the qualities traditionally relegated to women, such as the capacity to cooperate, nurture and show emotion, are extremely valuable to society. They complement, in fact, the instrumental and rational attributes assigned to men.[16] Rich and Daly take a more radical line. Celebrating feminine values, they regard masculine ones as not simply deficient but downright harmful. Daly identifies masculinity with a paradoxical fear and envy of the feminine which leads men to prey parasitically and destructively on women's energies.[17] The French feminist theorist Irigaray also, of course, depicts masculinity as parasitical. Adopting a perspective which is surprisingly close to Daly's, she describes woman as 'the very ground in which manifest [masculine] mind sets its roots and draws its strength'.[18]

The strategy which Bargate uses to assert the value of the feminine is strikingly simple. It hinges, as does Carter's novel, on the distinction between sex and gender. *No Mama No* opens with Jodie, the female hero, feeling isolated and oppressed by the exclusively male family enclave of her husband David, depicted as an aggressive bully, and her two little sons Matthew and Orlando. She longs passionately to give birth to a daughter and, unable to produce one by biological means, does the next best thing. She resorts to *cultural* methods. She dresses Matthew and Orlando in girls' clothes and, renaming them Rainbow and Willow, treats them as if they were girls, encouraging them to be gentle and graceful. The blurb on the cover of the Fontana edition of the novel describes Jodie's attempted transformation of the two boys into girls as a 'grotesque' act reflecting 'a nightmare obsession'. However, this in no way corresponds to Bargate's account of the event. She describes it, emphatically, as a

means to liberate the boys from the restrictive aspects of the masculine role. Matthew/Rainbow responds with evident pleasure to
being allowed to wear a dress. He gives an impromptu dance of joy
and happily 'mothers' Willow, his little brother/sister. The episode
is a delightful one, illustrating the *jouissance* of pre-oedipal motility
which momentarily disrupts the harsh dispensation of patriarchal
law. The ease with which the two boys adapt to being feminine
exemplifies Bargate's view that femininity is the behavioural norm.
Masculinity, on the contrary, emerges as an aberration. It imprisons
the subject in a rigid carapace, preventing him from expressing
feelings of tenderness and warmth.

Other features of Bargate's novel further this indictment of masculinity. The three chief male characters – Jodie's husband David, his
psychiatrist buddy McCoy, and Nathan the husband of Jodie's
friend Joy – are shown as ganging up together to enforce patriarchal
codes of conduct and keep women subservient. They take pleasure
in displays of penetrative aggression, both figurative and literal. In
social terms, they intrude on women's company and, by disrupting
their friendship with one another, stop them achieving any effective
degree of solidarity or group support. On a sexual level, they harass
and molest women. Jodie laconically remarks that David is 'quite
heavily into the Saturday night celebration of the penis'. In a tone
which is distinctly radical feminist, she observes that 'Millions of
women all over the country must be raped on Saturday nights in the
name of married love.'[19] Men's acts of violence against women are
described, in accord with the views of Daly and Irigaray, as originating in their fear and envy of the feminine. This accounts for David's
fit of punitive rage at Jodie's efforts to transform their two little sons
into girls. It also explains the irrational and obsessive hatred he feels
for the local male transvestite, a gentle, inoffensive individual nick-
named 'Toad'.

An important feature of the novel, one which prevents its grim
denouement from appearing unrelievedly bleak, is Bargate's introduction of two male characters who have reconstituted their masculinity on non-aggressive lines. As well as Toad, there is Jodie's friend
Jack. Jack behaves sympathetically and supportively towards her, in
contrast to the brutal measures adopted by David and the psychiatrist McCoy.

The various ideological contradictions apparent in the text hinge,
as is the case with Carter's novel, on essentialist attitudes to gender.
Though presenting masculinity as a construct, Bargate appears to see
femininity as an 'essence' – a 'natural', untainted substratum which
underlies all culturally constructed roles. Another problem with the
novel is that its affirmation of the value of feminine gentleness strikes

the reader on occasion as too extreme. We long for the female protagonists to assert themselves and challenge their male oppressors. In the Manichean scheme of values which characterizes Bargate's vision of reality, aggressive masculinity appears destined to invade and colonize forever the vulnerable, unresisting realm of the feminine.

Barfoot's *Gaining Ground* differs quite fundamentally from the two novels discussed above. She takes as her theme not the construction of femininity but, on the contrary, its deconstruction. Moreover, her description of the psychological transformation which Abra, the central protagonist and narrator, achieves owes more to psychoanalytic approaches to gender than it does to sociological ones. The central focus of the novel is the *sujet en procès* and its play of diverse, shifting identities.

The texture of the novel, as is generally the case with Barfoot's fiction, is both delicate and dense. In keeping with the psychological theme she treats, she creates a discontinuous first-person narrative, interweaving events from Abra's past life with episodes set in the present. The account Abra gives of her renunciation of the roles of middle-class wife and mother in exchange for a life of physical hardship and solitude in a cabin in the Canadian forest relates to several different facets of feminist theory. Her description of the alienating effect of the roles she casts off – they relegate her, she feels, to the status of 'robot'[20] and 'mannequin' (p. 69) – illustrates the psychoanalytic concept of 'femininity as masquerade'. As Irigaray observes, 'the masquerade ... is what women do ... in order to participate in man's desire, but at the cost of giving up theirs'.[21] Carter, in *The Passion of New Eve*, adopts a masculine point of view and depicts the masque of femininity from the outside, describing with obvious pleasure the exotic costumes and make-up Leilah and Tristessa use to seduce men. Barfoot, on the contrary, explores it from the inside. Taking the female viewpoint, she emphasizes the burdensome legacy of suffering and alienation which it imposes on women.

The transformation of personal consciousness which Abra experiences on leaving her family and liberating herself from the pressures of feminine role-play also connects with another strand of feminist psychoanalytic thought. The French theorist Cixous points out that, to avoid 'being reduced to the state of coded mannequin', we have to recognize that we are 'complex, mobile, open beings'. Commenting on 'the concert of personalizations called I', she observes that the identities we possess transcend gender divisions.[22] The discoveries which Abra makes about her psyche while living alone in the forest involve a similar set of perceptions. Dismissing the unitary self as an illusion, she comes to perceive that she possesses multiple, contrary identities. She describes these as 'the dreamer', 'the practical self', 'the new born child' who takes pleasure in the world of nature, and the censorious self who sits in judgement on the others. A liberating transformation of consciousness is not the only advantage Abra gains from her experience of rural solitude. The physical hardship she endures strengthens her mentally and physically, teaching her independence and survival skills. She finds the close observation of the natural world immensely pleasurable. One of the most attractive features of the novel is Barfoot's vivid descriptions of the animal life of the forest and the changing seasons – the birds, the squirrels and the melting snow. In this respect the novel contributes to the positive affirmation of the values of solitude, celibacy and meditative practices associated with the cultural feminist movement. Tricia Bickerton observes that, despite the obvious strains which a life of solitude involves,

> it is often a very positive experience for a woman to be alone. It may be the first time in her life she can discover what she wants, her own needs, without taking someone else into consideration. ... She may discover new possibilities, talents and horizons .... Indeed, perhaps she becomes stronger and attempts to do things that once seemed easier to avoid. She is free, as it were, to create herself.[23]

The discovery that she is 'free to create herself', which Abra achieves with pain and effort, enables her to gain a new, exhilarating perspective on life. It constitutes the central theme of Barfoot's sensitively written and enjoyable novel.

Femininity and its construction, as well as being a popular theme in novels by women, also features in a number of short stories. One of the most amusing and psychologically acute is 'Raymond's Run' (*Gorilla, My Love*, 1972) by the black American writer Toni Cade Bambera. Using the device of humour, Bambera analyses the oppressive facets of the feminine identity from the point of view of her child hero Squeaky (the girl's proper name is Hazel Elizabeh Deborah Parker). Squeaky has a well-deserved reputation for being a tomboy. She fiercely resents the efforts made by adults, her mother in particular, to get her to 'act like a girl for a change'.[24] As she breathlessly observes on the occasion of the May Day festivities, her mother, instead of being angry with her for refusing to pretty herself up in a frilly dress, ought to be pleased:

> You'd think she'd be glad her daughter ain't out there prancing around a May Pole getting the new clothes all dirty and sweaty and trying to act like a fairy or a flower or whatever you're supposed to be when you should be trying to be yourself, whatever that is, which is, as far as I am concerned, a poor Black girl who really can't afford to buy new shoes and a new dress you only wear once a lifetime 'cause it won't fit next year. (p. 27)

As is evident from this passage, Squeaky loathes play-acting. Remembering being forced to dance about acting a strawberry in a nursery school pageant of Hansel and Gretel, she objects with dignity: 'I am not a strawberry. I do not dance on my toes. I *run*' (p.28). Running is, in fact, her favourite occupation. The central event of the story is the efforts she makes to beat her rival, the stuck-up Gretchen, in the May Day race. Squeaky trusts Gretchen no more than she trusts the majority of girls. She associates girls – or ones who conform to the feminine stereotype, at any rate – with rivalry, bitchiness and deceit. The story concludes on a positive note. As well as winning the race, Squeaky manages to acquire a more honest understanding with Gretchen. Describing the momentary transcendence of the feminine role which they both achieve, she comments:

> We stand there with this big smile of respect between us. It's about as real a smile as girls can do for each other, considering we don't practise real smiling every day, you know, cause maybe we too busy being flowers or fairies or strawberries instead of something honest and worthy of respect ... you know ... like being people. (p. 32)

In marked contrast to the roles of 'flower' and 'fairy' which as a girl Squeaky is expected to play, are the liberating identities which she experiences in the moment of exhilaration prior to the race. In an image from her infancy she pictures herself as a 'choo-choo train, running through the fields of corn' and ecstatically describes how 'all the time I'm dreaming this, I get lighter and lighter till I'm flying over the beach again, getting blown through the sky like a feather that weighs nothing at all' (p.30). A striking feature of the story, as my choice of quotations indicates, is Bambera's brilliant rendering of the rhythms and colourful colloquialisms of young Squeaky's speech-patterns.

Woman: Nature, body

Another motif related to femininity and its construction which receives analysis in novels and short stories is the identification of woman with the realm of nature and the body. In exploring the different manifestations which this identification can assume, writers focus attention on its oppressive consequences and on the contradictions which it involves. They also depict women's responses, along with the strategies they use to resist and challenge it. Before we discuss the representation of these topics in particular texts, it will be necessary to outline some of the theoretical perspectives available to writers of fiction.

Theorists have come up with various explanations to account for the identification man: culture, mind/woman: nature, body which frequently operates in a phallocratic culture. Sherry Ortner suggests that it stems from the placing of an exaggerated focus on woman's reproductive capacities.[25] Although she is not, in fact, composed solely of womb and breasts, man tends to see her as such. Baker Miller and Susan Griffin, with differing degrees of radicalism, claim that the identification has its origin in the fact that men, internalizing a Platonic-Christian value-code, unconsciously relegate to women those facets of experience which they find degrading, feel guilty about and seek to deny.[26] These include sexuality and physical/emotional areas of existence in general. Whatever the source of the identification, the effects to which it gives rise are clearly oppressive. It excludes woman, theoretically at least, from participating in the sphere of culture and history. Irigaray, summing up the dehumanizing view of woman inherent in Western philosophical thought, writes: 'Woman does not take an active part in the development of history, for she is never anything but the still undifferentiated opaqueness of sensible matter.'[27]

A consequence of the identification which is particularly relevant to this study of women's fiction is the barriers it imposes to female creative activities and aspirations. This theme, explored by Sandra H. Gilbert and Susan Gubar from a theoretical point of view,[28] appears in fictional form in Michèle Roberts's novel *The Visitation* (1983). Helen, the central character, hopes to become a creative writer. However, she experiences difficulty writing since, whenever she puts pen to paper, her skin erupts in a mysterious rash. On coming across an old herbal in a shop, she looks up the entries under W, and finds the following words listed:

Womb: women's weeping therefrom; women in childbed; women's complaints, how to soothe; women's courses, how to stop, how to bring on; women's diseases; women's longings; women's pains.[29]

The list is depressingly predictable. In a phallocratic culture woman is defined by reference to the body and sexual reproduction, along with their polluting ailments, desires and 'pains'. Helen's rash can be explained by the fact that she has internalized the view of woman promoted by the dominant culture. Her body, responding accordingly, resists the attempts she makes to write and participate in the world of the intellect. Seeking a way out of her predicament, she resorts to the solution which many women writers have taken in the past. She strives to erase all awareness of her body and sex. Roberts describes with a note of irony how, in order 'to write, Helen always feels she has to cancel her body out, become pure mind. Genderless, transcendent, like a man' (p. 99). Men are, of course, neither 'genderless' nor 'transcendent'. The fact that Helen sees them in this way indicates her uncritical acceptance of a phallocratic scheme of values. She regards man as *self* and woman as his *other* – the polluted carrier of the experiences and desires which he seeks to shed.

Contemporary women writers treat the identification of woman with nature and the body in a variety of different ways. Carter, for example, exploits the potential the motif possesses for fantasy and the grotesque. Illustrations of this include her description of the mutant prostitutes, part-vegetable, part-woman, in *The Infernal Desire Machines of Dr Hoffman* (1972) and her exquisitely sensuous representation of the metamorphosis of woman into beast in the conclusion of her short story 'The Tiger's Bride' (*The Bloody Chamber*, 1979).

Atwood also makes use of the motif. Her approach, however, is more intelligent and discriminating than Carter's. Instead of using it uncritically for purposes of sensationalism and rhetorical display, as is unfortunately the case with Carter, she manages to convey to the reader a sense of moral horror, even outrage, at the brutally degrading treatment of women to which it gives rise. 'Polarities' (1971; *Dancing Girls*, 1977), one of her finest short stories, admirably illustrates this. In it Atwood takes the unusual line of presenting the equation woman: nature, body, from the point of view of a man. Morrison, an American who has recently taken up a post as teacher of literature at a provincial Canadian university, is presented as the chief focalizer of events. The story hinges on the devastating discoveries he makes about himself and his attitudes to women. His chauvinistic outlook, Atwood disturbingly suggests, is by no means unique to him. It reflects a deep-seated stratum of misogyny inherent in Western culture. The fact that it lies beyond his power to alter his attitudes makes him emerge, in fact, as the *victim* rather than the *villain* of the piece.

Morrison is presented from the start as something of an isolate. A typical academic, he appears more at home in the world of ideas than of people. Signs are planted in the text that indicate that he feels ill at ease both with his own body and the world of nature. While eager to find himself a girlfriend to relieve his physical isolation, he rejects propositioning the most obvious candidate available – his colleague Louise, a graduate assistant in the university department where he teaches. Not only does she fail to attract him sexually, but he finds her intelligence and efficiency positively intimidating. The kind of girl he is looking for is, he admits, very different from Louise. He pictures her as 'a nice, loosely structured girl, with ungroomed, seedy breasts, more thing than idea',[30] who will make no emotional demands on him and seek no commitment. Atwood suggests that Morrison, in fearing commitment and regarding women purely in sexual terms, relegates to them those aspects of experience which he himself finds problematic. Later in the narrative Louise is portrayed as suffering a mental breakdown. Her collapse is brought on, Atwood implies, by her inability to tolerate the fragmented, alienated nature of contemporary urban life. She is dumped in the local hospital where she is heavily sedated with drugs. These work a terrible transformation on her intellect and looks. Her muscles slacken, she puts on weight, and she starts to resemble an inert, sprawling doll. Morrison visits her there, and the climax of the story occurs in Atwood's account of his response to her changed appearance. He is appalled to discover that, far from being repelled by her degraded state, he finds it positively attractive. It is, he recognizes, 'the hopeless, mad Louise he wanted, the one devoid of any purpose or defence. A sane one, one who would judge him, he would never be able to handle' (p. 73). His despondent musings on this ironic conclusion to his quest for love foreground the polarities man: culture, mind/woman: nature, body, around which Atwood's indictment of masculinity in the story revolves:

> So this was his dream girl then, his ideal woman found at last: a disintegration, mind returning to its component shard of matter, a defeated formless creature on which he could inflict himself like shovel on earth, axe on forest, use without being used, know without being known. (p.73)

The passage is a deliberately disturbing one, intended to shock us. The words 'inflict', 'axe', 'use' conjure up male fantasies of rape and violence. The platonic dichotomy of body/mind, signalled by the phrases 'shard of matter', 'earth', 'formless' and 'know', corresponds to Irigaray's description of the phallocratic picture of woman as 'the opaqueness of sensible matter'. A phallocratic culture sees woman as a being who, though 'lacking in all power of logos', none the less 'offers unawares an all-powerful soil in which the logos can grow'.[31]

As is often the case with Atwood's fiction, her treatment of the polarities of self/other in the story goes beyond the realm of sexual politics to touch on the politics of race. Morrison's American nationality is important in this respect. So also is the episode in which he compares the spectacle of the degraded Louise to that of an Indian woman whom he encountered in the past. The latter was sitting outside a cheap hotel, taking off her clothes as an invitation to sex, enacting for a group of sniggering male Canadian onlookers a masquerade of their own guilt-ridden lusts. By referring to the Indian woman, Atwood makes the point that the position Louise occupies as the repository of inadmissible male desires is a stereotypical one. It is an entrenched and commonplace feature of Western culture.

The comparison Atwood draws between the women patients Morrison sees in the hospital and the caged animals at the local zoo extends the theme of polarities even further. It unsettles the reader, destabilizing our conventional assumptions about the borderline between the human and the sub-human.

Whereas Atwood's 'Polarities' explores from the male point of view the degrading effects of the identification of woman with nature and the body, other works of fiction investigate the self-destructive syndromes in which it frequently entraps women. The latter include certain novels and short stories which examine the situation of the female anorexic. Examples are Atwood's *The Edible Woman* (1969) and 'Agoraphobia' (1983) by the New York writer Emily Prager.

Anorexia is a condition which feminist theorists discuss in some detail. No longer is it interpreted as reflecting the female subject's efforts to conform to the image of extreme slenderness promoted by the fashion industry and media. Sheila MacLeod, on the contrary, describes the female anorexic as engaging in an unconscious protest at 'being identified solely or primarily with the flesh – and all the attributes of second-class citizenship which such an identification implies'.[32] Kim Chernin goes further. She suggests that the 'tempestuous warfare against the body'[33] which the anorexic wages, constitutes an attempt to erase signs of her sex while simultaneously representing a protest against women's lack of power. Denied power in the public world, the 'female hunger artist' (Chernin's name for the anorexic) retaliates by exerting control and practising creativity in the one arena where she does possess it – *her own body*. A fascinating portrayal of the anorexic as 'hunger artist', emphasizing the ambiguous pleasures and pains of her situation, is to be found in Sue Roe's novel *Estella, Her Expectations* (1982). Roe describes her eponymous hero as:

> the Estalla whose knees and whose shoulders were so boney, whose hip bones were so like birds' wings, who dressed so black, who ate so little and drank so much, that she, from her frail pedestal of control, could fashion and mould and sculpt a whole image of a painted self out there in the distance.[34]

A representation of woman as 'hunger artist' also occurs in Prager's 'Agoraphobia' (*A Visit from the Footbinder*, 1983). The story is a grotesque fantasy, sharpened – as is often the case with Prager's work – by a vein of blackly sardonic humour. Marian Root, the central character and focalizer of events, is an aspiring New York poet. She has won several prizes for her verse. Her situation is, however, beset with difficulties. Though wishing to apply for a grant to continue her modernization of the couplet form, she is incapable of writing the applications and sending them in. The reason is, she is anorexic and agoraphobic. The two conditions appear related. They reflect, she grimly admits, a self-destructive urge to make herself 'less and less physical'.[35] Marian relentlessly subjugates her body, denying it food, light, air and physical contact. She self-mockingly pictures herself as a weird-looking sci-fi monster, 'a giant head on a spindly weak little body, the first woman extraterrestrial on the upper West Side' (p. 113). Bizarre though the image is, it effectively epitomizes woman's position as 'other', at the same time illustrating the rift between body and mind which the anorexic often suffers. To quote Hilde Bruch, 'Many experience themselves and their bodies as separate entities, and it is the mind's task to control the unruly and despised body.'[36]

The chief strategy which Prager employs to explore the contradictions of Marian's situation is the creation of a fantasy dialogue between her and her imaginary companion and alter-ego named Dolores. It is no coincidence that Dolores first materialized when Marian, an infant at the time, was literally sitting in a pile of her own shit, having 'lost control'. In contrast to Marian, Dolores is portrayed as a sharp-tongued, pragmatic extrovert. She bullies and insults Marian, calling her 'Eve on a raft of insanity' (p. 120), and nagging her to pull herself together. As well as humorously illustrating Marian's schizoid state, the dialogue with Dolores highlights the knife-edge suspense drama of which every moment of the agoraphobic's life is composed. Will Marian, or will she not, succeed in summoning up the nerve to leave her apartment to go to a friend's party? If she does manage to set foot outside the door, will she or will she not ever get to the party?

The psychosomatic origins of Marian's condition are never fully explained. However, allusions to sexual violation surface in the text, and there are also hints that, in subjugating her body, she is rebelling against the phallocratic identification of woman with sex and reproduction. An image which plays a key part in the story is the absurdly horrific one of a model of a 'giant uterus, with red light ovaries that lit up to show the onset of menstruation' (p. 118). The model hangs in the Museum of Natural History where Marian remembers seeing it as a child. As well as symbolizing the concept of woman as breeding machine, existing merely to have sex and produce babies, it wittily and obscenely sums up her status as 'the defined sex'. As Irigaray and other theorists point out, woman is the object of interrogation and investigation by an army of male gynaecologists, sexologists and psychoanalysts, all eager to explore and illuminate the so-called 'dark continent'.[37] The image of the giant uterus and its symbolic significance clearly conflict with Marian's intellectual ambition as a poet. They help to explain the disabling, self-destructive conflicts she suffers.

Another aspect of the problematic relationship which, in a phallocratic culture, woman experiences with her body is the pressure put on her to conform to the images of feminine beauty promoted by the media and fashion industry. This motif also plays a key role in women's fiction. The problems and contradictions it involves, ones which form the ideological base of the treatment of the theme in novels and short stories, are explicated by Rosalind Coward in an essay which she ironically entitles 'The Body Beautiful'. Coward comments on the significance, in terms of sexual politics, of the model of extreme slenderness which has been fashionable for women since the 1960s. She points out that 'the shape is a version of the immature body' and is 'reminiscent of adolescence'.[38] Conveying an impression of dependency and powerlessness, it is totally unthreatening, which explains why, Coward suggests, men find it so attractive. Coward goes on to outline the choices which are available to women. We can either, she observes, make an effort to accommodate to the fashionably slender model of beauty and, sacrificing the image of strength and psychological power denoted by a well-built physique, achieve indirect access to social and material power by making ourselves attractive to men. Or we can reject the slender model, forgo the access to the material and social power which it confers, and rest content with a substantial body-image which, though unfashionable, denotes an impression of psychological power and strength. Here I need to point out that theorists such as Orbach and Chernin regard the act of putting on weight not as a sign of weakness and self-indulgence. On the contrary, Orbach describes it as 'a purposeful act' and 'a directed, conscious or unconscious challenge to sex-role stereotyping and the culturally defined experience of womanhood'.[39] It can also be, she points out, a method which women unconsciously adopt to neutralize their sexual identity. It enables them to avoid being treated as sex objects and subjected to sexual harassment by men.

The urgency of the problems which the contradictions summarized above pose for women is indicated by the frequency with which they form the theme of novels and short stories. Writers as disparate as Atwood, Consuelo Baehr, Fay Weldon and the London-based West Indian writer Barbara Burford all make them the centre of works of fiction.

Atwood's *Lady Oracle* (1977) is an experiment in comic Gothic. Structured on the theme of the fractured self, it investigates the multiple, contradictory identities available to women in contemporary society. When she is a child Joan Foster, the central character, goes with her aunt to visit the fair at the Canadian National Exhibition. Here she finds, among the usual side-shows, tents displaying various human spectacles. These include freaks, pleasure-loving dancing girls and – in addition – a fat lady. Atwood's choice of stereotypes is extremely apt since Joan is called on to play, on different occasions, all three roles. The identity of fat lady is one foisted on her both in childhood and adolescence – with predictably oppressive effects. Her rolypoly figure debars her from playing the graceful part of butterfly in the school ballet. Instead she is relegated to the ignominious one of mothball. To her immense distress she is unable to wear the pair of spangly wings she so much covets. As her teacher Miss Flegg logically remarks, 'Who ever heard of a mothball with wings?'[40] When Joan reaches puberty she continues to be overweight. Her binges of overeating, reflecting feelings of hostility towards her mother, exclude her from the world of teenage dating and sex. The only roles available to her are those of 'kindly aunt and wise woman' (p. 93), playing duenna and confidante to her slender, sexually attractive peers.

The contrary facets of the female identity which Atwood represents by the images of fat lady and dancing girl are treated by Burford in a more fantastic manner still. Donna, the fourteen-year-old black hero of the story 'Dreaming the Sky Down' (*The Threshing Floor*, 1986), leads a double life. By day she has to endure the dreary routine of a pupil at a London comprehensive school where she suffers frequent racist taunts. She is also, on account of her twelve-stone figure, subjected to jibes about her looks and gait. At night, however, Donna's situation undergoes a magic transformation. She is liberated from the physical burden of weight and the psychological burden of racist abuse by dreaming that she is flying – initially in the confined space of her bedroom and then, having managed by a feat of balancing to lift the window-sash, out into the summer night among the dusty trees. Combining the surreal with the mundane, Burford describes Donna's impressions of flight as follows:

> Beneath her bare feet, the leaves shifted, green as angelica; restored to springtime translucency by the lamp directly below her. She lightened and drifted carefully up the inner space of the tree, halting once to whisper, in response to startled bird cheeps: 'It's okay! I'm dreaming.'[41]

But is Donna really dreaming? The denouement to the story springs surprises on the reader. At this point Burford daringly challenges the conventional dichotomies of mind/matter, dream/waking, allowing fantasy and reality to merge. The story is strikingly original in its conception and execution.

A writer who has made an especially significant contribution to the fictional representation of the oppressive effects and contradictions of the model of femininity promoted by the fashion industry is, of course, Fay Weldon. Her two novels which treat this theme, *The Fat Woman's Joke* (1967) and *The Life and Loves of a She-Devil* (1983), differ markedly in narrative complexity and the degree of anger and indignation at woman's exploited position they convey. However, they also possess certain notable features in common. Both novels create inventive variations on the prescriptions and prohibitions for femininity listed by Orbach, along with the paradox they involve:

> Women are expected to be petite, demure, giving, passive, receptive in the home and, above all, attractive. Women are discouraged from being active, assertive, competitive, large and, above all, unattractive. *To be unattractive is not to be a woman.*[42]

The Fat Woman's Joke and *The Life and Loves of a She-Devil* also reveal general similarities of narrative design. Both are structured, in a manner reminiscent of myth and fairy tale, on the antithetical pair of female figures, good girl and shrew. While the former figure complies obediently with patriarchal expectations of feminine behaviour, the other resists and challenges them. This narrative device has the effect of exposing to the reader the divisions between women which a phallocratic culture promotes.

The narrative design of *The Fat Woman's Joke* is based on a straightforward contrast between Phyllis who, in order to satisfy her husband's sexist views about female beauty, allows her body to be mutilated by cosmetic surgery, and Esther, the eponymous fat woman, who rebels against the model of slenderness currently in vogue by deliberately over-eating. Esther's substantial build and enormous appetite for food represent symbolically both a protest against woman's lack of power and an attempt to achieve, in Chernin's words, 'a unified condition of the self'.[43] The latter is in marked contrast to the fragmented image of the female body as a collection of fetishized parts (breasts, legs, hips) circulated by the media and porn industry. Esther's most important function in the narrative, from an ideological point of view, is to draw attention to marriage and the female body as sites of woman's oppression and feminist struggle. She points out that men, motivated by misogyny, treat women as domestic slaves: by expecting them to look slim and fragile, they seek to reduce them to 'a piece of docile flesh'.[44] Susan, Esther's young rival who tries to steal her husband, ironically agrees with her analysis. She complains that, while men are admired for their solidity (physical and mental), women are always praised for the opposite. The reason why a slender, petite women is attractive to men is, she suggests, that her 'lack of flesh negates her. The less of her there is, the less notice he need take of her' (p. 50)!

The location of the novel in the era of 'the swinging sixties' is of vital importance. It was at this period, with the fashion model Twiggy achieving fame, that the ideal of an exaggeratedly slender figure started to tyrannize women's lives. And in the excessively sexist climate of the era rivalry between 'single girl' and 'married woman' was not only expected, it was positively encouraged.[45]

Many of the themes of *The Fat Woman's Joke* reappear in a more provocative and symbolically contrived form in Weldon's later novel *The Life and Loves of a She-Devil*. The latter is enlivened by a strongly radical feminist spirit. A passage from the essay 'Fashion as violence against women' by the British WAVAW group is an excellent introduction to my discussion of this novel:

> Under male supremacy women's status depends greatly on male approval. If we don't conform we pay heavy penalties. It means that many women mutilate and injure themselves, spending an enormous amount of time, energy and resources in the process. Fashion divides us into angels, whores, dolly-birds, and hags. This is important in the maintenance of male power. It prevents us seeing each other as allies, but sets us up as enemies, always in competition.[46]

The above passage pinpoints, with almost uncanny accuracy, the key motifs which form the ideological basis of Weldon's novel. The plot revolves around the decision made by Ruth Patchet, so-called She-Devil and hag, to take revenge on the petite, angel-like Mary Fisher, her rival in love, by engineering a complex act of role-reversal. Ruth devotes time, energy and resources to undergoing a series of surgical operations which transform her tall, substantial figure into a simulacrum of her rival's. By this method, she succeeds eventually in winning back the love of her faithless husband Bobbo. However, she does so at a heavy price. The surgeon who agrees to reconstruct her body along petite lines performs the operation unwillingly. Highlighting the assumptions of female inferiority in phallocratic ideals of beauty, he tells Ruth, 'You are asking to be made pretty: trivial, if you will forgive me.'[47]

The black comedy of revenge enacted in the novel draws attention to the fact that stereotypes of femininity, psychological as well as physical, are constructs created by men. It is the taunts and insults uttered by her husband Bobbo which initially goad Ruth to play the role of She-Devil. One of Weldon's achievements in the novel is to invert and valorize this abusive epithet, identifying it with female independence and resistance. This strategy is, of course, a typically radical feminist one. Joreen uses it in her famous radical feminist squib 'The Bitch Manifesto'.[48] She ingeniously subverts and valorizes the epithet bitch by identifying it with feminist strength, independence and rebelliousness.

Weldon's *The Life and Loves of a She-Devil* has been aptly described as an 'inverted fairy tale'[49] which re-works motifs from Anderson's *Little Mermaid* and Grimms's *Cinderella*. Her treatment of the Cinderella story, it is interesting to note, again reveals links with radical feminist approaches. It possesses strong affinities with Daly's interpretation. Daly sees the Ugly Sisters' mutilation of their feet to fit the glass slipper presented by the Prince as representing the self-destructive acts which patriarchal stereotypes of beauty encourage women to perform.

Images of femininity and the dominance of the male gaze

Another topic which is currently achieving a degree of prominence in women's fiction, one which relates to the theme of the female body-image and its construction, is the male gaze and the dominance which it exerts. Coward sums up the relevance of the polarized position of observer/observed to the relations between the sexes in the following terms:

> In this society, looking has become a crucial aspect of sexual relations, not because of any natural impulse, but because it is one of the ways in which domination and subordination are expressed. The relations involved in looking enmesh with coercive beliefs about appropriate sexual behaviour for men and women.[50]

The controlling effects of the male gaze are, of course, apparent in other areas besides personal relationships. A significant illustration of the power it wields is the circulation of images of women produced by the media and the advertising industry. The effects of this circulation are, on the whole, exploitative and oppressive. The proliferation of visual representations of femininity, while encouraging men to feel secure, makes women feel anxious. It pressures the latter into a narcissistic preoccupation with self-image and imposes indirect control on their behaviour. It simultaneously enables men to cope with the threat which feminity represents, allowing them, as Laura Mulvey suggests, to distance the image of woman, fetishizing her and regarding her voyeuristically as a 'spectacle'.[51] Women certainly do achieve a degree of narcissistic pleasure from their position as focus of 'the Look'. However, they pay a heavy price for it in terms of coercion and control.

The dynamics of the male gaze is analysed in a number of novels and short stories. Doris Lessing treats the topic in *The Summer Before the Dark* (1973). The central character Kate Brown, in her mid-forties, becomes oppressively conscious of the power which the gaze wields in dictating and controlling not only her appearance but also her identity and sense of self-worth. In the latter stages of the novel she is portrayed as deliberately experimenting with the image she projects. By means of frequent changes of dress, make-up and hair-style, she remodels herself into a series of contrasting images of woman – sexy and glamorous, or drab and down-at-heel. She studies the way men respond to these various images, and is appalled to discover the power the gaze possesses to confirm or erase her identity.

While Lessing centres her analysis on the actual gaze, other writers treat its symbolic substitute and extension – the lens of the camera or cine-camera. Marian, the central protagonist of Atwood's novel *The Edible Woman* (1969), finds herself the focus of her fiancé Peter's objectification and scrutiny. His attempts to dominate and control her reach extreme heights when, at their engagement party, he produces a camera and tries to 'shoot' her. Atwood encourages the reader to recognize the way the camera can function as an offensive weapon. Manipulated by a chauvinistic male, it possesses the capacity to objectify, dominate and control women.

Another writer who uses the image of the camera – in this case, film – to investigate the workings of the male gaze, is Rebecca Brown. Like Atwood's novel, Brown's story 'The Joy of Marriage' (*The Evolution of Darkness*, 1984) exposes the exploitative aspects of the cult of permissive sexuality associated with the 1960s. The title of the story, recalling that of the best-selling sex manual *The Joy of Sex*, signals to the reader the kind of issues Brown aims to explore. Introducing ideas reminiscent of Michel Foucault's, she reveals the way the contemporary cult of frankness about sex can result in personal relations becoming public property. The images of women and sexual practice circulated by the media, ostensibly for educational purposes, are shown to reflect a voyeuristic impulse. They satisfy men's obsessive need to distance woman, thus negating the threat which she represents.

Brown adopts a strategy of symbolic narrative to treat these ideas. In a series of surrealistic episodes recalling sequences from dream or film the nameless female narrator makes the disturbing discovery that the cottage where she is honeymooning with her husband has been inexplicably transformed into a set of vast rooms. No longer is the place secluded. It is teeming with strangers. Her husband sits encased in a glass-walled booth from which he projects a non-stop stream of sex-movies. The films, depicting him and herself making love, are watched by a large and admiring audience. The only time he ever emerges from the booth is to give an introduction to the films. This he does, the narrator notes, in the tone of 'an evangelical sinner saved by grace'.[52] The story concludes on a desperate note with the narrator condemned to lead a life of solitude among crowds. The only contact she now enjoys with her husband is in dreams. It is so long since she actually touched him that, as she strives in vain to tell him, 'I've forgotten what you look like in 3 D, the flesh' (p. 26).

One of the most complex analyses of the theme of the dominance of the male gaze and the circulation of images of woman which it produces occurs in *Estella, Her Expectations* (1982) by Sue Roe. I mentioned the novel earlier in relation to the topic of anorexia. The signifying practices of photography, film, dance and painting are all shown as contributing to the circulation. The novel centres on the twin motifs of seeing and image. Parodying Descartes, Roe observes, 'You are observed. Therefore you exist.'[53] The comment emphasizes the degree to which woman's identity and sense of reality in contemporary culture depend on her position as the focus of 'the Look'.

Roe skilfully exposes the contradictory aspects of woman's position as the object of the male gaze. Unlike the other writers discussed in this section, she pays particular attention to the pleasures it involves. Like the theorist E. Ann Kaplan,[54] Roe presents women's sexual and social pleasures as constructed around the process of objectification. Estella and her friend Mercy, though recognizing the ephemeral, narcissistic aspect of such pursuits, enjoy dressing up in picturesque, exotic clothes. They love parading in front of the mirror – both for their own delight and the photographer's. The Dickensian phrase 'What larks', uttered in *Great Expectations* by the innocent working-class Joe Gargery, is transferred by Roe to the sophisticated contemporary world of women's fashion. It is used in relation to the decadent games Estella and Mercy play, picturing themselves in 'wasp waist corsets dripping with ribbons' and other deliciously erotic items of dress. Like Angela Carter and Elizabeth Wilson,[55] Roe emphasizes the pleasurable aspects of 'femininity as masquerade' and the interest in fashion it involves. At the same time, however, she does stress the limitations of woman's position as object of the gaze. Mercy, in fact, rebukes Estella for being content to live in a claustrophobic, narcissistic world of fantasy; she impatiently commands her: 'Look for something outside your wretched mirror. Realise there's a very large frame of reference out there' (p. 88).

One of the most successful features of the novel is the illuminating way it relates the theme of the circulation of images of femininity to the motif of the *sujet en procès*. The sign woman is revealed to be composed of myriad shifting, conflicting images. Estella appropriates for herself a number of different identities from popular culture – *femme fatale*, bride, sad lady and dancer. Roe also explores new ground in the way she focuses attention on women's fantasy projections of men. The role of fashion photographer is portrayed as a princesses of himself' (p. 36). However, man is also described – more ominously – as playing the Gothic, death-related roles of 'executioner' and 'man in black'. The conflicting images of man which woman projects are brought to the reader's attention. The gentle image of the lover with 'the large tender face' is contrasted with the violent figure of the gypsy who makes brutal love. In showing Estella taking pleasure in the latter fantasy, Roe acknowledges the element of masochism which is involved in the construction of female desire.

The style of the novel, with its use of discontinuous narrative and impressionistic description of colour and texture, is admirably suited to the themes of image and seeing which it treats. Roe's style has affinities with Kristeva's account, articulated in relation to Virginia Woolf, of the tendency of women writers to focus on 'suspended states, subtle sensations and, above all, colours – green, blue.... Estranged from language, women are visionaries, dancers who suffer as they speak.'[56] The similarities between Roe's and Woolf's styles vividly illustrate the positive influence which the latter continues to exercise on contemporary women's fiction.

Conclusion

Interesting differences emerge between the approaches to femininity adopted by the writers whose works are discussed above. While many of them utilize ideas of the fractured self and the *sujet en procès*, they treat them in notably different ways. The attitudes they take to these topics, represent, in fact, a cross-section of the perspectives discernible in contemporary feminist theory. In Barfoot's *Gaining Ground* the release of multiple, heterogeneous identities achieved by the central character is clearly presented as a sign of psychic liberation. In Prager's 'Agoraphobia', in contrast, it is portrayed as an indication of her mental illness and her inability to function socially and intellectually.

Writers differ as to whether or not they present their characters as eluding or challenging phallocratic expectations of feminine behaviour. Further differences are apparent in the writers' attitudes to masculinity. Atwood and Roe, for example, present men and women alike as victims of the pressures of gender codes. Other authors, however, such as Bargate, portray man as the oppressor, and seek to analyse the structures of male-supremacist power. They illustrate the social and economic advantages which men possess and the abuses of authority in which they engage. These differences of outlook depend, to a degree, on whether the writer's view of gender is predominantly 'psychoanalytic' or 'radical feminist'. Psycoanalysis, as I pointed out in the Introduction, highlights the entrenched aspect of gender positions and tends to present both sexes as equally subject to their control. Radical feminism, on the other hand, foregrounding the dialectic of sex, focuses attention on the tension between male dominance and female acts of resistance and rebellion.

I have to admit that, despite the variety of the themes the writers treat, their novels and short stories do reveal certain serious omissions. They omit reference, on the whole, to themes of women's community and feminist collectivity. Even when they do describe acts of resistance to patriarchal power, as is the case in Weldon's novels, they present them as operating on a basis which is totally personal. In *The Life and Loves of a She-Devil* the protagonist's act of rebellion also involves an element of self-mutilation. In fact, far from stressing community and collectivity, many of the writers whose works have been discussed here present the relationship which the central character experiences with other women as one of alienation and even antagonism. She relates to other women at best as confidante, listening to their problems, and at the worst as rival for the favours of a man. This brings me to another limitation which the novels and short stories I have considered in this chapter reveal. This is their strongly heterosexual and, in certain cases, heterosexist bias. Motifs of woman-identification and erotic female relations are, on the whole, absent. This is especially apparent in the final section of the chapter which focuses on images of femininity and the male gaze. What, one wonders, is the effect if a woman controls 'the Look' and eyes another woman with desire or love? Is the relationship inevitably exploitative? Is it one of equality? Or – another possibility – is the scopic economy, as Irigaray suggests, a predominantly masculine one which has little significance to relations between women?[57] These questions, ones which theorists and writers of fiction are now starting to investigate,[58] are not raised in any of the novels and short stories discussed in this chapter.

These limitations of theme, as we shall shortly see, are amply compensated for by the focus on sexual politics in the works of Marilyn French, Marge Piercy and Nancy Toder. These three novelists, along with other writers whose works are explored in the following chapter, prioritize themes of female community, woman-identification and feminist struggle. Their decision to treat these topics, I hasten to point out, far from liberating their texts from narrative flaws and ideological inconsistencies, merely confronts them with a fresh and possibly more difficult set of problems to solve.

To the consideration of these we shall now turn.

Notes

1. *The Sadeian Woman: an exercise in cultural history* (Virago, 1979), p. 6.
2. See Hester Eisenstein, *Contemporary Feminist Thought* (Unwin, 1984), pp. 5-14.
3. See Toril Moi, *Sexual/Texual Politics* (Methuen, 1985).
4. Eisenstein gives a discussion of androgyny, op. cit., pp. 58-68.
5. Rosalind Coward gives a critique of the 'conditioning model' in *Patriarchal Precedents: sexuality and social relations* (Routledge & Kegan Paul, 1983), pp. 262-8. See also Jacqueline Rose, *Sexuality in the Field of Vision* (Verso, 1986), pp. 225-33.
6. Annis Pratt, *Archetypal Patterns in Women's Fiction* (Harvester Press, 1982), p. 29.
7. Carol Pearson and Katherine Pope, *The Female Hero in American and British Literature* (R. R. Bowker, 1981), pp. 16-60.
8. Mary Daly, *Gyn/Ecology: the metaethics of radical feminism* (Women's Press, 1979), pp. 56-7.
9. *The Feminine Mystique* (Gollancz, 1963), p. 66.
10. *Speculum of the Other Woman*, trans. Gillian C. Gill (Cornell University Press, 1985), p. 53.
11. 'Notes from the front line', *On Writing and Gender*, ed. Michelene Wandor (Pandora, 1983), p. 71.
12. '"Phallomorphic power" and the psychology of "woman"', *Ideology and Consciousness*, 4 (1978), pp. 4-36.
13. Moi, op. cit., pp. 150-73.
14. Daly, op. cit., pp. 67-8, 71-2; Janice Raymond, *The Transsexual Empire* (Women's Press, 1980).
15. Barbara Burris, 'The fourth world manifesto', *Radical Feminism*, ed. Anne Koedt et al. (Quadrangle Books, 1973), p. 355.
16. Jean Baker Miller, *Toward a New Psychology of Women* (Penguin, 1978).
17. Adrienne Rich, *Of Woman Born: motherhood as experience and institution* (Virago, 1977); Daly, op. cit.
18. *Speculum*, ed. cit., p. 225.
19. Op. cit. (Fontana, 1979), p. 61.
20. Op. cit. (Women's Press, 1980), p. 58. Subsequent references are to this edition and are in the text.
21. *Ce Sexe qui n'en est pas un* (Minuit, 1977), p. 131, quoted by Stephen Heath in 'Joan Riviere and the masquerade', *Formations of Fantasy*, ed. Victor Burgin et al. (Methuen, 1986), p. 54.
22. 'Sorties', trans. in Elaine Marks and Isabelle de Courtivron (eds), *New French Feminisms* (Harvester Press, 1981), p. 97.
23. 'Women alone', *Sex and Love: new thoughts on old contradictions*, ed. Sue Cartledge and Joanna Ryan (Women's Press, 1983), p. 164.
24. 'Raymond's run', *Gorilla, My Love* (Women's Press, 1984), p. 27. Subsequent references are to this edition and are in the text.
25. 'Is female to male as nature is to culture?' *Woman, Culture and Society*, ed. Michelle Zimbalist Rosaldo and Louise Lamphere (Stanford University Press, 1974), pp. 67-87.

26. Baker Miller, op. cit.; and Griffin, *Pornography and Silence: culture's revenge against nature* (Harper and Row, 1981).
27. *Speculum*, ed. cit., p. 224.
28. Sandra Gilbert and Susan Gubar, *The Madwoman in the Attic: the woman writer and the nineteenth-century literary imagination* (Yale University Press, 1979).
29. Op. cit. (Women's Press, 1983), p. 98. Subsequent references are to this edition and are in the text.
30. 'Polarities', *Dancing Girls and Other Stories* (Virago, 1984), p. 56. Subsequent references are to this edition and are in the text.
31. *Speculum*, ed. cit., pp. 162, 224.
32. 'The way of all flesh', *The Guardian* (21 June 1983), p. 8.
33. *Womansize: the tyranny of slenderness* (Women's Press, 1983), p.65.
34. Op. cit. (Harvester Press, 1982), p. 115.
35. 'Agoraphobia', *A Visit From the Footbinder* (Chatto and Windus, 1983), p. 113. Subsequent references are to this edition and are in the text.
36. *The Golden Cage: the enigma of anorexia nervosa* (Open Books, 1978), p. 55.
37. Relevant to this is Irigaray's comment: 'The speculum may, quite simply, be an instrument to dilate the lips, the orifices, the walls of the vagina so that the eye can penetrate the *interior*. ... Woman, having been misinterpreted, forgotten ... would now become the *object* to be investigated' (*Speculum*, ed. cit., pp. 144-5).
38. Rosalind Coward, *Female Desire: women's sexuality today* (Paladin, 1984), p. 41. See also Susie Orbach, *Fat is a Feminist Issue* (Hamlyn 1984), pp. 96-9.
39. Op. cit., p. 18.
40. *Lady Oracle* (Virago, 1982), p. 49.
41. 'Dreaming the sky down', *The Threshing Floor* (Sheba, 1986), p. 6.
42. Op. cit., p. 168.
43. Op. cit., p. 191.
44. *The Fat Woman's Joke* (Coronet, 1982), p. 105. Subsequent references are to this edition and are in the text.
45. See Rosalind Brunt, '"An immense verbosity": permissive sexual advice in the 1970s', *Feminism, Culture and Politics*, ed. Rosalind Brunt and Caroline Rowan (Lawrence and Wishart, 1982), pp. 143-70.
46. dusty rhodes and Sandra McNeill (eds), *Women Against Violence Against Women* (Onlywomen Press, 1985), p. 255.
47. *The Life and Loves of a She-Devil* (Coronet, 1984), p. 203. Weldon gives a devastating exposé of male manipulation and control of the female body in her short story 'And Then Turn Out the Light', Polaris (Coronet, 1978), pp. 107-17.
48. *Radical Feminism*, ed. cit., pp. 50-9.
49. Patricia Craig, *Times Literary Supplement*, 4, 216 (20 January 1984), p. 76.
50. *Female Desire*, ed. cit., p. 76.
51. Mulvey, 'Visual pleasure and narrative cinema', *Screen*, 16, no. 3 (1975), pp. 6-18; 'Feminism, film and the avant-garde', *Framework*, no. 10 (1979), pp. 3-10.
52. 'The Joy of Marriage', *The Evolution of Darkness and Other Stories* (Brilliance Books, 1984), p. 25. Subsequent references are to this edition and are in the text.
53. *Estella, Her Expectations* (Harvester Press, 1982), p. 14. Subsequent references are to this edition and are in the text.
54. 'Is the gaze male?', *Desire: the politics of sexuality*, ed. Ann Snitow et al.

(Virago, 1984), pp. 321-38.
55. See Carter's fiction, and her discussion of fashion in *Nothing Sacred* (Virago, 1982); and Elizabeth Wilson, *Adorned in Dreams: fashion and modernity* (Virago, 1985).
56. 'Oscillation between power and denial', *New French Feminisms*, ed. cit., p. 166.
57. *This Sex Which is Not One*, trans. Catherine Porter with Carolyn Burke (Cornell University Press, 1985), pp. 23-33.
58. See Linda Williams, 'When the woman looks', *Re-Vision: essays in feminist film criticism*, ed. Mary Ann Doane et al. (American Film Institute, 1984), pp. 83-99; and Sara Maitland's short story 'The Loveliness of the Long-distance Runner', *Mae West is Dead: recent lesbian and gay fiction*, ed. Adam Mars-Jones (Faber, 1983), pp. 217-26.

Chapter Three

Sexual Politics:
The Personal is Political

Indeed, one of the greatest achievements of the women's movement so far has been to challenge the division between public and private life imposed by bourgeois society, and to show that personal relationships are social and political.

Red Collective, *The Politics of Sexuality in Capitalism*, p.11

Sexual relations between men and women always render explicit the nature of social relations in the society in which they take place and, if described explicitly, will form a critique of those relations ...

Angela Carter, *The Sadeian Woman*, p. 20

Introduction: The politicization of personal life

Writing in the early 1970s in *The Fiction of Sex* the critic Rosalind Miles expressed disapproval at what she called 'the sheer parochialism' of novels by women. Confusing 'women's liberation' with 'sex equality', she complained that writers focus too much attention on sexuality and sexual relationships while ignoring the situation of women in paid work. She looked forward to the time in the near future when they would 'learn to avoid the specifically female' and 'widen their field of vision and experience' by rejecting 'a narrow concentration upon the minutiae of women's lives, the emphasis on domestic difficulties and sexual sorrows'.[1]

Miles's predictions make ironic reading today since, in actual fact, none of them has proved correct. As I indicated in Chapter 1, the reverse has occurred. Novels which treat the situation of women in paid work are relatively rare while themes relating to 'specifically female' areas of experience such as motherhood, woman-identified relationships and women's community are in fashion. The reason for this development is that, with the rebirth of feminism in the late 1960s, the 'private' domestic area which Miles disparages has received re-evaluation. No longer can it be dismissed as 'parochial'. The division between the 'private' and 'public' realms has been challenged and to a degree eroded by the feminist focus on sexual politics and the perception, integral to it, that 'the personal is political'. Both concepts require some explication before we consider their relevance to women's fiction. Eisenstein in her study of contemporary feminist thought defines sexual politics as 'the system of interpersonal power by means of which individual men dominated individual women'.[2] The theory gained currency in the political struggle centring on personal life waged by the American New Left in the 1960s. It is, of course, central to the writing of early feminists such as Kate Millett and Shulamith Firestone. The concept that 'the personal is political', often used as a feminist slogan, carries several different meanings. One of the most important, as Heidi Hartmann explains, is that woman's supposedly 'personal' problems, rather than reflecting her own inadequacy, stem from a collective oppression originating in the imbalance of power between the sexes. Observing that 'the great thrust of radical feminist writing has been directed to the documentation of the slogan *the personal is political*', Hartmann writes:

> Women's discontent, radical feminists argued, is not the neurotic lament of the maladjusted, but a response to a social structure in which women are systematically dominated, exploited and oppressed.... *The personal is political* means for radical feminists, that the original and basic class division is between the sexes, and that the motive force of history is the striving of men for power and domination over women, the dialectic of sex.[3]

Hartmann cites a number of different areas where male domination operates – the family, sexual relations, the labour market, the media, the medical profession and clinical psychology. These provide in some cases the context for the novels and short stories discussed in this chapter. They are regarded, of course, by radical feminists as sites of feminist struggle. It is, in fact, this conviction which gives radical feminism its 'radical' force. The intense and sometimes painful analysis of personal experience which took place in the consciousness-raising groups in the early 1970s was neither academic nor primarily therapeutic in aim; it was intended, to quote Mica Nava, 'to raise political consciousness so that people would act to change their lives'.[4] In keeping with this emphasis, many of the works of fiction discussed in this chapter treat themes which are overtly political, illustrating women's struggles to transform their lives and resist male power.

The topics I have chosen to organize my discussion of texts are ones of major importance. The first, sexual relations as the site of feminist struggle, is the area which theorists such as Kate Millett and Anne Koedt took for their analysis of sexual politics in the early years of the Women's Movement. It presents writers of fiction with certain problems and pitfalls. Sexuality and sexual relations, as Frankie Rickford states, are extremely difficult to write about successfully – especially for feminists. Addressing fellow authors, she humorously points out: 'You have to pick your way through a theoretical minefield, avoiding both voluntarism and determinism without being trapped by liberalism.'[5] The problems which writers of fiction encounter in treating aspects of sexual politics vary considerably. They are structural and stylistic, as well as ideological.

The concept that 'the personal is political' and assumptions about the politicization of private life which it implies, do not, of course, go unchallenged. Socialist feminists have been critical of their validity and political efficacy from the early 1970s.[6] Another topic I have thus decided to explore, one especially relevant to the present decade when these critiques have gained momentum, is the interrogation and debates these ideas have provoked among feminists. Some of the questions which women ask hinge on the theme of voluntarism and its limitations.[7] Are relations with men invariably oppressive, or are men capable of reconstructing their sexuality along non-macho lines? To what degree are we able to modify and transform our personal lives and living structures to conform to feminist principles? If we do succeed, what will be the practical result? Will it alter, to any noticeable extent, the imbalance of power between the sexes in the public sector of the labour market and the economy? Disputes about class and about the implications of Feminist Therapy and the Women's Peace Movement have promoted other questions. These issues are controversial and, to make space for their discussion, a new type of fiction has recently emerged: 'fiction of debate'. The writer, engaging in polemics and articulating contrary points of view, encourages the reader to weigh up the merits and demerits of the case and formulate her own response.

Writers themselves bear witness to the liberating effect which the re-evaluation of the domestic and sexual areas to which women have traditionally been relegated has had on their creative energies and ability to write. The black American writer Grace Paley recalls how prior to the Women's Movement women tended to regard such areas as too trivial to merit representation in fiction:

> I didn't really think I was shit, but I really thought my life as a woman was shit. Who could be interested in this crap? I was interested in it, but I didn't have enough social ego to put it down.... Women who have thought their lives were boring have found they're interesting to one another.[8]

Now, however, as the theorist Chernin remarks, 'our sense of what is important and worthy of understanding is enlarged and seriously transformed.' Areas of life previously regarded as purely 'personal' in import, such as sexual relations, marriage, childcare and domestic violence, 'come increasingly to be examined for the larger meaning in our culture's treatment of women.'[9] Unlike the works of fiction considered in the previous chapter, many of which are written in an anti-realist mode and focus on the fractured self, the majority discussed here are examples of so-called realism. However, as I argued previously, since their interest is primarily ideological and polemical, a more suitable term for them is 'fiction of ideas'. To appreciate and fully understand them, one needs to approach them in the light of the radical and socialist feminist theories which they appropriate and re-work. Indicative of this is the way that the comments voiced by theorists clarify and illuminate the narrative strategies which the writers utilize. Millett in her influential work *Sexual Politics* describes coitus as representing 'a charged microcosm of the variety of attitudes and values to which culture subscribes'.[10] Writers of fiction, adopting a similar perspective, take a microcosmic unit of society (one particular sexual relationship, one particular family) and use it as a spy-hole into a wide network of social, cultural and political structures. Nancy Hartsock, commenting on the workings of a consciousness-raising group, explains, 'we drew connections between personal experiences and political generalities about the oppression of women: we took up our experience and transformed it through reflection.'[11] Writers of fiction make connections between similar areas of life. The linking of the personal and the political, practice and theory, as well as being a tenet of radical feminist thought,[12] is also a significant facet of the creative writer's craft. The source of inspiration which radical feminist ideas provide for writers on the level of both content and narrative-strategy will become apparent in the following pages.

Sexual relations as the site of feminist struggle

A crucial problem facing authors who seek to treat in fictional form ideas relating to sexual politics, especially those writing in the early years of the Women's Movement, is how to convey to the uninformed reader their meaning and implications. The novels of Marilyn French, Marge Piercy, Nancy Toder and Gillian Hanscombe, which constitute the focus of discussion in this section, reveal the urgency of this problem. The four authors, though writing for a predominantly female audience, are not addressing a specifically feminist one. They cannot rely on the average woman reader being familiar with details of feminist theory. They adopt, as we shall see, a variety of different strategies to clarify and explain them.

French, in her feminist version of the popular genre of the romance, *The Bleeding Heart* (1980), utilizes a characteristically direct but somewhat unsubtle method. Determined that the reader shall have no excuse for failing to understand the ideas of the dialectic of sex and 'the personal is political' around which her text revolves, she gives her pair of lovers, Victor and Dolores, a dialogue focusing specifically on their discussion. The position which the two figures occupy in this dialogue (and a very tempestuous one it is!) are not the stereotypical ones of 'victor' and 'suffering victim' which the heavy symbolism of their names leads us to expect. As in other episodes of the novel, an element of role-reversal occurs. Dolores is an independent career woman who teaches at Emmings College, Boston. She possesses a knowledge of feminist theory which Victor, a mere male executive with typically chauvinistic attitudes, lacks. This gives her the edge of power – in intellectual, verbal terms at least – over him. The dialogue opens, in fact, with her occupying the dominant role of teacher, lecturing him on the imbalance of power between the sexes, while he is relegated to the subordinate roles of pupil and stooge. The insensitive rejoinders he makes to her comments are clearly intended to exemplify male ignorance about sexual politics and the politicization of personal life. He rudely accuses her, 'You see male domination everywhere', and, claiming that 'what people do in the privacy of their own home is their business', criticizes her for confusing personal and public areas of life. He goes on to remark that, since the domestic realm is a trivial one anyway, it makes an unworthy topic of conversation for an intellectual lady like herself. This feeble attempt at flattery understandably acts as a red rag to a bull. It provokes Dolores to rage, giving her the cue to educate him – and simultaneously, of course, the reader – in the principles of radical feminist theory. Insisting that both personal and public areas are sites of male dominance, she launches into a fierce attack on her lover, one which demonstrates the importance of sexual and domestic spheres:

> It's the fucking future of the world, you dolt! On the relations between men and women rest everything else: the well-being or not of the children, ... the character of the society, the future of the society, the character of the entire culture! It just happens to be, Victor Morrissey, the most profound subject there is!'[13]

Victor is unimpressed by this tirade. He insists that, if women genuinely want equality with men, they should accept the values of capitalist enterprise and compete with them in the professional world of business. Dolores, of course, disagrees. She affirms a commitment to a woman-centred perspective. Her goal, she claims, is to change the world and 'make it a place where women's way of seeing, thinking, feeling, is as valid as men's' (p. 309).

In the episode discussed above, French handles ideas from radical feminist theory somewhat clumsily. She resorts to setting up a teacher/pupil relationship between her two romantic leads. On other occasions, however, she treats them with considerable skill. She incorporates the concept of the dialectic of sex cleverly into the format of the romance she writes, making it the motivating force for the eventual tragic separation of the two lovers. Instead of feuding families, the machinations of jealous rivals or differences of class or religion prising the two apart, it is the contradiction of power and interest between the sexes that does so. French presents this, in accord with radical feminist perspectives, as the central contradiction at the hub of a phallocratic culture. Victor and Dolores do indeed occupy the position of 'star-crossed' lovers – though in a very different manner from the traditional meaning of the term!

Another feature of *The Bleeding Heart* which merits comment is the inconsistency apparent in French's treatment of sexuality. While presenting every other aspect of male/female relations as culturally constructed and the site of a shifting power struggle, she treats heterosexual sexual practice in thoroughly essentialist terms. She presents it to the reader as both 'natural' and unproblematic. Her uncritical acceptance of it is curiously at odds with the radical feminist stance which she adopts in other areas of the text.

French's failure to place heterosexuality in the context of sexual politics and to subject it to any form of critique is amply compensated for by the three novels I shall now discuss. Marge Piercy's *Braided Lives* (1982), Nancy Toder's *Choices* (1980) and Gillian Hanscombe's *Between Friends* (1982) all treat different aspects of the problematization of heterosexuality which is a feature of contemporary feminist thought. In fact, each novel focuses attention on a different stage in this process. The novels are also of interest from the viewpoint of narrative strategy and design. The writers adopt widely different solutions to the problem which, as French's novel illustrates, can prove troublesome. This is, how to explicate and convey to the reader the meaning of ideas of sexual politics without resorting to methods of prosy exposition and instruction.

The concept of the problematization of heterosexuality which forms a thread linking the three novels has its basis in the perception that sexuality and sexual practice, rather than being 'natural', are cultural constructs. To quote Angela Carter's witty analysis:

Our flesh arrives to us out of history, like everything else does. We may believe we fuck stripped of social artifice; in bed, we even feel we touch the bedrock of human nature itself. But we are deceived. Flesh is not an irreducible human universal.[14]

The recognition of the cultural construction of sexuality carries, of course, profound implications for women. It opens our eyes to the control which a male supremacist culture exerts on the sexual aspects of our lives. It enables us to perceive that, in the words of Patricia Duncker, 'there is no natural sexuality and that the codes within which women and men operate are in fact male sexual ideologies masquerading as natural law.'[15] In exploring male dominance in the area of sexuality Piercy, Toder and Hanscombe all take a radical approach. They treat sexual intercourse and the primacy accorded to it in contemporary society as the cornerstone of male supremacy. In this they agree with Millett and other radical feminist theorists whose argument 'describes sexuality, with variations along a continuum of masculine aggression (from the celebration of penetration to the brutality of rape), as the site in which male power and male supremacy are expressed'.[16] The three novelists also make reference to feminist critiques of male-defined theories of sexual pleasure. Anne Koedt's acclaimed essay 'The Myth of the Vaginal Orgasm'[17] is one of the earliest and most influential of these. Koedt points out that since knowledge (sexual knowledge in particular) is controlled by men, it is they who define and describe female sexual response. The consequence is, emphasis is placed on vaginal penetration while the importance of clitoral sex is marginalized or even ignored. A male-supremacist culture, Koedt points out, finds the idea of clitoral sex extremely threatening since it enables women to be sexually independent of men.

Piercy's *Braided Lives* is set in the mid-1950s at the start of the 'Sexual Revolution'. Focusing on the experience of Jill and her cousin Donna, two undergraduates at an American university, she investigates the contradictions in the feminine position in this era. Jill and Donna become trapped unawares between the conflicting discourses of the new cult of 'permissive sexuality' which foregrounds the coital imperative, and the puritanical sexual discourse of the older generation. The latter prohibits access to contraception and abortion, expecting a girl to remain a virgin until she marries.

The strategies which Piercy uses to signal to the reader the connections between 'personal' and 'political' areas of life are considerably more subtle than the ones adopted by French. Piercy avoids giving prosy expositions of radical feminist ideas. Instead she plants signs in the text, relying on the reader (envisaged as female with some knowledge of feminism) to interpret them correctly. Here, her use of a 'framing device' plays a vital function. The main body of the novel, set in the 1950s, is framed by episodes set in the post-feminist 1970s.

The latter give us a feminist perspective from which to interpret the events which occur earlier. The concluding episodes of the novel make overt reference to feminist ideas of collectivity and sisterhood. When Donna suffers a tragic and untimely death from an illegal abortion, Jill transmutes the grief and anger she feels to political ends, and with the assistance of friends she sets up a feminist help-line and abortion service for women in a similar predicament to Donna's. Jill's response to Donna's death is significant to the novel's ideological design. It illustrates how, with the advent of the Women's Movement, women began to recognize the political import of sexual relations and, transcending the limitations of subjectivism, formulated a theory of collective oppression. Uniting in feminist struggle, they strove to challenge male control of sexuality.

The narrative strategies described above are underpinned by another method Piercy uses to stress the links between 'personal' and 'political' dimensions. This is her relentless accumulation of episodes illustrating male exploitation and brutalization of women. Knowledge (especially sexual knowledge) is shown to be a construct reflecting male control. Male-defined criteria of literature operate in the college where Jill and Donna study. Thus, Jill's male tutor dismisses the poems she writes as mere 'personal outcries' since they treat topics taken from the devalued realm of female experience and woman-identification. Sexual discourse and practice emerge as similarly male-defined. Among the college students a hierarchy of sexual practices operates with, to quote Rickford, 'sexual intercourse, supposedly the king of the erotic castle'.[18] Clitoral sex is disapproved of; a woman's desire for it is interpreted as proof that she is 'sexually immature', 'not a real woman'.[19] Piercy successfully demystifies sexual intercourse by revealing it to mean different things to different people, depending on their sex and access to power. To the male characters it signifies not only pleasure but, in accord with radical feminist views, a means to control women and recruit them into their service. It functions also as proof of manhood – something to brag about to one's buddies in the dorm. For the female characters, on the other hand, intercourse is associated with romantic love and self-sacrifice. It signifies the ultimate act of self-surrender – one undertaken at great personal risk, since contraception, if you are unmarried, is difficult to obtain. It also carries risk of male violence, as illustrated by the occasion when Donna is raped by a student she dates. In treating this event, Piercy again takes a radical feminist approach. She challenges the line of demarcation between conventional intercourse to which a woman consents and sexual molestation or rape. In a society in which men dominate women the concept of 'consent' is shown to have little or no meaning. The hetero dating system, around which college life revolves, to quote

Andrea Dworkin, 'sets up every woman as a potential rape victim'.[20] Piercy also exposes the hypocrisy of male attitudes to sex. Jill's college friend Theo describes how her analyst took advantage of her sexually. He justified the act on the grounds that it would help cure her of her 'sexual problems' (lesbian tendencies). However, while emphasizing male exploitation, Piercy takes pains not to present masculinity in an essentialist light. Josh, the man with whom Jill eventually sets up home, treats her as an equal, accepting her desire for independence.

Although most of the narrative strategies which Piercy employs are highly successful, a few emerge as awkward and predictable. Her handling of the commonplace device of structuring the novel around a pair of female figures with contrasting personalities is an unfortunate example of the latter. Jill and Donna remain rigidly fixed in the stereotypical roles of 'independent strong woman' and 'self-destructive narcissist'. No element of role-reversal or play of shifting identities is introduced to enliven their polarized positions and attitudes.

Whereas Piercy focuses primarily on the politics of coitus, exposing woman's vulnerability to sexual exploitation in the pre-feminist era of the 1950s, Toder and Hanscombe treat a subsequent stage in the process of the feminist problematization of heterosexuality. They investigate the politics of the clitoris. As well as highlighting the challenge which the lesbian feminist identity and way of life pose to a phallocratic culture, they elucidate connections between lesbianism and feminism. Both their novels constitute examples of 'lesbian feminist fiction'. The category is, of course, an imprecise and problematic one. Does it denote fiction written *by* lesbians, *about* lesbians, *for* lesbians — or all three?[21] Another feature which makes it difficult to define is that writers are increasingly choosing to bring together lesbian and hetero protagonists within the frame of a single text. Hanscombe's novel, as we shall see, illustrates this particular trend.

One reason why Toder's *Choices* merits inclusion in this study is that it draws on an unusually wide range of lesbian feminist theory. Accounts of the marginalization and erasure of clitoral sex, formulated by theorists such as Koedt and Gayatri Chakravorty Spivak, form the ideological basis of the novel. Spivak develops the philosophical and semiotic aspects of Koedt's initial analysis. Describing the clitoris as a signifier of female sexuality, she presents its erasure, either literally by means of clitorectomy or symbolically by banishing it from sexual discourse, as a key symbol of women's oppression. The erasure of the clitoris, she argues, represents an attempt by a phallocratic culture to excise the significance of female sexuality as non-reproductive, autonomous pleasure.[22] Theories arguing the links between lesbianism and feminism produced by Adrienne Rich and Charlotte Bunch are also relevant to Toder's novel. Rich enumerates the various different forces – social, sexual and economic – which recruit and coerce women into hetero relations. She also discusses the political value of woman-identified relationships and acts of marriage resistance.[23] Bunch illustrates the value of lesbian feminist politics to the Women's Movement as a whole. She demonstrates that it gives 'a political critique of the institution and the ideology of heterosexuality as a cornerstone of male supremacy'.[24] This, she points out, is useful to all women, whatever sexual identification they adopt.

The strategy Toder uses to embody these ideas is the strikingly simple one of question and reply. The first half of her novel raises a question which the second half effectively answers. The first half, set in the pre-feminist era of the early 1960s, focuses on the friendship and sexual relationship which develops between Sandy and Jenny in their college days. Their involvement is beset with difficulties from the start. The heterosexist climate of college life, which erases knowledge of clitoral sex and lesbianism, initially blinds the two to the fact that women are capable of relating sexually to one another. Then, when eventually they do embark on an affair, the stigma attached to lesbianism and the need for secrecy it promotes, have a predictably disruptive effect. Jenny feels especially isolated. In order to prove she is a 'real woman' and to enjoy a social life, she starts to date boys. She leaves the anguished Sandy trapped in a contradiction which, since she is ignorant of feminist analyses of sexual politics, she lacks the tools to solve. Though convinced that her relationship with Jenny is vitally important to them both, she none the less perceives that it has disintegrated. All she can do is ask herself miserably, 'Why does it have to be like this?' This, as Toder observes emphasizing its significance, is a 'question which neither of them understood, nor would understand for many years'.[25]

The second half of the novel answers Sandy's question by giving a critique of male control of sexual knowledge. Years have elapsed and Jenny is now married. Sandy, in contrast, has refused to marry and, with the advent of the Women's Movement, identifies herself as lesbian feminist. She works as a clinical psychologist and, on being given the opportunity to speak at a national conference, chooses as her topic the problems encountered by gay teenagers. In the dicussion following her presentation, she addresses the topic of the non-objective nature of scientific discourse, citing as an example the labelling of homosexuality as deviant and the erasure of the clitoris from sexual discourse in the 1950s and 1960s. Now, however, as she tells her audience, women are challenging these ideas and starting to define their sexuality for themselves. Certain other episodes in the novel also foreground the connection between the coital imperative and women's oppression. These substantiate practically the theoretical points which Sandy makes in her conference paper. The design of Toder's novel, with its dialectic of question and answer, is on the whole very successful. However, she does encounter problems of a narrative kind. The device of encapsulating an explication of the politics of the clitoris into Sandy's conference presentation is a clumsy one. It results in passages of undiluted polemic which bore the reader. And the contrast Toder draws between Sandy (the brave, politically right-on lesbian) and Jenny (the vacillating bisexual easily recruited into hetero relations) emerges as schematized and biased. Like Jill, the hero of Piercy's *Braided Lives*, Sandy belongs to the 'role-model' tradition of women's fiction.[26] Her attributes of courage and leadership make her something of a 'lesbian superwoman'. An idealized portrayal of lesbianism, as Elizabeth Wilson observes,[27] is a common fault in works of fiction treating its political significance. The novel does reflect, in fact, a pronounced element of lesbian chauvinism. In portraying the two figures, Toder treats the lesbian position as morally superior, while failing to recognize the reality of the bisexual's. Like many feminist writers, she makes the mistake of dismissing bisexuality as a cop-out, presenting it as a form of 'failed lesbianism'.

The representation of lesbianism as an ideologically superior position, discernible in Toder's *Choices*, is certainly not a feature of Hanscombe's *Between Friends*. On the contrary, adopting a line of argument similar to that of the theorist Beatrix Campbell,[28] she seeks to challenge lesbian chauvinism and separatist extremism. Like Campbell, she aims to heal the rifts between hetero and lesbian feminists brought about by the Politicial Lesbian Movement,[29] by encouraging the two groups to explore and build on the common political ground they share.

In order to achieve this, Hanscombe takes as her focus a group of four women, two of whom are lesbian and two hetero. She compares their different attitudes to the politics of vaginal penetration, the motif around which the narrative revolves. The first half of the novel gives a theoretical analysis of the topic. Interestingly it is not Meg, the lesbian central character, but Amy her friend, who identifies as hetero and lives with a man, whom Hanscombe chooses to articulate the oppressive effects of the coital imperative. Amy writes in a letter to Meg:

> About vaginal penetration: quite simply we should think about giving it up. Not participate in this act. Unless we are *deliberately* planning to become pregnant. In this way we can isolate the actual meaning of vaginal intercourse, which is reproduction.... When men want or-

gasms, there is plenty of other ways they can have them. Penetrating a woman represents the invasion of her body-space and her psychological space as well, just as penetrating *anything* represents invasion.[30] In keeping with these sentiments, Amy insists on a relationship of equality with her boyfriend Tim. She refuses to marry him, be financially dependent or engage in penetrative sex. Far from being apologetic about living with him, however, she regards the relationship as politically valid. She believes that, since men form half the population, it is vital that feminists try to educate them and find ways of coexisting with them which are non-oppressive. She criticizes the Political Lesbian Movement and its advocacy of total separatism as bigoted and impractical.

The two other female figures in the novel, Jane and Frances, take polarized positions as regards to men and penetrative sex. Jane supports the Political Lesbian Movement. At the start of the novel she is committed to separatism, even criticizing Meg for bringing up a son. Frances, on the contrary, is hetero and cannot be described as feminist. She uncritically accepts male domination, allowing her macho lover Jim to exploit and bully her.

In the second half of the novel the oppressive effects of the coital imperative, up to now a matter of theoretical debate, suddenly become horrifyingly real. Meg is sexually molested by Jim, Frances's egotistical boyfriend. The event functions as a catalyst. It forces the four women to clarify and articulate their attitudes about men, male violence and female friendship. To Meg's distress, Frances refuses to credit her account of the rape – and an inevitable rift occurs between the two. Jane and Amy, on the other hand, both behave extremely supportively. The novel concludes with a shift from the personal to the public realm. Meg and Amy plan to bring together lesbian and hetero feminists by organizing a campaign focusing on marriage resistance.

An interesting feature of *Between Friends*, one which certainly merits reference, is that it is an epistolary novel. Hanscombe's choice of the traditional format of an exchange of letters to investigate contemporary feminist debates about sexuality strikes one, on first consideration, as inappropriate and bizarre. In fact, the format suits her polemical purposes admirably. Her use of it reveals interesting links with seventeenth- and eighteenth-century contributions to the genre. The exploration of personal consciousness and intense preoccupation with niceties or moral conduct which, as Ruth Perry points out in her study,[31] are experienced by the female characters of the epistolary fiction of earlier periods, are effectively transferred by Hanscombe to an analysis of moral attitudes and an equally intense discussion of sexual politics on the part of present-day feminists. The concluding episodes of the novel centring on Meg's rape also reveal

affinities with the fiction of earlier eras. As Perry points out, epistolary fiction in the past often hinges on an act of sexual violence committed against the person of the heroine. It is this, Perry suggests,
which provides the characters with the motive for an exchange of
letters since 'it produces the anguished consciousness that needs the
release of writing letters'.[32] The situation in Hanscombe's novel is
very similar. The event of Meg's rape and the dilemma it places her
in *vis-à-vis* her friendship with Frances, prompt her and her friends
to communicate their responses and offers of support in letters.

Despite the serious nature of the topic she treats, Hanscombe
weaves into the novel a refreshing strand of wit and humour. She
plays amusingly with the contradictions and irrationalities of desire.
Meg the non-separatist lesbian and Jane the dogmatic separatist,
though disagreeing on Political Lesbianism, the raising of sons and
almost every other ideological issue, find to their astonishment that
they are sexually attracted. By the end of the novel they are involved
in a passionate relationship – and are even making plans to live
together.

As well as exploring the different ideological positions open to
women, Hanscombe also examines – though in less detail – some of
the stances available to men. Tim, Amy's lover, succeeds in reconstructing his attitudes to conform with principles of sex equality. In
this, he forms a striking contrast to Jim, Frances's bully of a boyfriend

As a postscript to the novels discussed above, it is worth pointing
out that certain facets of the political project championed by the
writers and the theorists whose ideas they appropriate have been
achieved – to a degree, at least. In the Women's Movement the oppressive effects of the coital imperative are perceived and (despite
the occasional scapegoating of lesbians) the connections between
lesbianism and feminism recognized. Other facets, however, have
been markedly less successful. The proposal, presented by Campbell
in theoretical terms and Hanscombe in fictional form, that hetero and
lesbian feminists unite to challenge the primacy of penetrative sex
and affirm 'a positive commitment to female eroticism'[33] has received little support. As Elizabeth Wilson points out in her critique,
'the statement is utopian' because it fails to take into account the
psychological complexities of the construction of sexual desire and
'ignores the actual homophobia of existing society, or at least evades
the political consequences of the actual persecution of homosexuals'.[34] Lesbianism may be the preferred form of sexuality in some
feminist circles but it is certainly not so in society at large. Hetero and
lesbian feminists do frequently succeed in burying their differences
and working together on common projects (the Peace Movement,

Women's Centres, and Women's Studies courses are examples) but their positions in the public world cannot be described as equal. In the labour market and in custody cases lesbians suffer discrimination and penalization. The lesbian identity is caricatured or erased by the popular media. TV soap operas, one notes, while introducing the token male homosexual, invariably portray all female protagonists as hetero. These factors, combined with the failure of hetero feminists to define for themselves any form of collective sexual politics, help to explain why Campbell's and Hanscombe's recommendations have tended to fall on deaf ears.

Attempts to reclaim heterosexuality and bisexuality for feminism

As is evident from the novels discussed in the previous section, sexuality and sexual practice are controversial issues in the Women's Movement. On the one hand, socialist feminists point sympathetically to the 'sense of grievance ... among heterosexual feminists who've felt outcast – they're the Fifth Form Remove, the bad girls who smoke in the changing room and go with men.'[35] They attribute the failure of heterosexual women to assert their presence in the Movement – very unfairly in my opinion – to what they dismissively call 'the hegemony of radical feminist rhetoric'. On the other hand, radical feminists draw attention to the contradictions which relations with men involve for feminists. They also argue that, since heterosexual women are in the majority and enjoy the endorsement of society as a whole, they have no reason to seek sympathy. They have only themselves to blame for failing to articulate a sexual politics – and have no right to hold radical feminists responsible.

Yet, despite the failure of heterosexual feminists to work out a sexual politics on a collective basis, many women, as Angela Hamblin points out in her essay 'Is a feminist heterosexuality possible?', have of course made a personal attempt to transform their relationships with men. Commenting on the difficulties of this project, Hamblin points out that 'feminists in heterosexual relationships have to grapple with male definitions, male assumptions and male power in one of the most intimate areas of our lives, involving some of our deepest feelings.'[36]

Writers who treat in fictional form the kind of issues Hamblin discusses are relatively rare. One is Michèle Roberts, whose novel *The Visitation* (1983) has been described as undertaking the project of 'reclaiming heterosexuality' for feminism.[37] In exploring the different attachments which her hero Helen, a convent-educated Londoner from a middle-class home, forms with men and women, Roberts seeks to balance the claims of heterosexuality versus female friendship.[38] Roberts takes a predominantly psychoanalytic approach to sexuality and gender. Focusing on the motif of the fractured self, she incorporates into the text ideas of the androgynous subject appropriated from Jung. Unfortunately, however, as the critic Duncker comments, the novel, while containing vividly impressionistic depictions of personal experience, reveals too weak a grasp of sexual politics for Roberts's projects quite to succeed. Her portrayal of Helen and her twin brother Felix as victims of restrictive gender codes in the early stages of the novel is sensitive and convincing. However, as is often the case with writers who take a psychoanalytic aproach to gender, she never directly confronts the question of male privilege and power. Her relatively uncritical attitude to the coital imperative and her weak grasp of sexual politics are especially apparent in the latter stages of the work where Helen attempts to form relationships with men while simultaneously establishing herself as a creative writer. And, as some of the university students with whom I have discussed the novel complain, the male characters emerge, on the whole, as unmemorable. They are a group of indistinguishable stereotypes. This is a serious fault in a text that aims to reappraise heterosexual relations.

Another aspect of Roberts's novel which is worth commenting on is the marked contrast it presents to the novels of Piercy, Toder and Hanscombe discussed above. The contrast between the two kinds of fiction illustrates very clearly the rift between mainstream critical approaches and radical feminist ones. *The Visitation* is a text which is thoroughly acceptable to the dominant, university-based tradition of literary criticism. Roberts's skilful manipulation of the device of intertextuality (illustrated by her re-working of motifs from myth and fairy-tale), her use of discontinuous narrative to create an interplay between past and present, and her sympathetic analysis of heterosexual relations in the light of Lacanian and Jungian ideas, are all features of the novel likely to please academic critics. The texts of Piercy, Toder and Hanscombe, on the contrary, are obviously less acceptable. The writers' critique of the oppressive effects of the coital imperative, along with their affirmative representation of woman-identified and lesbian relationships, are unlikely to appeal to the average academic. Their use of an apparently 'realist mode' (I say 'apparently' because their chief interest lies in discussing ideas not in constructing images of life) and the focus they place on the social and political value of a stable, 'unified' identity, lead their novels to be dismissed as 'transparent'. This simplistic and, in my view, faulty judgement is, of course, understandable given the male-dominated composition of the majority of departments of English Studies in colleges and universities. Only when there is a larger proportion of women teaching-staff in them – not just women, but women with feminist and lesbian feminist perspectives – will texts of this kind receive a fair hearing. As my analysis of them indicates, they do provide, in fact, plenty of scope for critical analysis. The writers' handling of ideas from feminist theory, and the narrative strategies and transactions with the reader in which it results, are both daring and inventive.

Another topic related to sexual politics which feminists have tended to ignore or treat dismissively is bisexuality. Commenting on the problematic situation of the bisexual in contemporary society, Deborah Gregory writes:

> There are many more feminists than ever I suppose who identify privately as bisexual. Few of them seem pleased about it. Many feel they are bisexual by default, as they seem to be neither lesbian nor heterosexual. Many fear their feelings for particular male lovers are a contradiction of their emotional and political commitment to women.[39]

Issues of the kind raised above are investigated by Aileen La Tourette in her story 'Passing' (Mae West is Dead, 1983). The story is a model of eloquence and brevity - only four pages long, in fact! While exploring the situation of the bisexual, La Tourette also confronts a number of important questions about sexuality in general. They are similar to those asked by Rosalind Coward in a theoretical essay. Does the individual possess a single 'true' sexual identity, or does she possess several? Is desire subject to voluntary control? Can she switch from hetero to lesbian involvements at will? Are involvements with men necessarily oppressive? If they are, which particular facet is it that makes them so – the act of intercourse or, to quote Coward, 'the structures of desire and expectations surrounding the sexual act in a culture such as our own?'[40] The psychoanalytic approach on which La Tourette structures her narrative is also similar to Coward's.

The central theme of 'Passing' is the contradictions and unpredictable nature of sexual desire. The nameless female narrator has been engaging secretly in lesbian relations for a number of years. She welcomes the advent of the Women's Movement because it enables her to relate openly to women and express what she sees as her 'true' lesbian identity – only to find, herself, unexpectedly, feeling intensely attracted to a man. The object of her desire, a young foreigner called Marc, reciprocates her feelings, and the two become lovers. La Tourette fully exploits the humour and irony of the situation. The narrator, having spent her pre-feminist years having affairs with women while passing as hetero, now finds herself doing the opposite. She is having an affair with a man while passing to her friends in the Movement as lesbian. Once again, she feels herself to be 'a person without integrity, a sexual double agent, a half-caste'.[41] Forced by her predicament to recognize the limitations of voluntarism, she admits that her attraction to men is much more deep-seated than she had supposed. In a delightfully witty pasage, comparing heterosexuality to an item of clothing, La Tourette examines the flaws in the 'conditioning model' of sexuality accepted by many feminists in the early years of the Movement:

> We called heterosexuality 'conditioning' in our long-ago Consciousness-Raising sessions, minimizing and maximizing it at the same time, so that it became responsible for all our ills and was simultaneously external to us, like an archaic article of lingerie, tight as a second skin but always possible to remove, could you but find the hooks and eyes; but it was actually something far more stubborn, piecemeal and subtle. (p. 178)

The narrator's discovery that she is capable of relating erotically to men as well as women also, of course, challenges the concept of a unitary sexual identity. It reveals the structures of desire to be multiple and heterogeneous.

Another question La Tourette examines in the story is whether relationships with men are invariably oppressive. In considering this, she again takes an unorthodox line. Presenting the narrator and her lover Marc as examples of role-reversal, she cleverly deconstructs the binary opposites man: self, dominant, articulate, and woman: other, dependent, silent. Marc, a foreigner with little English, emerges as emotionally and verbally dependent on the narrator. His gorgeous 'ink-blue eyes', 'long tassel-like fringes of eye-lashes' and alluring French accent make him the stereotypical object of desire. He does not exploit her, she exploits him! The aspect of the relationship the narrator does find oppressive and that leads her, regretfully, to end it is not personal but cultural. She knows that if she stays with Marc she will become trapped in the oppressive hetero roles of wife and mother. It is this that prompts her to leave him and return to her lesbian way of life. She chooses, as she wryly puts it, to play 'the clown', not 'the bride'.

Two 'messages' emerge from this perceptive and amusingly recounted story. First, La Tourette acknowledges the fact that neither the Women's Movement nor mainstream society has a place for the bisexual who acts out in her personal life the contradictory, multiple facets of desire. Both distrust and cold-shoulder her, regarding her as a disruptive influence. Secondly, she grudgingly admits that the lesbian feminist identity and way of life are the best of the unsatisfactory alternatives available to women at present. Though in psychological terms a simplification, they are at any rate preferable to the roles of wife and mother which patriarchal society foists on women. Many of us, of course, agree with this point of view, and choose to identify as lesbian for a similar set of reasons.

Fiction of debate

A distinctive feature of contemporary feminism, one which historians of the Movement emphasize, is the variety of theoretical perspectives which it has produced. This proliferation of theory has been accompanied by, and no doubt helped to accelerate, the fragmentation of the Movement into a number of divergent, and to a degree shifting, ideological positions and tendencies. A sign of this is that the categories 'radical', 'socialist' and 'liberal feminist' initially used in the 1970s, are no longer adequate to define women's disparate, conflicting points of view. Other types of feminism have also emerged. These include cultural feminism, lesbian feminism, political feminism, revolutionary feminism, feminism with a psychoanalytic emphasis, and several other kinds, each possessing its own subdivisions and subcults. Commentators give different reasons to explain the proliferation of theory and the accompanying fragmentation of the Movement. Jo Freeman attributes them largely to the Movement's structureless and decentralized methods of working. The unit of the 'small group', around which the activities of the Movement revolve, is extremely fertile in producing 'debates', 'disputes and ideas'[42] and is effective in carrying out short-term, localized projects. It fails, however, to promote either continuity or 'a sense of direction'. Other theorists, scapegoating lesbians and radical feminists, blame the fragmentation of the Movement on 'opposing attitudes to heterosexuality and to the significance of violence against women'.[43]

The negative effect of the rifts and ideological divisions outlined above are painfully apparent to us all. They result in a wasteful replication of labour and energy, and promote antagonisms between women. More seriously, they have a disabling effect on collective feminist action at a national level, destroying our hopes of a speedy improvement in women's material circumstances. On the positive side, however, they undoubtedly contribute to the intellectual vitality of contemporary feminism, illustrating the capacity it possesses for growth and change. In this respect, they have had a generative influence on fiction and its production. They create a constantly changing pool of ideas for writers to draw on, and also give them the opportunity to intervene in the disputes of the Movement. As I mentioned in Chapter 1, in the Movement's present fragmented, amorphous state, novels and short stories assume a new cultural and social importance. They provide a valuable channel of communication, and create a forum for both airing and debating ideas. The writers whose works are discussed in this section all contribute to this process. They either interrogate and problematize in their fiction issues of interest to feminists or, engaging in full-scale polemic, they debate them.

Valerie Miner's *Movement* (1982) illustrates the former trend. One of Miner's achievements in the novel is to interrogate the radical feminist assumption of an unproblematic correspondence between personal and political areas of experience. The title of the novel signals this to the reader, in the respect that it is applicable to both areas. Susan, the central character, is a journalist and freelance writer. The term 'movement' denotes, at the most obvious level, the trips she makes around the world in pursuit of her career. It also signifies the changes of personal consciousness she experiences – and, on a public level, the political movements of the 1960s and 1970s which influence them. In still more general terms, 'movement' implies life envisaged as a process of flux and change – both for the individual and society as a whole.

Susan is portrayed as a socialist and feminist, and in exploring this aspect of her life Miner deliberately highlights the discrepancies she experiences between practice and theory, the actual and the ideal. Women's community and lesbian relationships, though recognized as providing a temporary source of solace and support, are depicted as unstable and ephemeral. Divisions and hostilities between women, stemming from differences of economic privilege and marital status, are rife. The life of a woman who embarks on the contradictory project of trying to live independently of men in a male-dominated society is revealed to be a constant struggle. Miner's description of the problems Susan encounters on leaving the secure haven of her middle-class marriage to fend for herself, corresponds closely to the analysis of the situation of the unmarried woman articulated by the theorist Barbara Haber. Haber observes that:

> although employment makes possible the economic survival of large numbers of women outside of marriage ... it does not offer solutions to the problem of social isolation, lack of gratifying work, absence of intimacy and sexual closeness, or the threat of male violence.[44]

The various hardships and threats which Haber enumerates are all experienced by Susan at some point or other in her life. In a passage towards the end of the novel Miner allows her forcefully to voice a number of unpalatable truths which feminists generally prefer not to confront. Sitting alone at night in the office of the Rape Crisis Centre,

Susan ponders the contradictions which a commitment to women's liberation involves, and the lack of tangible rewards it brings the individual:

> Where was the sisterhood now? Susan wondered sometimes if feminism was the ultimate in female masochism because there seemed to be nothing beyond the struggle. She had been retained as a good fighter, a prolific petitioner. Now, brittle with fatigue, she contemplated how she gave her loneliness to group consciousness, her anger to organized protest, her oppression to revolutionary retribution. So what if she were free from sexist family, teachers, husband, boss, critics? What was salvation if there was no afterlife?[45]

Despite the frustrations and disappointments expressed here, the novel does not have a depressing effect. Miner's stance is, on the whole, positive. She celebrates Susan as a survivor.

A striking feature of the text, one which is very relevant to this study of the interrelation between narrative practice and feminist theory in women's fiction, is the strategy Miner adopts to foreground the connections between personal and political areas of experience. Interspersed with events from Susan's personal life are other episodes which, relating to the main story-line on a purely thematic basis, explore the experiences of a number of other peripheral female figures. The reader thus has the impression of a collage of women's day-to-day activities, linked by the unifying thread of sexual politics.

Writers who debate the controversial issues which perplex and divide feminists at the present time, experiment with a variety of different strategies. One of the simplest and most obvious is the structuring of the narrative around a pair of female figures, each of whom represents and argues on behalf of an alternative point of view. Miner's fiction also provides us with an example of this device. The issue at stake in her novel *Blood Sisters* (1981) is the conflicting attitudes of Irish women to the struggle for national liberation – and the vexed question, should they adopt a separatist or a non-separatist position? Focusing on the relations between the two Irish cousins Beth and Liz, Miner explores the contrary choices they make. Beth, regarding matters of race as taking precedence over those of gender, decides to take an activist stance and work with men in the Provisional Wing of the IRA. Liz distrusts male-defined structures and rejects violence; she joins a radical feminist, separatist group. Interweaving events from the lives of the two women, Miner succeeds in giving a critique of both their positions. The politics of the IRA, as well as being condemned as brutal, are indicted for making no concession to women's needs and interests. However, nor does the politics of the radical feminist small group escape unscathed. Beth scornfully dismisses the middle-class lesbian feminists with whom Liz mixes as a 'lace ghetto',[46] one which unwisely excludes the male population. She accuses them of being out of touch with working-class women and their economic situation. The critiques she offers are socialist feminist in emphasis. They resemble the interrogation of radical feminist priorities expressed by the theorists Mitchell, Oakley and Segal.[47] The tensions informing the relationship between the two cousins form the emotional core of Miner's novel. The women's involvement with each other runs the gamut from scenes of trust and affection to ones of recrimination, distress and anger.

Another novel which treats an ideologically contentious topic, and can loosely be described as an example of 'fiction of debate' (an unsuccessful one, in my view) is Lisa Alther's *Other Women* (1984). The issue she explores is the merits and demerits of the Feminist Therapy Movement and its political implications for women.[48] Like Miner, Alther structures the novel around a pair of female figures each of whom supports and champions an opposing point of view. The focus of the text is a series of encounters between Caroline, a lesbian mother, and her heterosexual analyst, Hannah Burke. At the start the two argue fiercely, adopting polarized ideological attitudes. Caroline champions the radical feminist concept of the politicization of personal life, and argues for a socialist commitment to the attempted transformation of society. Hannah, on the other hand, pessimistically regards the violent state of present-day society as irreversible. Recommending a policy of 'personal adjustment', she advises Caroline to stop concentrating on instances of 'injustice, brutality, war, hunger', and focus instead on 'the incredible beauty and intricacy of life'.[49] As Caroline works as a nurse in a casualty hospital where she comes into daily contact with victims of violent crimes, many of which are perpetrated by men, she understandably finds this mawkishly sentimental counsel very difficult to accept! Curiously, however, Alther appears intent on discrediting and ridiculing Caroline's feminist and socialist ideals. She uses them as a source of cheap humour, while endorsing Hannah's point of view. Like her earlier novel *Kinflicks* (1976), *Other Women* reveals numerous confusions and inconsistencies. Alther's use of humour, rather than being radical in its emphasis, has the effect of blurring the political issues she treats. The novel can also be criticized for giving unfair representations of the principles and aims of the Therapy Movement. Alther does the Movement a marked disservice by parodying and distorting its ideas.

A much more inventive and successful example of fiction of

debate is a recently published novel by the British writer Nicky Edwards. It carries the harshly monosyllabic and deliberately anti-glamorous title *Mud* (1986). Edwards's project, one which is overtly polemical, is to investigate the strengths and weaknesses of the Women's Peace Movement as illustrated by its famous manifestation, the Greenham Common Peace Camp.[50] The strategies which Edwards utilizes are, as we shall see, much more complex and ambitious than the simple confrontation between the two characters with opposing viewpoints adopted by Miner and Alther. A device which Edwards uses with exceptionally good effect is that of historical comparison. She compares and contrasts the dilemma and contradictions confronting modern women peace protestors with the different but equally troubling ones which the men and women involved in the First World War faced. The title of the novel brings together these disparate periods and political areas. It denotes both the mud of the First World War battlefields[51] which, as Edwards emphasizes, sometimes proved fatal to combatants, and the muddy terrain of Greenham Common, a source of hazard and discomfort to the women living there. It also carries symbolic meaning, signifying the confusions and contradictions discernible in the commitment to violence on the part of soldiers, and the commitment to *non*-violence by modern peace protestors. Why should men in 1914 have volunteered to join the army to end up 'in a muddy ditch in a Belgian winter being shot at'?[52] Why should British women have agreed to work in factories making munitions which would widow German women? And why should modern-day peace protestors allow themselves to be brutally and sometimes sadistically manhandled by members of the police and army? These are some of the important questions which Edwards raises in the novel.

Another device she adopts to discuss issues relating to the Peace Movement is to make the psyche of Jo, a lesbian feminist, the main arena of the debate. Jo is an ex-Greenham Common woman. Various reasons have prompted her to leave the Camp. As well as feeling herself a 'burnt-out case', she has started to have serious doubts about the value and political efficacy of non-violent methods of protest. At the start of the novel she is trying to give expression to these doubts by writing a play which brings together in symbolic interaction 'a modern woman pacifist and a dead First World War infantryman' (p. 5). The debate about Greenham which takes place in her head is underpinned by the contrary points of view voiced by her friends. Her ex-comrade Kate tries to persuade her to return to the Camp to take part in further action. Her lover Beryl, in contrast, is fiercely opposed to the Peace Movement. She regards it as a diversion which, by 'keeping potential trouble-makers locked in an unwinnable confrontation with the police and army' (p. 81), debilitates the

Women's Movement, preventing women from participating in specifically feminist issues. She also accuses it of promoting patriarchal stereotypes of women as 'good wives and mothers' and 'baby loving nurturers'. Jo dismisses the latter criticism as prejudiced and naive. She values the Greenham Common experience as a successful experiment in feminist communal living. It is the press and media, she points out, which are to blame for rendering invisible the strong lesbian feminist presence there and presenting the protestors in a conventional light. The reason she refuses to return to the Camp is that she has doubts about the value of non-violent protest and the position of female moral superiority which it implies. Admitting that she found the violent treatment she received from the police and army personally damaging and felt strongly tempted to fight back, she complains:

> We hamstrung ourselves by getting into violent confrontation with men and telling ourselves that we are non-violent. So they could do what the hell they liked, while we tied ourselves with all these absurd rules designed to give us some kind of abstract moral half-nelson on them. Who needs it? (p.125)

Both she and the Infantryman John Gower, whose diary she reads while researching the play she plans to write, arrive at conclusions which, though contrary, have interesting parallels. He comes to perceive the futility of engaging in *violent* combat on the battlefield. She, on the other hand, recognizes the pointlessness of pursuing a policy of *non-violent* action at Greenham.

A few faults blemish this very interesting novel. These centre on the method of historical comparison which Edwards employs. The situations of a First World War infantryman and a modern woman peace protestor are, perhaps, too different to make suitable material for comparison. Whereas the former was forced to remain on the battlefied by threats of court martial and a firing-squad, the latter is free to leave Greenham if she so chooses. And, though the mud at Greenham is certainly uncomfortable, it has not – as far as I know – proved fatal to any of the protestors. Edwards also experiences problems in the characterization of Jo and her feminist friends, and the mode of speech she gives to them. All too often they appear 'cliquish' and arrogant, conversing in 'tough guy' monosyllables and phrases reminiscent of Hemingway heroes. The novel is, none the less, an adventurous one – both from a political point of view and as regards its narrative design. Edwards's account of the Peace Movement and the paradoxes which it presents to women is certainly well worth reading.

Conclusion

Fiction treating themes of sexual politics is, as we have seen, remarkably vital, possessing an exceptional capacity for growth and development. It reveals a notable degree of responsiveness and sensitivity to shifts in current feminist thought and practice. Texts exploring sexuality as the site of feminist struggle and examining different aspects of the politicization of personal life, with the increasing fragmentation of the Women's Movement in the 1980s, have been followed by ones which are overtly polemical in emphasis. The writers of the latter seek to problematize, interrogate or debate issues pertaining to sexual politics and related topics. The claim that relations with men are invariably oppressive for women has been re-scrutinized and, in some cases, challenged. Attempts have been made to reclaim heterosexuality and bisexuality for feminism. Disputes between radical and socialist feminists, along with arguments over the merits and demerits of Feminist Therapy and the Women's Peace Movement, have also found a place in works of fiction.

The examination of a selection of novels and short stories focusing on these ideas has enabled us to re-evaluate the so-called 'realist' mode of fiction, one which academic critics with an interest in psychoanalysis and deconstruction generally ignore or disparage. It has given us the opportunity to reappraise and appreciate the complexity and diversity of the texts' design and structure, as well as the ideas they incorporate.

Some of the most significant aspects of sexual politics, ones which I in fact cited in the introductory section, have received little or no attention here. Relations between men and women in the family, the labour market, the law and politics, have been scarcely mentioned. The topic of male violence, though receiving some degree of analysis, has been given nothing like the attention which – as is evident from the primacy that writers of fiction accord it – it deserves. The following chapter, however, will give an opportunity for these topics to be discussed. Concentrating on patriarchal relations, it again takes as its focus a number of novels and short stories treating the dialectic of sex. In this respect, it forms a continuation of the themes discussed in this chapter. As we shall see from French's *The Women's Room*, Fairbairns's *Benefits* and Weldon's *The President's Child*, patriarchal relations is a topic which prompts writers to make connections between a variety of institutions and social structures, and to introduce a wide range of characters.

Notes

1. Op. cit. (Vision Press, 1974), p. 197.
2. *Contemporary Feminist Thought*, ed. cit., p. 11.
3. 'The unhappy marriage of Marxism and Feminism: towards a more progressive union', *Women and Revolution*, ed. Lydia Sargent (Pluto, 1981), p. 13.
4. Mica Nava, 'From Utopian to scientific Feminism? Early feminist critiques of the family', *What is to be Done about the Family?*, ed. Lynne Segal (Penguin, 1983), p. 67.
5. 'No more sleeping beauties and frozen boys', *The Left and the Erotic*, ed. Eileen Phillips (Lawrence and Wishart, 1983), p. 139.
6. See Juliet Mitchell and Ann Oakley (eds), *The Rights and Wrongs of Women* (Penguin, 1976), pp. 7-15.
7. For a discussion of the topic see Nava, op. cit., pp. 66-90.
8. Kathleen Hulley, 'Interview with Paley', *Delta*, 14 (1982), p. 27.
9. Op. cit., pp. 1-2.
10. Op. cit., (Abacus, 1972), p. 23.
11. 'Political change: two perspectives on power', *Building Feminist Theory: essays from Quest, a feminist quarterly*, ed. Charlotte Bunch et al. (Longman, 1981), p. 7.
12. See Gail Chester, 'I call myself a radical feminist', *No Turning Back: writings from the women's liberation movement 1975-80*, ed. Feminist Anthology Collective (Women's Press, 1981), pp. 67-71.
13. *The Bleeding Heart* (Sphere, 1980), p. 307. Subsequent references are to this edition and are in the text.
14. *The Sadeian Woman*, ed. cit., p. 9.
15. Op. cit., p. 44.
16. Michèle Barrett, *Women's Oppression Today* (Verso, 1980), p. 44.
17. *Radical Feminism*, ed. Anne Koedt et al. (Quadrangle Books, 1973), pp. 198-207.
18. Op. cit., p. 140.
19. *Braided Lives* (Penguin, 1983), p. 231.
20. *Our Blood: prophecies and discourses on sexual politics* (Women's Press, 1982), p. 43.
21. See Bonnie Zimmerman, 'What has never been: an overview of lesbian feminist criticism', *Making a Difference: feminist literary criticism*, ed. cit., pp. 177-210.
22. 'Displacement and the discourse of woman' in Mark Krupnick (ed.), *Displacement: Derrida and after* (Indiana University Press, 1983), pp. 169-95; and 'French feminism in an international frame', *Yale French Studies*, 62 (1981), pp. 181, 184.
23. *Compulsory Heterosexuality and Lesbian Existence* (Onlywomen Press, 1981).
24. 'Not for lesbians only', *Building Feminist Theory*, ed. cit., p. 68.
25. *Choices* (Persephone Press, 1980), p. 53.
26. See Toril Moi, *Sexual/Textual Politics* (Methuen, 1985), pp. 42-9.
27. 'I'll climb the stairway to heaven: lesbianism in the seventies', *Sex and Love*, ed. cit., pp. 191-5.

28. Anna Coote and Beatrix Campbell, *Sweet Freedom: the struggle for women's liberation* (Pan, 1982).
29. See *Love Your Enemy? The debate between heterosexual feminism and political lesbianism* (Onlywomen Press, 1981).
30. *Between Friends* (Sheba, 1983), p. 29.
31. *Women, Letters, and the Novel* (A.M.S. Press, Inc., 1980).
32. Ibid., p. 22.
33. Coote and Campbell, op. cit., p. 231.
34. 'I'll climb the stairway to heaven', op. cit., p. 191.
35. Beatrix Campbell, 'A feminist sexual politics: now you see it, now you don't', *Feminist Review*, 5 (1980), p. 1.
36. *Sex and Love*, ed. cit., p. 105. Other theoretical works which attempt to reclaim heterosexuality include Betty Friedan, *The Second Stage* (Abacus, 1983) and Lynne Segal, *Is the Future Female?*, ed. cit. Friedan seeks to reclaim the family while Segal recommends feminists to make alliances with male-dominated political parties.
37. Patricia Duncker, 'Writing and Roaring: in search of the truly political feminist novel', *Trouble and Strife*, 6 (Summer 1985), p. 44.
38. 'Questions and answers', *On Gender and Writing*, ed. cit., p. 67.
39. 'From where I stand: a case for feminist bisexuality', *Sex and Love*, ed. cit., p. 143.
40. 'Sexual politics and psychoanalysis: some notes on their relation', *Feminism, Culture and Politics*, ed. cit., p. 172.
41. 'Passing', *Mae West is Dead*, ed. cit., p. 179. Subsequent references are to this edition and are in the text.
42. Jo Freeman, *The Politics of Women's Liberation* (Longman, 1975), p. 145.
43. Lynne Segal, *Is the Future Female?*, ed. cit., p. 65.
44. 'Is personal life still a political issue?', *Feminist Studies*, 5, no. 3 (1979). pp. 426-7
45. *Movement: a novel in stories* (Methuen, 1985), p. 180.
46. *Blood Sisters: an examination of conscience* (Women's Press, 1981), p. 21.
47. Mitchell and Oakley (eds), op. cit.; Segal, *Is the Future Female?*, ed. cit.
48. For a defence of therapy, see Sheila Ernst and Lucy Goodison, *In Our Own Hands: a book of self-help therapy* (Women's Press, 1981), pp. 1-7. For a critique, see Sara Scott and Tracey Payne, 'Underneath we're all lovable: therapy and feminism', *Trouble and Strife*, 3 (Summer, 1984), pp. 21-4.
49. *Other Women* (Penguin, 1985), p. 69.
50. For an affirmative account of the Peace Movement, see Barbara Harford and Sarah Hopkins (eds), *Greenham Common: women at the wire* (Women's Press, 1984). For a critique, see frankie green et al., *Breaching the Peace: a collection of radical feminist papers* (Onlywomen Press, 1983).
51. For reference to the mud see Mary Borden, 'The song of the mud', *The Forbidden Zone* (Heinemann, 1929), pp. 179-82; and Vera Brittain, *Testament of Youth* (1933; Virago, 1978), Virago edition, p. 370.
52. *Mud* (Women's Press, 1986), p. 5. Subsequent references are to this edition and are in the text.

Chapter Four

Patriarchal Relations

The 'exchange of women' is a seductive and powerful concept .... Women are given in marriage, taken in battle, exchanged for favours, sent as tribute, traded, bought, and sold. Far from being confined to the 'primitive' world, these practices seem only to become more pronounced and commercialized in more 'civilized' societies.

Gayle Rubin, 'The traffic in women: notes on the "political economy" of sex', *Toward an Anthropology of Women*, ed. Rayna R. Reiter (Monthly Review Press, 1975), p. 175.

She's afraid of men and it's simple, it's rational, she's afraid of men because men are frightening.

Margaret Atwood, *Bodily Harm* (1981; Virago, 1983), Virago edition, p. 290.

Introduction: Concepts of patriarchy

Patriarchy has proved to be a notoriously problematic term among theorists. Its chief drawback, as Sheila Rowbotham[1] points out, is that it gives a simplistic and inexact impression of women's relations both with men and with one another. Presenting women's relations with men as invariably antagonistic, it treats their oppression in a transhistorical light, ignoring those occasions in history when the sexes have worked together as allies. At the same time, by presenting women *en masse* as a unified interest-group, it fails to take account of the social and economic differences dividing them. Another problem with the term which theorists complain about is that it acquires different meanings in the different discourses and academic disciplines in which it plays a part. Psychoanalysts, sociologists and anthropologists all use it to mean different things.[2] This, of course, affects the feminist usage of the term, making it similarly imprecise and shifting. Veronica Beechey succinctly defines the most important meanings the term assumes among feminists. These are relevant to the works of fiction discussed below. Radical feminists such as Millett, Beechey remarks, use patriarchy in the popular sense of 'male domination and the power relationships by which men dominate women'.[3] Marxist feminists like Hartmann, on the other hand, give it a narrower and more precise interpretation, using it to denote the relations between women's subordinate position and the organization of capitalist modes of production. Feminists writing in a psychoanalytic vein such as Juliet Mitchell employ the term in yet another manner.

Patriarchy signifies to them a society in which the father enjoys either actual or symbolic power, with women relegated to the subordinate roles of property and object of exchange.

Concepts of patriarchy and patriarchal relations hold an immense appeal for writers of fiction. They are successfully appropriated by them as the ideological base for numerous novels and short stories. Interestingly, the very imprecision and confusing diversity of meanings which cause theorists headaches, prove a source of inspiration for creative writers. They give them scope and opportunity to create complex, multifaceted representations of male dominance. Inspiring a plethora of inventive strategies and designs, they enable writers to convey to the reader an impression of both the ubiquity and the intricacy of systems of male power. It is, in fact, as a vehicle for the depiction of the workings of male power that concepts of patriarchy and patriarchal relations are most effective. There can be few women who, at some time or other in their lives, have not experienced the frightening sense of being trapped in a conspiracy of male domination either in the workplace or the private domain of the home. The men whom they expect to protect their interests fail to do so. They gang up together and side with superiors while the women to whom they look for support insist on upholding the male hierarchy on which they depend for survival, preferment and social recognition. In material terms this notion of a 'conspiracy' may be a simplification and exaggeration. As a projection of imaginative reality, however, a description of the way many women feel living in a phallocraticc culture, it possesses an element of undoubted truth. And it may not be, in fact, the exaggeration which it at first appears. According to anthropologists such as Lévi-Strauss the whole edifice of kinship structures and civilized society as we know it is built on the keystone of the subordination and exchange of women. As Gayle Rubin observes, discussing Strauss's theories, 'As long as the relations specify that men exchange women, it is men who are the beneficiaries of the product of such exchanges – social organization.'[4]

Social organization is, indeed, a central theme in the novels and short stories under review in this chapter. In exploring ideas of patriarchal relations and male supremacy, writers focus particular attention on the interaction between public and private realms of experience. Here again they take their cue from theorists. The latter give conflicting explanations of the origins of male power. The radical feminist Brownmiller locates it in the biological differences between the sexes, the psychologist Dinnerstein in the asymmetrical rearing of boys and girls, and the sociologist Barrett in economics and ideology.[5] All these theorists agree, however, that, once in existence, the structures of male domination tend to be ubiquitous and all-encompassing. They pervade sexual, psychological, social and economic areas of life. They inform all the major institutions of society – politics, the law, the police, medicine and the universities. Writers of fiction as different as Atwood, French, Piercy and Weldon concur in emphasizing the all-encompassing nature of patriarchal power. They examine the interrelation between the different institutions and structures in which it is invested. The problematic position of the female protagonist trapped in their grasp and the efforts she makes to struggle free is a topic which writers also treat.

A question which provokes disagreement among theorists is to what degree, if any, women collude with men in oppressing and exploiting their own sex.[6] At one end of the spectrum is Daly, who sees women as innocent, 'spell-bound' victims helplessly caught in the toils of a patriarchal plot, a conspiracy deliberately constructed by men. At the other end are Dworkin and Griffin. In their analyses of the ideological differences dividing women, they acknowledge the part they play in colluding with male oppressors. Psychoanalytic theorists such as Mitchell and Kristeva take yet another approach. Avoiding the issue of male power, they present men and women as equally subject to psychological and cultural pressures, enacting scripts learnt from infancy. They present male-defined structures and institutions rather than men *per se* as responsible for women's subordinate status. Writers of fiction, as we shall see, reveal a similarly wide range of attitudes and responses to the vexed question of collusion.

An indication of the inspirational role which concepts of patriarchy and male supremacy play in women's fiction is the wealth of images and symbolic locations which they generate in novels and short stories. Locations and structures as diverse as the university, the pathology lab, the dream-city, the hunt, the puppet theatre and the circus ring all appear in texts.[7] They function as literal or symbolic settings for the enactment of the multiplex, tension-filled drama of the patriarchal power-struggle between the sexes.

Representations of patriarchal relations in four novels

Commenting on the numerous different methods which men employ to dominate women, Rich comes to the conclusion that 'we are confronting not a simple maintenance of inequality and property possession, but a pervasive cluster of forces, ranging from physical brutality to control of consciousness.'[8] The idea of a 'pervasive cluster of forces' which work together to enforce male domination in the private and public areas of life sums up very accurately the topic which links the four novels discussed in this section. The authors, while differing radically as regards the particular aspect of patriarchal power they choose to emphasize, display a common concern to foreground its ubiquity, vigour and interrelated facets. They adopt a variety of strategies to emphasize its tentacular structures, along with the struggles women wage to elude them.

The four novels which form the centre of analysis here have been chosen with the aim of illustrating the fictional treatment of some of the most important meanings of the term patriarchy. French in *The Women's Room* (1977) interprets the term in the popular radical feminist sense of male domination of women. Weldon, in contrast, structures *The President's Child* (1982) around the meaning it has acquired in anthropological and psychoanalytic discourse: the patrilineal system of kinship structures based on the Law of the Father. Carter in *The Magic Toyshop* (1967) and Emma Tennant in *Hotel de Dream* (1976) appropriate psychoanalytic interpretations of a somewhat different kind. Carter investigates the reproduction of male supremacist structures in the arena of the family, while Tennant explores, in humorous manner, the manifestations they assume in the collective unconscious.

As well as illustrating the ramifying structures of patriarchal power, the four novels under review all share a common focus on the family unit. The writers' choice of this particular location for their study of male supremacy is, of course, understandable. Described by Millett as 'a patriarchal unit within a patriarchal whole',[9] the family is the topic which radical feminists writing in the early 1970s chose for their initial analyses of women's oppression and the dialectic of sex. In the novels considered here it features, alternately, as the site of women's unpaid domestic labour and childcare services; the place where the Law of the Father is inculcated and the positions of masculinity and femininity learnt; and the arena where acts of male violence, including battery, rape and incest, are perpetrated.

French's *The Women's Room*, the novel with which I open my discussion, has received a number of unfavourable reviews from critics. Yet to dismiss the novel as 'a transatlantic blockbuster' manifesting a 'turgid tone',[10] as one British reviewer does, is to ignore the skilfully subversive treatment of certain popular genres and conventions which French achieves. Her account of the progress Mira makes from adolescence through marriage and divorce to academic studies at Harvard University reveals obvious connections with the *bildungsroman*. In Mira's case, however, as with the heroines of novels from earlier periods,[11] the reader's expectations of the process are inverted. Mira experiences physical maturity and marriage not in positive terms as 'growing up' but, on the contrary, as a negative 'going down, or even drowning'.[12] The novel reveals even more interesting connections with the popular genre of soap opera – ones which French herself advertises. Apologizing to the reader for failing to tell 'exciting adventure tales' and to treat 'important things' such as politics, she admits that she intends 'to drag you through an afternoon of soap-opera' (pp. 188-9). The apology is, of course, a rhetorical device to challenge the accepted belief in the value of the public realm of life and the downgrading of the personal and domestic, while simultaneously affirming the value of the latter. French utilizes the format of soap opera very cleverly, putting it to subversive use. Her episodic delineation of family life, amatory involvements and relations between parents and children is aimed not at the celebration of family values and romantic love, as is generally the case in soap opera. On the contrary, it exposes both areas as the site of male power and women's oppression.

French's representation of relations between men and women is strongly radical feminist in spirit. Like the theorists Millett and Firestone, she portrays women as constituting a different 'class' and 'culture' from men whom they are described as serving as 'slaves' in the home. Social and economic differences between women are presented as minor in comparison to the dialectic of sex. French even gives Mira a thoroughly radical feminist reason for deciding to get married. Mira marries her boyfriend Norm not for reasons of romantic love or economic security, the usual motives in works of fiction, but because she (mistakenly) believes that marriage will protect her from rape and male violence. This, of course, agrees with Susan Brownmiller's description of the threat of rape as one of the chief means men adopt to establish control over women and recruit them into their service.[13]

A feature of French's novel which at once strikes the reader is the focus she places on the *all-encompassing* nature of male power. As Mira herself divulges to us half-way through the text, she and her women friends use a code-word to denote the relentless bullying and exploitation they suffer from men and the institutions they control:

> By this time, all of us had a word. It was THEM, and we all meant the same thing by it: men. Each of us felt done in by one of them, but that wasn't it. Because each of us had friends, and our friends were also being done in by them. And each of our friends had friends ... (p. 293)

The syntax of the above passage, with its network of accumulative clauses and phrases, effectively represents and enacts the tentacular web of male power-structures in which the female characters feel themselves trapped. The device of accumulation – of episodes and events as well as clauses – is, in fact, the major strategy which French employs to emphasize the ramifying, all-pervasive nature of male power. The device enables her to substantiate the radical feminist indictment, central to the novel, that, to quote Millett, 'the military, industry, technology, universities, science, political office and finance – in short, every avenue of power within the society, including the coercive force of the police, is entirely in male hands'.[14] French moves from describing acts of exploitation and violence perpetrated by individual men in the private domain of the home to depicting analogous ones carried out by the public institutions of medicine, the university, the law and the police. Emphasis is placed on the way male-dominated institutions support and back up individual men in their attempts to subjugate women. Lily, incarcerated in a mental clinic by her husband who wants her out of the way, has her imprisonment ratified by male doctors who torture her with ECT. The police, interrogating Chris about the rape she has suffered, treat her almost as callously as the rapist. Val, in a concluding episode, has her body pumped full of bullets by the police, the supposed guardians of law and order. The interest French reveals in demonstrating the grasp exerted by male power in every area of life, along with the range of different characters, institutions and locations she introduces to make her case, are typical of novels written in the 1970s. Writers in the 1980s are more likely to adopt a narrower canvas and concentrate on one particular area or aspect of patriarchal power.

French's decision to structure *The Women's Room* on devices of accumulation and repetition, though having a compelling effect in the early stages, in the long run becomes rather tedious. It also strikes the reader as simplistic. As well as dismissing the entire male population as a bunch of villains and creeps, it raises awkward questions about female stupidity. Why, if the tactics of male domination are as blatantly obvious as French makes them appear, do women continue to be fooled by them? Although she gives a convincing exposé of the vigour and force of patriarchal power, she can be accused of seriously underestimating its intelligence, cunning and duplicity.

For a fictional analysis which takes into account these latter attributes, we need to turn to a novel which utilizes narrative strategies of a more complex and subtle kind. Weldon's *The President's Child* is the perfect example.

The plot of Weldon's novel has its germ in an actual historical incident, the brutal murder of the mistress of President Sukarno of the Philippines and the son she bore him, to prevent the son from becoming a 'political inconvenience'[15] to the state. Treating a similar incident in the West, Weldon describes the struggle waged by Isabel Acre to keep possession of the illegitimate son she has born Dandy Ivel – an American presidential candidate – and to survive the attacks on her life perpetrated by him and his henchmen. As Isabel is forced to recognize, 'when male power and prestige is at stake the lives and happiness of women and children are immaterial' (p. 160). The battle between Dandy and Isabel for possession of their son Jason is a vehicle for Weldon to explore the theme, one which (as is signalled by the heroic names of some of the characters) the novel shares with Greek tragedy, of the patrilineal inheritance system. This system represents the traditional form of patriarchal relations as we know it in the West. In it, woman is relegated to the roles of bearer of children (preferably sons who will inherit the father's name and property) and object of exchange cementing bonds between men.[16] Moreover, as Kristeva points out, though she is expected to bear her husband sons, the fact that they are regarded as his property debars her from ultimate possession of them. In certain extreme cases the part she plays in the act of procreation is not even acknowledged.[17] In accord with this focus, Weldon interprets the dialectic of sex as hinging on the struggle between the sexes to gain control of woman's reproductive capacities and the sons she bears. The lethal contest waged between Dandy and Isabel emerges as a twentieth-century enactment of this archetypal conflict.

By organizing her novel around the theme of patrilineal kinship structures, Weldon opens the way for the investigation of one of her favourite themes – the contradictions of vulnerability and power which women's reproductive capacities involve. Isabel's bearing of a son to Dandy, the presidential candidate, as she herself dimly perceives, alters her status in a male-dominated society. The fact that 'she had a womb, and it worked' (p. 160), while making her prey to male manipulation and endangering her life, is simultaneously a source of power. In Lacanian psychoanalytic terms, it gives her direct access to the phallus. In struggling to keep possession of her son, she temporarily transcends woman's designated role as object of exchange. She intervenes in and disrupts the male supremacist structures of history – in this case, the contest for the American Presidency.

Unlike French, who seeks to describe merely the ubiquity and force of male power, Weldon gives a devastating exposé of its cunning, hypocrisy and ruthlessness. To emphasize these particular attributes, she uses not the simple strategies of accumulation and repetition, but those of an intrigue plot. Devices associated with the thriller such as disguised identity, concealed motivation, suprise and suspense, play an integral part in the narrative. An ingenious feature of Weldon's novel, one which deserves comment, is the symbolic element apparent in the design. The narrative plot she uses mirrors and enacts the mechanics of the 'patriarchal plot', the conspiracy devised by Dandy and his henchmen to destroy female opposition and achieve total power. The concept of a 'patriarchal plot' features, of course, in the writing of certain radical feminist theorists. The best-known of them is Daly. Weldon's use of the motif reveals, in fact, marked similarities to Daly's ideas. The maze-like conspiracy concocted by Dandy and his supporters to trap and subjugate Isabel resembles Daly's description of 'the man-formed mythic maze' that is constructed to confuse and dominate women in general.[18] Weldon's views about masculinity also have a lot in common with Daly's. Like Daly, she portrays men as cementing bonds with their fellows by means of the exchange and violation of women. As well as being obsessed with displays of ritual and 'processions', they maintain power through the accumulation of nuclear weapons. They also successfully manipulate reality by means of language and myth. Weldon's and Daly's perspectives are, however, by no means identical. The two differ fundamentally, for example, over the issue of female collusion. Whereas Daly presents women as innocent victims of male dissimulation, Weldon takes a more cynical approach. She shows female characters colluding with men in order to injure and betray other women.

Angela Carter's *The Magic Toyshop* and Emma Tennant's *Hotel de Dream* are two novels which both take a psychoanalytic approach to gender. They form a decided contrast to the works of French and Weldon discussed above. Both novels are anti-realist in style, making inventive use of elements of fantasy. The two writers also have in common the representation of femininity as a problematic, disruptive presence within the phallocratic social order. This order, they illustrate, is only to be maintained by the strict subordination of woman and the realms of the emotions and the maternal which, in existing culture, she represents.

Carter takes as the location for her study of patriarchal relations in the *Magic Toyshop* the family unit. The particular household she treats belongs to the despotic Uncle Philip, toymaker and puppetmaster. The adolescent Melanie and her little sister are forced to take up residence there when their parents are killed in an air crash. Uncle Philip's household is an extremely gloomy one. It is fraught with psychological tensions and conflicts. He is a tyrannical figure, demanding total obedience from his young wife Margaret (symbolically portrayed as dumb), her brothers Finn and Francie, and Melanie herself. When not making toys or bullying his relatives, he stages performances in his puppet theatre. He recruits Melanie against her will into playing a contributory part in the entertainment, ironically assigning to her the typically feminine roles of nymph and victim of rape.

Uncle Philip's household, centring on his toyshop, emerges as a microcosm of patriarchal relations. It is the place where the Law of the Father is inculcated, and the masculine and feminine positions learnt. It is also the site of male violence and the arena of the oepidal conflict between father and son – or, in this case, Uncle Philip and his young brothers-in-law Finn and Francie. Carter makes effective use of the device of intertextuality, weaving into the text allusions to locations of patriarchal power taken from earlier myths and fictions. The biblical Garden of Eden, the family unit as described by Freud and the puppet workshop of Dr Coppelius in *The Tales* of E. T. A. Hoffmann are motifs she introduces, superimposing them on the central location of Uncle Philip's household.

Whereas the atmosphere of the cluttered interior of Uncle Philip's toyshop is oppressively claustrophobic, entangling characters and reader in the close-knit mesh of family life, that of Tennant's *Hotel de Dream* is, in contrast, agoraphobic. The novel plunges the reader into a maelstrom of fantasy. The dreams experienced by the characters interweave, creating a grotesquely comic form of 'collective unconscious'. The setting of the novel is the Westringham Hotel, a shabby London establishment with pretensions to gentility. An assortment of lonely, eccentric people live there, watched over by the officious proprietor Mrs Routledge. The dreams they experience are obviously escapist in function, compensating for the drab nature of their everyday lives. Mr Poynter, a conservative figure who upholds principles of law and order, visits in his sleep a rigidly organized city-state where he occupies the position of president. The state possesses many of the features which theorists such as Daly, Rich and Woolf identify with a male-supremacist culture. Military rule prevails, accompanied by a focus on discipline, hierarchy and hygiene. The women who live there are regarded as inferior, categorized as wives, virgins or whores. Humorous features include frequent performance by brass bands, to whose music Mr Poynter is particularly partial, and the symmetrical design of the architecture and landscape. To ensure that the straight line of the horizon is maintained and 'the sky come[s] down firmly to meet the land', he makes certain that 'any burial mound, copse or hillock rising above that level had been lopped or cut down'.[19] To relax from his presidential duties, he pays surreptitious visits to the red light district of the city. Here he allows his favourite prostitute to whip him and shove spoonfuls of tapioca pudding down his throat – masochistic pleasures reminiscent of his boyhood experiences at prep school!

Tennant, however, does not allow Mr Poynter to enjoy the pleasures of his dream-city in peace. One of the themes of this novel, as of her others, is femininity presented as a source of disruption and problems. In order to pursue this, she makes the dreams experienced by Miss Scranton, another resident of the Westringham Hotel, run amuck and collide with Mr Poynter's – with unexpectedly comic effect. Miss Scranton's dreams are matrilineal in character. They take the form of an encounter with a group of vastly proportioned Amazons whom she comes across bathing in the sea. While travelling across country to take part in their annual mating rite, the women accidentally trespass on Mr Poynter's city-state. They tread sand into the presidential palace and dirty the immaculate carpet with wet footprints. Eventually captured and imprisoned in the dungeons below, they further disturb the patriarchal peace and quiet with loud sobs. Tennant portrays them as 'subterranean sirens, chained in dungeons beneath the foundations of the City, giving voice to their despair and grief in a language as familiar as echoes from the cradle and as impossible to understand' (pp. 77-8).

In this passage Tennant wittily presents femininity as the buried 'unconscious' of the patriarchal order. The Amazons' sobbing also has connotations of Kristeva's concept of 'semiotic babble' which has its origins in the bond between mother and child in the pre-oedipal stage.[20] Mr Poynter finds what he rudely calls the women's 'intolerable keening' disturbing in the extreme. Tennant, ridiculing the psychological defences men create to keep the feminine and the maternal from intruding on their lives, ironically comments: 'he realized he had constructed his City precisely in order to be removed from this sound forever' (p. 80)!

Interlocking structures: Gender, class, race

Commenting on the complexities of woman's position in present-day society, the theorist Hartsock points out that 'each of the interlocking institutions of capitalism, patriarchy and white supremacy conditions the others'.[21] The writers whose works I discuss in this section, rather than merely exploring the structures of male supremacy, examine the interaction they reveal with the pressures exerted by class or race. They adopt a similar set of priorities to Karen Kollias, who recommends that feminists take an interest in other issues besides gender. She reminds us that, though

> the women's movement has been defined as an educated, white, middle-class one ... if a truly representative feminist organization is to be created, then we must find concrete ways to incorporate class and race issues in a clear ideology.[22]

Zoë Fairbairns's *Benefits* (1979) and Marge Piercy's *The High Cost of Living* (1978), the two novels I shall consider first, both take as their theme the interaction between the dialectic of sex and the dialectic of class. The theme is traditionally a socialist feminist one. Socialist feminist ideas thus provide an appropriate context for discussing the novels.

Fairbairns's novel makes a fascinating comparison with French's *The Women's Room*. The two works reveal obvious similarities of design and structure. Like French, Fairbairns focuses attention on women's community, introducing a large cast of female characters from different walks of life. She also takes as the chief focalizer of events a woman with liberal feminist attitudes, as opposed to radical feminist ones. The aim of this strategy is, presumably, to win the sympathy and interest of the average woman reader. Both French and Fairbairns, moreover, centre their analysis on the family unit, presenting it as the principal site of women's oppression and exploitation. Here, however, significant differences emerge between their attitudes. French interprets women's unpaid labour in the home in a radical feminist light, depicting housework and childcare services as being done for the benefit of *men*. Fairbairns, on the contrary, adopts a socialist feminist perspective. She describes women as working not only for men but also for the *state*.

Fairbairns's novel is set in the Britain of the future, and possesses a strong element of the dystopic. It describes the attempts made by a right-wing government to impose control on women's domestic labour and reproductive capacities by paying them, on a selective basis, a financial 'benefit'. The consequences of the scheme are, as one might expect, disastrous. Large numbers of women lose their independence, they are driven back into the home – and a predictable escalation in domestic violence occurs. The chief source of tension in the novel is the struggle that takes place between the Women's Movement, spearheaded by a group of radical feminists, and the male establishment of politicians and social workers. The facet of feminist theory to which the novel relates is the controversial recommendation put forward by Maria Dalla Costa and Selma James on a socialist feminist platform that the state should pay women wages for housework.[23] Fairbairns gives an intelligent critique of the proposal, illustrating its numerous flaws. She appears to agree with the theorist Barrett that, far from improving women's situation, it serves to 'confirm women in low-paid work and institutionalize their regulation to the home'.[24]

Benefits has rightly been praised by critics for giving women's fiction 'a wider political dimension'.[25] Unfortunately, however, Fairbairns's style fails to do justice to the importance of the topic she treats. It is too uniformly pedestrian and low-key fully to engage the reader's interest. The novel lacks the sheer imaginative vitality and the capacity to involve the reader's emotions which French's *The Women's Room*, imperfect though it is in many ways, possesses.

A much more dynamic and inventive representation of the interlocking structures of male supremacy and capitalism is to be found in Piercy's *The High Cost of Living*. As well as giving a convincing exposé of the oppressive effects of patriarchal power, Piercy also – as the title of the novel signals – focuses attention on the economic pressures which harass women's lives. The novel is set in the city of Detroit. It describes the struggle waged by the hero Leslie, a graduate assistant with a working-class background, to achieve upward mobility in the middle-class, male-dominated world of the university. Leslie identifies as lesbian feminist, and emphasis is placed on the intense conflict she experiences between her allegiance to the feminist community, symbolized by the local rape-crisis line, and her involvement in the university and its values. The novel is enlivened by an element of personal experience. In an autobiographical essay Piercy describes Detroit as 'a violent place to grow up in'. In a sentence that vividly sums up a view of city life many of us share, she writes, 'as a woman I experience a city as a minefield. I am always potential quarry or target or victim.'[26] Both these remarks could aptly have been voiced by Leslie, the central figure in Piercy's novel. She too regards the city as a place of violence and, in an attempt to arm herself against attack, takes lessons in karate. The expertise she achieves is presented as the only realm of her life which is both truly satisfying and morally unsullied.

Piercy's analysis of the ambiguities of Leslie's social position is subtle and extremely poignant. Leslie discovers that, on occasion, class ties can prove stronger than ones of gender. She feels that she has more in common with her male friend Bernie, who like her has working-class roots and identifies as homosexual, than she does with many of her middle-class feminist friends. As she sardonically reminds him, they have both experienced a similarly painful struggle to reconstitute their personalities and attitudes along middle-class lines:

> We're both wiggling upward, Bernie, we've shed our class. We've flayed ourselves bare and plastered over our bleeding flesh with accents and books and classes and everything we weren't and wanted to be.[27]

One reason for the remarkable success of the novel – and I would rate it as Piercy's finest work to date – is the element of savage irony informing its design. Leslie's progress upwards in terms of class is perceived as a journey downwards where moral integrity is concerned. In her desperate quest for professional security and success, she continues to cling to the patronage of George, the professor in charge of the History Department where she works, despite the fact she recognizes his attributes of ruthlessness and corruption. The cost of living is, she discovers, high in moral as well as economic terms. A similar element of irony informs Piercy's characterization of George himself. She portrays him not as a stereotypical villain but as a charismatic charmer. Like many university professors who tyrannize their departments, bullying and exploiting their subordinates and making their lives utter misery, he has a reputation for having possessed radical tendencies in his youth!

Piercy's delineation of patriarchal relations differs from those of the writers discussed previously in this chapter. Instead of introducing a number of male characters and institutions, each of whom represents a different facet of male supremacy, she allows the figure of George to epitomize them all. He dominates the lives of all the main characters in the novel. He controls Leslie as employer, Honor the girl she loves as seducer, and his wife Sue as husband. He is, in fact, the pupper-master, manipulating all the strings. Intellectual, economic and sexual power are invested in his person. The symbolic dimension which he acquires is illustrated by the reference to him as 'the mysterious George' and by the semi-humorous comment that he is more 'some act of God ... a fictional person like a corporation' (p. 127) than a flesh-and-blood human being.

Piercy is not, of course, the only writer to bring together a number of different facets of male power in the figure of a single character, allowing him thus to emerge as a symbolic embodiment of male dominance. Jan Clausen makes effective use of the device in her short story 'Daddy' (*Mother, Sister, Daughter, Lover*, 1980). The story is a feminist classic. It gives a brilliant study of a father's successful attempt to alienate his young daughter's affections from her mother in a lesbian custody battle. Narrated from the daughter's naive point of view, it movingly contrasts the affluent, secure way of life Daddy enjoys with Mommy's insecure, financially deprived circumstances.

Another writer who makes use of the device is Glen Tomasetti in her humorous novel *Man of Letters* (1981). There must be something about the chauvinistic climate of university life that brings out the monster in men for, like Piercy, Tomasetti chooses to make her representative of male power an academic. The novel, a satiric portrayal of the male ego and its eventual collapse, is narrated by the pompous Dorton Serry. He is a professor of philosophy – the epitome of male arrogance. He prides himself on both his intellectual gifts and the sexual appeal he holds for women. Tomasetti describes the various blows his ego receives as the women in his life rebel and step out of line, refusing to play the roles of romantic idol and humble helpmeet which he expects of them.

It is interesting to compare the accounts of university life and the professors who dominate it in the works of Piercy and Tomasetti with 'the campus novel', a genre of fiction popular with male writers in the 1960s and 1970s. Contributors include Randall Jarell, Kingsley Amis, Malcolm Bradbury and David Lodge. The women novelists' acerbic wit and insight into sexual politics give them, in many respects, the edge over their male peers. Male writers tend merely to emphasize the comic aspect of university life. Women writers, in contrast, express anger at the injustices of the male-dominated educational system.

The complaint voiced by many feminists that the Women's Movement's preoccupation with gender has led it to ignore other factors in women's lives such as class and sexual orientation has been extended in recent years to include *race*. Audre Lorde writes: 'By and large within the women's movement today, white women focus upon their oppression as women and ignore differences of race, sexual preference, class and age.'[28]

The exploration of the interrelated pressures exerted by male supremacy, class-division and racism, as well as being a topic which theorists are starting to discuss, also occupies an important place in women's fiction. Certain white women writers such as Dorothy Bryant and Nadine Gordimer have contributed to the treatment of the theme. Bryant in *Miss Giardino* (1978) investigates the effect of these pressures on the life of a San Francisco teacher who has recently retired from her post at Camino Real High School. The novel reflects the trend current among contemporary women writers to focus attention on the lives of older and elderly women whose experiences the dominant culture tends to ignore. It also undertakes the more unusual project of representing the experiences of a woman in paid professional work.

Anna Giardino, the eponymous hero of the novel, is the unmarried daughter of working-class Italian immigrants to the USA. At the start of the novel, she is lying in a hospital bed, recovering from a mugging inflicted on her outside the school gates. As she strives to recollect the identity and name of her assailant, memories of her experiences both inside the classroom and outside it drift through her head. Her situation as a student of education and school-teacher has been a solitary one, revealing contradictions regarding race, class and sex.

When she was a young girl, struggling to acquire an education, her Italian father treated her with typical chauvinism. He resented the fact that she learnt to speak fluent English, regarding her linguistic proficiency as a threat to his authority and a sign of discontent with her working-class roots. At the same time however, recognizing aspects of himself in her, he felt a grudging sense of admiration for her qualities of independence, ambition and drive. On entering the teaching profession, Anna encounters a different set of problems. Like many women pursuing a career, her situation is extremely lonely. The dialectic of sex separates her from her colleagues, the majority of whom are male. Her independence and child-free status, on the other hand, divide her from other women whose lives centre on marriage and the family.

Bryant's novel is cleverly constructed. Indebted to the thriller in its design, it makes effective use of tension and suspense. The discoveries which Anna makes about the identity of her mysterious assailant – and more especially about herself and emotional conflicts – take the reader quite by surprise.

It is, of course, black women and women of colour who have made the most significant contribution to the representation of the interplay between gender, class and race. The theme is central to Burford's short stories. Several of these such as 'Miss Jessie' and 'Coming of Age' (*The Threshing Floor*, 1986) hinge on the tension existing between the personal attitudes and experiences of the individual black protagonist, and the collective cultures of the race to which she belongs. The London-based Jamaican writer Joan Riley and the American Toni Cade Bambera also focus attention on a similar set of topics.

Possibly the most famous study of the interaction between the factors of gender, class and race by a black woman writer is Alice Walker's *The Color Purple* (1982). Despite the public acclaim the novel has received, certain of its features have proved highly controversial. Criticism has been levelled at Walker's treatment of 'the unitary self'; at her celebratory depiction of the family unit (albeit an extended family and one which is not exclusively heterosexual); and at the element of 'utopian fantasy' apparent in the novel's design.[29] The plot, as Rachel Bowlby observes, is structured on a series of fortunate coincidences which provide the central character Celie with both personal fulfilment and economic security. Commenting on this particular feature of the novel, Bowlby complains that: 'Rather than posing residual problems that thwart her growing aspirations, Celie's world falls into place to meet them, presenting her as in the best commercials with a dream house and a successful small business' (p. 125). The novel does have, however, a number of defenders. Anselma

Jackson, replying to the criticism that Walker models her characters on the humanist concept of the unitary self, points to the strongly *collective* focus which she none the less achieves. Jackson claims, rightly in my view, that 'the autobiographical element that informs the text is not one of individual singularity, but that of the Black western woman' (p. 143). And, in response to the accusation that Walker fails adequately to address the 'determinants of patriarchy and capitalism as they work within the United States' (p. 117), she draws attention to her description of the cruelties of rape, incest and forced marriage which the female characters suffer. These are, of course, crimes perpetrated by men– and the major part they play in the novel indicates Walker's interest in investigating the structures of male power. Her treatment of the theme is illuminated by Lorde's analysis of the brutalizing effect which racial oppression has on black masculinity: 'Exacerbated by racism and the pressures of powerlessness, violence against Black women and children often becomes a standard within our communities, one by which manliness can be measured' (p. 120). Lorde's comments have obvious relevance to Walker's representation of the violent behaviour of the male protagonists in the early stages of the novel. As Sofia laconically remarks: 'A girl child ain't safe in a family of men.'

One of the most remarkable features of Walker's writing is the concise way she brings together the oppressive effects of male supremacy, economic deprivation and race oppression, highlighting their interrelation. Celie, expressing distress at the grim alternatives that await her sister Nettie, says; 'It nearly kill me to think she might marry somebody like Mr—— or wind up in some white lady kitchen' (p. 17). The sentence is typically dense in meaning. It summarizes in miniature the interplay between sex, economics, race and gender as it affects black women's lives. Sexual exploitation by a man of one's own race or domestic servitude to a white female employer are presented as equally grim alternatives.

Violence against women

Acts of violence perpetrated by men against women have featured in a number of the novels and short stories reviewed in the previous pages. However, the primacy which the topic assumes both in theory and fiction clearly makes it merit a separate, individual discussion. The topic is the focus of controversy among feminists. Radical feminists draw attention to the ubiquity and diversity of male crimes of violence. Their prevalence, they claim, supports their argument that 'men, collectively and as individuals, have an interest in maintaining women's oppression'.[30] Emphasizing the significance of the topic as the basis for feminist struggle, they point out that it is the one issue which, in the present fragmented state of the Women's Movement, concerns and is capable of uniting all women, whatever their political allegiances.[31] Socialist feminists, on the other hand, eager not to offend the male-dominated political parties with which they seek to form alliances, accuse radical feminists of exaggerating its importance. They claim that, by so doing, they alienate men, while relegating women to the roles of helpless victim or morally superior being.[32]

As is the case with the other themes discussed in this study, such as women's community, it is the radical feminist approach, not the socialist feminist one, whose influence is apparent on women's fiction. This, I would suggest, is understandable considering the validity of the radical feminist point of view – one which is cogently expressed by Liz Kelly in the journal *Trouble and Strife* (11, Summer 1987, pp. 23-8). Male violence, as well as being a common motif in women's fiction today, is also, as radical feminists argue, one which concerns all women. It creates a thread linking realist and anti-realist texts, novels which adopt a 'liberal feminist' slant and ones which are overtly political in emphasis. On occasion the writer's introduction of it can give a work, which in every other respect is politically conservative, a radical feminist edge, one which conflicts with its dominant ideological gist. This is the case with Alther's *Other Women*, a work I discussed in the previous chapter. The most convincing feature of this novel (an ideologically confused work if ever there was one!) is Alther's powerful description of the instances of male violence which Caroline encounters in her job as nurse and the disturbing effect which they have on her psyche.

My decision to include the discussion of male violence in the chapter of this study treating patriarchal relations reflects the radical feminist assumption of the connection existing between the two topics. This connection is clearly manifest in the case of rape, the form of violence to first receive theorization by contemporary feminists.[33] Feminists regard rape as a crime which, rather than illustrating the imperative of the male sex drive, has its origin in the male urge to control and dominate women. They challenge the notion that men are violent by nature, pointing out that in a phallocratic culture male sexual behaviour is constructed so as to be violent. From a feminist perspective, the crime of rape illustrates the inequalities between the sexes, while at the same time helping to perpetuate them. It has the effect of cementing bonds between men, simultaneously subjugating women by keeping them in a state of constant fear. Rape functions, to quote Griffin, as 'a male protection racket'.[34] In keeping with these ideas, feminists challenge the view of the rapist as a psychopath with a deviant mentality. He is more likely, they suggest, to be a familiar and trusted figure — a work colleague, boyfriend or husband.

Before proceeding to discuss the relevance of the ideas summarized above to works of fiction, I need to mention some of the problems which the representation of rape and other forms of violence pose to writers. They are diverse and challenging. How can the writer, while emphasizing the horror of the crime, avoid sensationalizing and glamorizing it? How can she succeed in depicting the complex response of the victim — her feelings of terror, humiliation and isolation during the act and her contradictory feelings of guilt and anger afterwards? An even greater problem centres on the writer's portrayal of the figure of the rapist or aggressor. If she gives a detailed analysis of his personality and motivation, she runs the risk of implying that he is a special 'deviant' case. If, on the other hand, she presents him as an unindividuated stereotype, she risks making him appear unconvincing. The New York writer Kathy Acker, it is pertinent to note, has been accused by critics of the first of these faults.[35]

In connection with these issues, it is interesting to look at the two incidents of rape which Piercy introduces into her novel *Small Changes* (1973). Both are positioned extremely carefully in the narrative. Rather than emerging as 'special cases', they serve to underpin the other kinds of exploitation and victimization (social and economic) which women encounter. The rape of Beth, one of the two central characters, illustrates this. At the very moment when she appears to have extricated herself from the pains of an unhappy marriage and is establishing a new life for herself independent of men in a woman's commune, her past suddenly catches up with her. Her husband manages to track her down. He kidnaps her, takes her back to Syracuse his home town and, having locked her in the bedroom, rapes her. Piercy's representation of the event is radical feminist in tenor. The husband's assault on Beth is motivated, she indicates, not by sexual desire but by the impulse to punish and humiliate her. Beth's contradictory response to the ordeal is movingly delineated. 'Why must she hate herself for being hurt,'[36] she wonders – and instinctively compares the experience with the beatings her father used to give her when she was a child. She catches herself envying women who have taken the precaution to learn the art of self-defence.

The other incident of rape in the novel is unusual in the respect that it is presented from the viewpoint of the male aggressor. Phil, an ageing 1960s hippie, looks back on the occasion in his youth when he and his buddies carried out a gang rape. He regards the event with mixed feelings. He himself did not participate physically in it, his disgust preventing him from getting an erection. As Piercy makes clear, the male perpetrators viewed the act as a means to prove their manhood and strengthen their ties with one another by dominating women. To quote Phil's description, 'It had been a ritual, it was feeling powerful and being men together.' He admits, however, that the event turned out in practice very different from his fantasies:

> It wasn't like he thought it would be, it wasn't like the daydreams where the woman yields and likes it and it's groovy. It was like four of them beating up on her. It was like his old man breaking his mother's jaw. He felt scared. He felt they could kill her. It would be all the same ... (p. 287)

Yet even though he feels guilty at condoning the event, he experiences a sense of shame at his failure to make a physical contribution: 'Part of him mocked the idea of manhood that consisted of torturing a girl in an alley and part of him judged with his peers that he was less a man for not being able to get it up when they could' (p. 289). Piercy's focus on the significance of rape as a proof of male virility agrees with Dworkin's observation that, in a patriarchal society, 'the norm of masculinity is phallic aggression'.[37]

Other writers besides Piercy describe the act of rape as cementing links either between individual men or male-dominated institutions. French represents the rape of Chris, Val's teenage daughter, in *The Women's Room* as having this effect. The event, combined with the brutal interrogation of Chris by the police, eventually drive Val to terrorism. She starts to see all men as enemies, 'a bunch of rapists' (p. 586). Carter in *Heroes and Villains* (1969), a work of specular fiction investigating the part played by ideology and force in maintaining a male-supremacist culture, explores the function of rape as a tool for subjugating women. Jewel, the son of the tribe, utilizes it to gain possession of Marianne and force her to marry him. He tells her triumphantly, 'I've nailed you on necessity, you poor bitch.'[38] He further explains the act as motivated by his fear of women. This agrees with the interpretations put forward by the theorists Daly and Irigaray.

Sara Maitland's *Virgin Territory* (1984), a novel analysing patriarchal power-relations in the Roman Catholic Church, is another work which focuses on the topic. It opens with the rape of a nun from a South American mission house. The event has a disturbing effect on Anna, one of the sisters at the mission. It prompts her to interrogate and criticize the Church's attitudes to female sexuality and the position of women. The voices of the Church Fathers, with their message of female sin and subservience, echo in her head. They function as a powerful symbol of patriarchal authority at its most oppressive and traditional.

Other works of fiction, including novels by Kathy Page and Pat Barker, focus particular attention on the responses and emotions of the victim of rape. Page in *Back in the First Person* (1986) explores the effect of the ordeal on Cath, a young school-teacher. Cath is molested by her ex-boyfriend who seeks to punish her for terminating the relationship. The failure of her friends to understand her situation combined with the callous attitudes of the police and lawyers, force her to retreat temporarily into an isolated world of silence and fear. As the title of the novel indicates, Page creates interesting shifts of narrative, moving from first-person to third and back again. The device is a vehicle to represent the temporary breakdown of Cath's capacity for autonomy and self-determination which the experience of rape causes. Barker, in the episode focusing on Kelly Brown in *Union Street* (1982), describes the effect of rape on the consciousness and behaviour of an adolescent girl from a working-class home. Barker movingly traces the ambiguous interplay of shame, 'self-mutilating and aggressive' tendencies[39] which characterizes young Kelly's response to the event.

Rape is, of course, not the only form of male violence to receive attention from theorists and writers of fiction. Battery in the home, brought into prominence both by feminist analyses and the setting up of Women's Refuges around the country, is another theme which writers treat. *Peeling* (1986), by the Australian Grace Bartram, focuses on an older woman's experience of working in a Women's Refuge. Moira Duff in *The Vocation of Pearl Duncan* (1982) explores the topic from a more personal angle, giving a raw and unsentimental account of the situation of a woman trapped in a violent marriage. Rejecting myths of female superiority, she emphasizes the speed with which Pearl grows accustomed to a life of violence as well as the way she colludes emotionally with her aggressor. She also highlights the social and economic difficulties Pearl encounters in trying to extricate herself and her sons from their predicament.

Black women writers have also made a significant contribution to the treatment of the theme of violence against women. Alice Walker's short story 'Porn' (*You Can't Keep a Good Woman Down*, 1971) examines the role of woman as object of sexual exchange, cementing bonds between men. The novel *The Unbelonging* (1985) by the Jamaican writer Joan Riley, based in Great Britain, focuses on the topics of incest and racial violence. Both writers, it is important to recognize, place emphasis on their protagonists' capacity to survive and resist acts of exploitation and aggression. They are by no means passive victims but make an effort to challenge or elude such acts.

One of the most memorable studies of male violence by a black woman writer is Toni Cade Bambera's short story 'Talkin Bout

Sonny' (*Gorilla, My Love*, 1972). Bambera is an exceptionally talented writer with an acute political awareness and here, as is generally the case, she uses her wit for radical purposes. She gives a savagely ironic indictment of the consequences of the cultural stereotyping of man as aggressor and woman as victim, the 'natural' target of his abuse. The story, intended to shock the reader, centres on the reception by Sonny's buddies of the news that he has just killed his wife. The murder, an exceptionally brutal one, is condoned by the men on the grounds of the male urge to violence: 'It's not his fault.... Something just came over him.' It is further justified on the grounds that the wife was 'a bitch' who 'maybe had it coming ...'. In their enthusiasm, they carry the acceptance of phallocratic codes of aggression to its logical conclusion. They transform the crime from a murder to an act of heroism, celebrating it as 'maybe ... the most beautiful thing Sonny has ever done in his whole life'![40]

The works of fiction previously discussed in this section have in common the fact that they all focus attention on one particular form of male violence. The 1980s, however, have seen the appearance of a new kind of novel. Treating violence against women as *the* distinguishing feature of a male supremacist society, it seeks ambitiously to investigate the interrelation between a variety of different forms and manifestations. Barker's *Blow Your House Down* (1984) and Atwood's *Bodily Harm* (1981) are two noteworthy examples of this trend. The two novels are linked by their comprehensive and deliberately disturbing treatment of themes of violence. They differ totally, however, in every other respect. Barker, using the mode of socialist feminist 'realism', takes as her focus a group of prostitutes in the recognizable, closely documented setting of a town in the North of England. Atwood, on the contrary, creating an anti-realist text centring on the fractured self, places her characters in the alien, sleazily exotic setting of a Caribbean island. Her novel exploits a number of features commonly associated with the Gothic mode. It also takes on, in the latter stages, the nightmarish quality of dystopian fiction, a facet which links it to her subseqently published work *The Handmaid's Tale* (1985).

The events recounted by Barker in *Blow Your House Down* are based on the incident of the 'Yorkshire Ripper', the sex-murderer Peter Sutcliffe who in recent years terrorized the North of England.[41] An interesting feature of Barker's novel is that it succeeds in bringing together both radical feminist and socialist feminist perspectives on prostitution. Her representation of the prostitutes' experience of victimization by the sex-murderer has affinities with the analysis of the prostitution system formulated by the revolutionary feminists Sheila Jeffreys and Maureen O'Hara. Central to Barker's account is the idea that prostitution both promotes and perpetuates male dominance. As well as reinforcing the division of women into 'pure' and 'impure', it gives men the licence, in exchange for the payment of a fee, to exploit them sexually and brutalize them. Prostitution enables men, in Jeffreys's vivid phrase, 'to feel more poweful over all women by abusing one'.[42] The comments voiced by O'Hara are also relevant:

> All women who work as prostitutes are treated as the legitimate prey of male sexual violence. The institution of prostitution creates a group of women who are social outcasts, whom men can freely abuse and degrade.[43]

The view of prostitution expressed in the above quotation is, in fact, extremely close to Barker's.

While Barker's representation of the prostitute's position as victim of male violence is radical or revolutionary feminist in spirit, her analysis of their economic situation is socialist feminist. She explores, for example, the interaction existing between the women's lack of financial security in the home, where they are expected by the authorities to survive on a male wage (one which is often non-existent), and their exploited position in the local factory where many of them have work experience. It is their failure to survive by these 'respectable' methods, she suggests, which drives them to earn a living on the streets. Once there, they become vulnerable to the abuse of men in general. They are treated as 'legitimate prey' not only by their clients but also by the police. They are 'objects of exchange' in the most literal sense, used to cement bonds and work out antagonisms between different groups of men. The police, instead of trying to protect them from the sex-murderer, use them as bait to catch him. Barker parallels the acts of sexual violence the women encounter from their clients to the domestic violence they suffer from husbands and boyfriends in the home. She also emphasizes the lack of a clear demarcation-line between 'violent sex' and the kind of sexual practice which society regards as acceptable.

Baker reinforces her representation of the workings of male power by a striking, if somewhat heavy, use of symbolism. The local chicken factory where some of the women work emerges, through the emphasis on the division of labour operating there, as a microcosm of patriarchal power-relations. The men are assigned the violent task of killing the birds while the women are allocated the menial, though equally unpleasant job, of plucking and gutting. The chicken carcases lying on the factory bench, their 'plump, naked, white thighs spread wide',[44] function as an image of the women's role as the helpless victim of aggression and exploitation, both sexual and social.

Despite the grimness of the theme she treats, Barker's portrayal of the prostitutes' lives contains a number of positive features. Optimistic elements include the sense of community which – in the face of fearful odds – they succeed in fostering among themselves.

Like Barker's *Blow Your House Down*, Atwood's *Bodily Harm* investigates woman's position in a male supremacist culture, focusing particular attention on the roles assigned to her of victim of male violence and object of sexual exchange. The aspect of sexuality on which Atwood concentrates, however, is not the prostitution system but the cult of permissive sexuality. She traces the progress her hero Rennie makes from a libertarian approach to sex, in which she accepts her boyfriend Jake's reassurances that sadistic portrayals of women in pornography and an element of violent sex-play are healthy, harmless fun, to an unwilling recognition of the dangers they involve. As Atwood remarks, commenting on Rennie's growing nervousness about relations with men, 'She's afraid of men and it's simple, it's rational, she's afraid of men because men are frightening.'[45] Rennie is an ambitious young journalist who prides herself on her lack of moral scruples and hedonistic view of life. She is very unwilling indeed to admit to anything as unfashionable as being scared of men. A number of different events force her to do so. An operation for breast cancer in which a male surgeon wields the knife is followed by a series of mysterious attacks on her person. Her managing editor also plays a part. He instructs her to inspect a collection of sadistic pornography, held in police custody, with the aim of writing a feature about it. The collection includes what is laconically described as 'a couple of sex-and-death pieces' (p. 210). The objects in the collection are referred to by one of Rennie's acquaintances as 'raw material' (p. 209). The phrase is the subject of mordant punning, a device in which the novel abounds. With a growing sense of horror, Rennie comes to perceive its applicability to herself. In the binary system woman: nature/man: culture, operating in a patriarchal society, she herself constitutes a piece of 'raw material'. She exists to be experimented upon, psychologically moulded or literally carved up according to the whim of the next aggressive male she meets.

Atwood does not present the motif of sadistic pornography to the reader in isolation. On the contrary, it constitutes the hub of her analysis of male violence. The theorist Dworkin connects the prevalence of pornography in existing society to the violent practices of a male-supremacist political system: 'Pornography reveals that male pleasure is inextricably tied to victimizing, hurting, exploiting; that sexual fun and sexual passion in the privacy of the male imagination are inseparable from the brutality of male history.'[46]

Atwood makes a similar connection between the two areas. Her decision to shift the location of the action in the second half of the novel from urban Canada to the rural setting of a Caribbean island is the vehicle by which she achieves this. Whereas the first half of the novel explores the significance of pornography and violent sex to the 'privacy of the male imagination', the latter half, describing the ruthless political struggles taking place on the island, focuses attention on 'the brutality of male history'. The political struggles on the isle epitomize, in fact, patriarchal relations at their most stark. The men compete in drug smuggling, gun running and violent electioneering, leaving to women the roles of child-bearer, drudge and object of exchange. Watching two men haggling over her life, Rennie is pressured by the terror of the moment to deconstruct the elevated position which the romantic love-code assigns to woman and perceive her true status: 'Rennie can see what she is now: she's an object of negotiation. The truth about knights comes suddenly clear; the maidens were only an excuse. The dragon was the real thing' (p. 258). As Rennie is forced to recognize, the real business of life, including competition, bargaining, confronting danger, takes place in the male world. To quote Dworkin, 'all credible transactions of power, authority, and authenticity take place among men.'[47]

Atwood deliberately denies the reader the comfort of dismissing Rennie's fear of male violence as idiosyncratic or perverse by giving her, in the concluding stages of the novel, a female companion Lora whose views are, if anything, more extreme. Lora is a native of the Caribbean, and her experience of male brutality quite puts Rennie's in the shade! The situations of the privileged white woman and the underprivileged woman of colour, though different, are shown to involve a similar terror of male aggression.

As mentioned above, *Bodily Harm* reveals pronounced affinities with the Gothic. The Gothic genre, traditionally noted for its representation of woman as victim, becomes in Atwood's hands the perfect medium for depicting contemporary woman caught unaware in the 'rape culture'[48] which pervades society. Motifs associated with the genre which Atwood introduces include: the ingenuous heroine as the victim of male manipulation and attack; an intrigue plot in which the male protagonists compete for power; the collapsing of conventional boundaries between external/internal and animate/inanimate; and the reference to certain socially taboo topics – in this case, cancer and sado-masochistic sexual practice.[49]

Underlying Atwood's analysis in the novel of woman's situation as the victim of male violence is a motif which forms the basis of many of her works of fiction. This is, woman's position in a phallocratic culture as the 'other' of man. The representation of woman as 'raw material', the prevalence of which Rennie comes with horror to recognize, portrays her, in philosophical terms, as the ground upon which man constructs his violent fantasies. This agrees, of course, with the perceptions of the French theorist Irigaray who points out that in a phallocratic culture:

> Woman is the reserve of 'sensuality' for the elevation of intelligence, she is the matter used for the imprint of forms, the representative representing negativity (death), dark continent of dreams and fantasies ...[50]

The topic of pornography which Atwood treats in the first half of the novel is admirably suited to exposing the disturbing truth about woman's role as the victim of male acts of violence, at both a personal and a cultural level.

Conclusion

The theme of patriarchal relations, whether treated in terms of the individual family unit or of the structures of society as a whole, has proved to be a major source of inspiration to women writers. As illustrated by the novels and short stories I have reviewed in this chapter, writers differ considerably in the perspectives they adopt to the topic and in the narrative strategies and devices which they utilize. Novels taking a radical feminist approach to patriarchal power exist side by side with ones which explore the interlocking structures of male dominance, class and – on occasion – race. Black writers, as one would expect, have made an especially vital contribution to the latter theme. Psychoanalytical studies of male supremacy, exploring woman's roles as object of exchange and as the ground of male fantasies and dreams, coexist with accounts which are sociological, foregrounding the economic and social aspects of woman's subordinate status. Male violence against women also plays a significant part in fictional representations of patriarchal power. All in all, the topic of patriarchal relations emerges as one of the most central in women's fiction today.

Notes

1. 'The trouble with patriarchy', *No Turning Back*, ed. cit., pp. 72-8.
2. See Rosalind Coward, *Patriarchal Precedents* (Routledge & Kegan Paul, 1983).
3. 'On patriarchy', *Feminist Review*, 3 (1979), p. 66.
4. 'The traffic in women: Notes on the "political economy" of sex', *Toward An Anthropology of Women*, ed. Rayna R. Reiter (Monthly Review Press, 1975), p. 174.

5. For a discussion of the topic see Eisenstein, *Contemporary Feminist Thought*, ed. cit., pp. 15-26.
6. Ibid., p. 112.
7. Marge Piercy, *The High Cost of Living* (Harper and Row, 1978); Sandy Boucher, 'The cutting room', *Mae West is Dead*, op. cit., pp. 182-94; Emma Tennant, *Hotel de Dream* (Gollancz, 1976); Mary Dorcey, 'A country dance', *Girls Next Door*, ed. cit., pp. 159-75; Angela Carter, *The Magic Toyshop* (Heinemann, 1967) and *Nights at the Circus* (Chatto and Windus, 1984). I include an analysis of the latter two novels in my essay on Carter's fiction in *Women Reading Women's Writing*, ed. Sue Roe (Harvester Press, 1987), pp. 179-205.
8. *Compulsory Heterosexuality and Lesbian Existence*, ed. cit., p. 12.
9. *Sexual Politics*, ed. cit., p. 33.
10. Anne Duchêne, review, *Times Literary Supplement*, 3,968 (21 April 1978), p. 433.
11. Annis Pratt, *Archetypal Patterns in Women's Fiction* (Harvester Press, 1982), pp. 29-37.
12. *The Women's Room* (Sphere, 1978), p. 63. Subsequent references are to this edition and are in the text.
13. *Against Our Will: men, women and rape* (Penguin, 1976).
14. Op. cit., p. 25.
15. *The President's Child* (Coronet, 1983), p. 161. Subsequent references are to this edition and are in the text.
16. For reference to woman's role as object of exchange, see Rubin, op. cit., and Irigaray, 'Women on the market', *This Sex Which is Not One*, ed. cit., pp. 170-91.
17. *About Chinese Women*, trans. Anita Barrows (Marion Boyars, 1977), pp. 17-24.
18. *Gyn/Ecology*, ed. cit., p. 402.
19. *Hotel de Dream* (Picador, 1983), p. 8. Subsequent references are to this edition and are in the text.
20. *About Chinese Women*, ed. cit., pp. 17-33.
21. 'Fundamental feminism: process and perspective', *Building Feminist Theory*, ed. cit., p. 37.
22. 'Class realities: create a new power base', *Building Feminist Theory*, ed. cit., p. 125.
23. *The Power of Women and the Subversion of the Community* (Falling Wall Press, 1973).
24. Op. cit., p. 244.
25. Alison Light, review, *Spare Rib*, 91 (February 1980), p. 46.
26. 'The city as battleground: the novelist as combatant', *American Urban Experience: essays on the city and literature*, ed. Michael C. Jaye and Ann Chalmers Watts (Manchester University Press, 1981), pp. 210, 211.
27. *The High Cost of Living* (Harper and Row, 1978), p. 135. Subsequent references are to this edition and are in the text.
28. *Sister Outsider* (Crossing Press, 1984), p. 116. Subsequent references are to this edition and are in the text.
29. Brighton L.T.P. Group, 'Problems of the progressive text: *The Color Purple* by Alice Walker', *Literature Teaching Politics 6: Conference Papers, 1985*, pp. 117-46. Subsequent critiques of Walker's novel refer to this publication. Quotes from the novel refer to the Women's Press edition, 1983.
30. Liz Kelly, 'The new defeatism', *Trouble and Strife*, 11 (Summer, 1987), pp. 23-8.
31. Sabina Lovibond, *New Statesman*, 112, no. 2888 (1 August 1986), p. 19.

32. See Segal, *Is the Future Female?* ed. cit.
33. See Brownmiller, *Against Our Will*, ed. cit.
34. 'Rape: the all-American crime', *Women: a feminist perspective*, ed. Jo Freeman (Mayfield Publishing, 1975), pp. 24-39.
35. *Feminist Review*, 6 (1986), p. 48.
36. *Small Changes* (Fawcett, 1974), p. 306. Subsequent references are to this edition and are in the text.
37. *Our Blood*, ed. cit., p. 46.
38. *Heroes and Villains* (Penguin, 1981), p. 56.
39. *Union Street* (Virago, 1982), p. 46.
40. *Gorilla, My Love*, ed. cit., p. 84.
41. A feminist analysis of Peter Sutcliffe's murderous crimes is provided by Nicole Ward Jouve's study *The Streetcleaner: the Yorkshire Ripper case on trial* (Marion Boyars, 1986).
42. *Women Against Violence Against Women*, ed. cit., p. 69.
43. Ibid., p. 72.
44. *Blow Your House Down* (Virago, 1984), p. 141.
45. *Bodily Harm* (Virago, 1983), p. 290. Subsequent references are to this edition and are in the text.
46. *Pornography: men possessing women* (Women's Press, 1981), p. 69.
47. *Our Blood*, ed. cit., p. 104.
48. See Eisenstein, *Contemporary Feminist Thought*, ed. cit., p. 104.
49. See Rosemary Jackson's analysis of Gothic motifs in *Fantasy: the literature of subversion* (Methuen, 1981).
50. *Speculum*, ed. cit., p. 141.

Chapter Five

Motherhood
and Mothering

Motherhood is not only a core human relationship but a political insti-
tution, a keystone to the domination in every sphere of women by men.
Adrienne Rich, *On Lies, Secrets and Silence: selected prose 1966–1978*
(Virago, 1980), p. 216

Introduction: Shifting approaches to motherhood

A memorable episode in Roberts's *A Piece of the Night* (1978), a novel
exploring relations between mothers and daughters which will be
discussed subsequently, presents Julie and her mother Claire engaging in a heated argument about feminist attitudes to motherhood.
Julie regards the Women's Movement as a source of positive support
to mothers; she insists: 'Feminism's about mothers. It's about back-
ing them up.' Claire, however, is sceptical. 'You could have fooled
me!', she retorts, adding with great bitterness, 'As far as I can see, you
hate everything that I believe in.'[1]

The dispute between Julie and Claire makes a suitable starting-
point for my discussion of themes of motherhood and mothering in
contemporary women's fiction, since it epitomizes very clearly the
contradictions and conflicting viewpoints which feminist approaches
to the topic display. These are just as apparent in novels and short
stories as they are in theoretical works. In fact, a striking feature of the
fiction considered in this chapter is the polarized attitudes to motherhood which they display. A number of novels, chiefly ones written
in the 1970s, foreground the oppressive aspects of motherhood. They
depict women's reproductive capacities as making them vulnerable
to male control, and describe childbirth and the raising of children as
painful, burdensome experiences. Other novels written in the 1980s,
in contrast, treat the topic in a distinctly celebratory light. They

present motherhood as a source of pleasure and ambiguous power. One novel at least succeeds in bringing together these two contrary perspectives. This is Atwood's much acclaimed work *The Handmaid's Tale* (1985). An example of dystopian fiction, it achieves the feat of focusing attention on both the personal and the political facets of motherhood. The modes of writing which the authors adopt also reveal marked differences. Realism, anti-realism and fantasy all play a part in the spectrum of styles.

The past fifteen years have seen a radical shift in the theorization of motherhood and mothering in feminist thought. In the early 1970s attitudes were, on the whole, negative. In that period, to quote Eisenstein, 'that feminism and motherhood were in diametrical opposition had seemed almost axiomatic'.[2] Theorists presented the bearing and rearing of children as a form of drudgery. They held them culpable for keeping women tied to the home, thus preventing them participating in the public sphere of paid employment and political struggle. Radical and socialist feminists alike devoted their energies to thinking up means to 'liberate' women from the practice and ideology of motherhood. Firestone advocated the replacing of biological birth processes by artificial methods of reproduction while the socialist feminist Mitchell recommended collective childcare and abortion on demand.[3]

The predominantly negative approach to motherhood, adopted by feminists in the early years of the Movement, coincided – very unfairly – with expressions of resentment and hostility towards the figure of the mother herself. Castigated as the tool of patriarchy, she was attacked for the part she played in socializing children into traditional gender roles, thus perpetuating the positions of male dominance and female subordination. Negative attitudes to motherhood are, of course, closely related to a negative view of femininity. As M. Rivka Polatnick remarks, '*mothering* behaviour is not very different from *feminine behaviour*'.[4] It was, in fact, only when traditional feminine attributes such as the capacity to nurture, cooperate and show emotion started to receive re-evaluation in the works of Baker Miller and others that a reappraisal of motherhood and the mother began to take place. Only then did a more just and complex analysis of both topics become possible. The connection between concepts of 'motherhood' and 'femininity' are clearly discernible in certain works of fiction. The contradictions of power/vulnerability inherent in the maternal position is a theme which Tennant and Weldon treat. The two writers also emphasize the disruptive threat which femininity and motherhood pose the phallocratic social order and its values.

The reinterpretation of ideas of motherhood and mothering which has taken place among feminists depends to a large degree on the interest in the topic of the pre-oedipal bond between mother and child shown by both American and French theorists. Adrienne Rich's study *Of Women Born: motherhood as experience and institution* places motherhood firmly in the context of sexual politics, presenting it as an arena of feminist struggle. By distinguishing the *institution of motherhood*, as constructed by a male-dominated culture, from the *experience*, she highlights the control which patriarchy exerts on women's reproductive capacities. At the same time, she recognizes the potential for pleasure and self-fulfilment inherent in the bearing and rearing of children. As Rich herself comments, though for many women 'mothering has been penal servitude, *it need not be*'.[5]

Two other American theorists who focus attention on the pre-oedipal bond are Nancy Chodorow and Dorothy Dinnerstein. Though adopting different viewpoints, each discovers in childcare arrangements under patriarchy the psychological roots of woman's relegation to the private domain of the home and her relative exclusion from the public one of paid professional work and politics. The theories of Rich, Chodorow and Dinnerstein are especially relevant to two of the themes which form the basis of my discussion of fictional texts – *The politics of reproduction* and *Relations between mothers and daughters*.

French theorists have also made an important contribution to the analysis of motherhood. Cixous and Kristeva each makes connections, though of a very different kind, between writing, femininity and the pre-oedipal. Cixous describes *écriture féminine* as a form of writing, with its inspiration in the body, which originates from the mother's voice.[6] Though available to both sexes, in a phallocratic culture it most frequently occurs in texts written by women. Kristeva associates motherhood with the attribute of *maternal jouisance* and the potential for disruption which it possesses. This *jouissance*, she points out, is both feared and devalued by a phallocratic culture which recognizes the threat it constitutes to the status quo.[7] In my opinion, it is impossible to relate the theories of Cixous and Kristeva to the stylistic aspect of works of fiction by British writers in any systematic way. However, the identification of femininity with an experimentally fluid form of writing which subverts the reader's expectations of linear, rational discourse, merging identities and ego-boundaries in a manner similar to that which occurs in the pre-oedipal mother–infant bond, is a feature of several of the novels considered here. Eva Figes's *Days* (1974) and Roberts's *A Piece of the Night* (1978), discussed in a subsequent section, are fascinating examples of it.

Attitudes to motherhood current among feminists at the moment reveal a number of inconsistencies and confusions. Appalling contradictions exist between practice and theory. For example, the prominence the topic enjoys in academic discussion and works of fiction has done little if anything to improve the actual situation of mothers. Their social status remains as low and their economic circumstances as underprivileged as ever. This appears to be the case not only in society at large but also unfortunately in the Women's Movement. A contributor to a recently published collection of feminist essays complains bitterly of 'the discrimination, degradation, hatred, ignoring and excluding'[8] meted out to mothers by feminists who are child-free. As the quotation indicates, the issue of motherhood and its political implications is a very contentious one among feminists today. Radical and socialist feminists criticize cultural feminists for promoting a cult of motherhood that serves to reaffirm the stereotypical view of women as 'the eternally feminine nurturer and peacemaker'.[9] Lynne Segal moreover suggests that the popularity of motherhood in contemporary culture (fiction no doubt included) has its origins in the lack of satisfaction available to women in other areas of life:

> In my view, the new focus on mothering, the maternal revival in feminism, has come partly from feminists' disappointment that our aspirations to engage in creative and rewarding work, to struggle for social change, to build warm and supportive communal spaces and friendship networks – as well as to choose to have children – have proved so often difficult, stressful or transitory.[10]

The fact that it is themes of motherhood and mothering which are in fashion in novels and short stories at the moment, and which constitute the topic of discussion here, rather than themes of women's experience of paid employment and political struggle in the public world, appears to support Segal's point.

It is difficult to determine whether the primacy accorded to motherhood in contemporary fiction serves to draw attention *to* or deflect attention *from* the problematic position of actual mothers. The analysis of fictional texts in the following pages will give the reader ample opportunity to ponder this intriguing and important question.

The politics of reproduction

Feminist theorists with an interest in motherhood differ markedly as to the particular aspect of the maternal processes which they choose to emphasize – biological, psychological or domestic. A point on which they all do agree, however, is the immense importance the topic bears to the domain of sexual politics and the dialectic of sex. Thus Rich, writing in radical feminist vein, observes that 'motherhood is not only a core human relationship but a political institution, a keystone to the domination in every sphere of women by men'.[11] And Oakley, in a socialist feminist study, points out, 'how reproduction is managed and controlled is inseparable from how women are managed and controlled.'[12]

The analysis of the sexual politics of motherhood also plays a major part in works of fiction. In this study we have already come across one example of a novel focusing on this area. This is Weldon's *The President's Child*, with its representation of woman's complex position in the system of patrilineal inheritance. The contradictions of power/vulnerability which the capacity to bear and rear children confers on women, a major theme in Weldon's novel, also dominate a number of other fictional texts. The four novels I discuss in this section illustrate some of the different perspectives and narrative strategies which writers adopt in treating the topic. Walker's *Meridian* (1976) illustrates the way childbearing makes women vulnerable to male control and manipulation. However, the novel also introduces certain positive perceptions. Walker affirms woman's ability to challenge the restrictions of the maternal role and, having extricated herself from them, achieve independence. Weldon's *Puffball* (1980) and Tennant's *Alice Fell* (1980), two novels which possess a number of features in common, take a very different approach. Both adopt a 'cultural feminist' viewpoint, identifying woman with nature and the body. Their perspectives, in this respect, may be criticized as ideologically regressive. Both writers none the less succeed in presenting motherhood in a light which is deliberately ambiguous. On the one hand, they celebrate and to a degree idealize the processes of birth and reproduction; on the other, they present them as the hub of a fierce battle between the sexes. Atwood's *The Handmaid's Tale* (1985), the novel I consider last, is the most ambitious of the four in intellectual scope and narrative design. It also gives the most comprehensive and balanced analysis of themes of motherhood and reproduction. As indicated earlier, Atwood succeeds in bringing together both personal and political, positive and negative, facets.

The contradictions of power/vulnerability which childbearing involves for women, the topic which unites the four novels under discussion, is one which theorists have explored in detail. Rich, for example, commenting on the mother's ambiguous position, suggests that there exists 'a basic contradiction throughout patriarchy: between the laws and sanctions designed to keep women essentially powerless, and the attribution to mothers of almost superhuman power (of control, of influence, of life-support)'.[13] The dichotomy of maternal power/female powerlessness is also, of course, central to the argument Dinnerstein puts forward in *The Mermaid and the Minotaur*. It is, she claims, the immense power which mothers wield over their children in the private sphere of the home which accounts, paradoxically, for the subordinate role assigned to women in other areas of life. The patriarchal social order responds to the threat which maternal power represents by imposing strict control on women's activities and restricting their access to the public sphere. A question over which feminists disagree is, is the power which the mother wields in the home more illusory than real?[14] Psychoanalytic theorists have formulated, in fact, the concept of 'the phallic mother' to denote the fantasy image of the omnipotent mother which the infant projects. The term signifies, to quote Ruth Mack Brunswick, the image of 'the all-powerful mother, the mother who is capable of everything and who possesses every valuable attribute'.[15]

These theories and ideas, as we shall see, do much to illuminate the perspectives of the four novelists discussed below.

Walker's decision to highlight the oppressive aspects of the maternal role in *Meridian* is in consonance with the dominant theme she seeks to delineate. This is the struggle waged by black women to liberate themselves from the private sphere of the family and achieve access to the public world of education and political struggle. Meridian, the hero, eventually succeeds in achieving this goal. Having left school and borne a son, she is subsequently politicized by an encounter with a group of Civil Rights workers. Braving the ridicule and abuse of her fellow townsfolk, she decides to give away her son in order to free herself to leave home and go to college. After completing her college education, she proceeds to commit all her energies to Civil Rights.

Walker's most striking achievement in the novel is to examine the ideology of motherhood as it affects black American women, exposing its oppressive aspects. As Barbara Christian remarks in her cogent commentary, Walker 'scrutinized that tradition which is based on the monumental myth of Black motherhood', including 'the true stories of sacrifice Black mothers performed for their children'.[16] The theme of maternal self-sacrifice and its unhappy consequences is especially relevant to the episodes depicting Meridian's relations with her mother, Mrs Hill. Mrs Hill is portrayed as giving up her career, her professional ambitions and her peace of mind in order to marry and raise a family. Her experience of the trials of childcare make her increasingly bitter and depressed: 'She could never forgive her community, her family, his family, the whole

world, for not warning her against children.'[17] The chain of guilt
linking mother and daughter, once forged, is difficult to break.
Meridian, as a child, perceives sadly that she and the other children
are a burden to their mother: 'It was for stealing her mother's
serenity, for shattering her mother's emerging self, that Meridian felt
guilty from the very first, though she was unable to understand how
this could possibly be her fault' (p. 41).

The sense of frustrated ambitions and loss of selfhood experienced
by Mrs Hill as she finds her time and energies consumed by child-
rearing activites are felt equally strongly by Meridian herself on the
birth of her own son. She becomes fiercely resentful of the double
standard. Whereas she is expected to devote her whole life to
childcare, her husband is required merely to make the occasional
appearance in the home. At one point she is driven to despair by
isolation and frustrated hopes; she contemplates killing her son and
taking her own life. Walker's description of Meridian's anguished
state of mind in this episode, and of the brutal abortion she
subsequently undergoes, reveals affinities with Rich's analysis of the
more distressing aspects of maternity in her study *Of Woman Born*.
By giving away her child and refusing to bear another one, Meridian
does succeed in breaking the chain of the 'reproduction of mothering'.
She also challenges the stereotype of maternal self-sacrifice. However,
she pays a heavy price for this. As well as social stigma, she suffers
guilt-feelings induced by the moralistic attitudes of her family and
the community. They condemn her as a heartless monster.

Meridian, though written primarily in a realist mode, contains a
number of features verging on the symbolic. These include the choice
of the name Meridian for the hero; the account of the history of the
Sojourner magnolia tree; and the parable-like nature of several of the
chapter headings. These features draw attention to the political
significance of the novel. The principle of irony informing several of
the episodes prevents the reader from taking refuge in complacent
assumptions of 'historical progress'. The Sojourner tree, a symbol of
black liberation, is destroyed by a group of students rioting in the
cause of 'freedom'. The Sacred Serpent Park, when eventually the
black community is allowed entry to it, no longer possesses any
historical meaning for them.

In marked contrast to Walker's vivid account of a black woman's
struggle to liberate herself from the oppressive facets of the maternal
role in the context of the Civil Rights Movement of the 1960s, are the
celebratory delineations of motherhood created by Weldon and
Tennant. Identifying woman with nature and the body, and portraying her as ruled by hormonal and physical processes, the latter two

writers emphasize the pleasurable aspects of domesticity and mother–child relations. At the same time, however, they depict the home as the site of a power-struggle between the sexes. Their two novels also have in common an atmosphere of a privileged, upper-middle-class existence of a particularly British kind. Weldon interweaves into her text references to the folklore and superstitions of the Gloucestershire countryside, while Tennant alludes to myths of British Empire and the Suez Crisis. The idealized and romanticized representations of reproduction and childcare which both writers construct raise interesting questions of interpretation. Does one praise them for valorizing aspects of woman's life which are generally disparaged and marginalized, or criticize them for concealing their drudgery and tedium under a veneer of false glamour?

The central theme of *Puffball* is a woman's reproductive capacities. The novel opens with Liffey and Richard, a young couple who undertake what proves to be the hazardous project of moving from the city to the country, deciding to start a family. Then, in a series of chapters amusingly and accurately entitled 'inside Liffey', Weldon proceeds to describe the perils and triumphs of conception, pregnancy and childbirth. *Puffball* is not, of course, the first of Weldon's novels to introduce a heroine who is pregnant. *Down Among the Women* (1971), published nine years earlier, gives a far less lyrical and celebratory account of the topic. Poor Scarlet lies in bed 'swollen and monstrous',[18] the object of her women friends' ambivalent attention. While envying her for having 'left the girls and joined the women', they simultaneously pity her, thinking 'there but for the grace of their hormones, the chancy consideration of men, go they' (p. 20). Central to the novel is the dictum: 'A good woman knows that nature is her enemy. Look what it does to her' (p. 61). Technology and culture, in contrast, are shown in general to be her friend. This is true both of the 'packet of frozen fish fingers ... and spoonful of instant mashed potato', convenience foods which simplify the chore of cooking, and the diaphragm contraceptive which the unmarried Helen wisely has fitted. *Puffball*, like *Down Among the Women*, focuses at least to a degree on the value of technology and culture. An attempt at natural childbirth, disastrously mismanaged, results in Lally producing a stillborn child. And it is a caesarian section, performed by a male surgeon in a modern hospital, which saves Liffey's and her baby's lives. However, on the whole it is *nature*, not culture, which Weldon chooses to foreground and celebrate in *Puffball*. The celebration is, however, ambiguous, since 'Mother Nature' is portrayed as a contradictory goddess.[19] Though exercising a benevolent influence on Liffey's pregnancy, she is none the less acknowledged to be 'a bitch', blind to the fate of the individual and concerned only with the survival of the species.

In presenting sexual reproduction as the hub of the battle between the sexes, Weldon explores the key question: is woman's ability to bear children a source of power or of vulnerability? Her answer is equivocal. Liffey discovers, on becoming pregnant, that her power in the *public* world decreases. She loses her money and becomes socially and economically dependent on her husband Richard. She also becomes vulnerable to the manipulation of Mabs and Tucker, the ominous farming folk whom she encounters in the countryside. At the same time, however, she gains new *psychic* powers – 'Liffey, now, had powers of her own' (p. 142), Weldon announces triumphantly. These, represented by Liffey's ability to communicate with her unborn child and its 'singing', are described as strong enough to compete with Mabs's witchcraft and noxious potions. Mabs's powers, also stemming from her maternal status, are depicted as similarly ambiguous. They wax and wane, in Lawrentian manner, with the cycle of day and night.

In terms of genre, *Puffball* is very clearly a pastoral comedy. It can be read, in fact, as a fascinating exercise in intertextuality – an innovatory, 'feminine' version of Shakespeare's *A Midsummer Night's Dream*. Like the lovers in Shakespeare's play, Liffey and Richard move from the city to the countryside. Here, under the influence of Mab and her potions, they commit a series of follies, engaging in a hectic change of sexual partners. Order, in the form of marital monogamy, is eventually restored and the couple return to the city. The image of the moon, with its connotations of change, the feminine and the erotic, is a dominant one. There is even an echo of Shakespeare's verse in Weldon's description of the puffballs – 'Three white globes ... stood blindly sentinel' (pp. 18-19).

Whereas Weldon concludes *Puffball* with a description of the event of a birth, Tennant opens *Alice Fell* with an account of one. Alice, the eponymous heroine, is born and reared in an English country house. The house functions as more than a mere setting for events, becoming in the course of the text an ingeniously contrived image of the patriarchal social order. The upper storey is inhabited by the Old Man, a mysteriously despotic figure with associations of Old Testament God, paterfamilias and elder statesman. He lives as a recluse, sustained by memories of the British Empire. He finds a degree of companionship in his menagerie of animals (recalling the creatures in the Garden of Eden); the group of 'immortals' (ghosts of male intellectuals of the past, including Freud and Jung); and his cousin George, a figure resembling Hoffmann's Dr Coppelius who constructs automata and marionettes. The old Man is cared for by Mr and Mrs Paxton, a local couple from the village. They are of inferior social status – and live on the ground floor of the mansion.

The central theme of the novel, as in Tennant's other works, is the disruptive effects of femininity on phallocratic culture. The patriarchal order, represented by the Old Man, is disturbed first by the appearance of Molly and Pam, sterotypes of 1920s womanhood, and secondly and more drastically by the birth of Mrs Paxton's daughter, Alice. The birth, described as an occasion of transgressive *jouissance* in accord with Kristeva's ideas, is celebrated in a series of elaborate conceits linking microcosm and macrocosm. Mrs Paxton's heaving body becomes a 'farmyard', teeming with animal life. The water flowing from her womb is depicted as a flood which threatens to drown the public, male supremacist world and its representatives:

> Mrs Paxton groaned, and water came from her. Newspapers were flooded and Mrs Grogan [the midwife] rushed to change them: Suez Crisis and Woman's Own and in the last rush an old Picture Post. Winston Churchill was pushed under Mrs Paxton's monumental legs and lay in the water. His face frowned, and dissolved ...[20]

As is evident from this quotation, sexual reproduction emerges in the novel as the hub of the power-struggle between the sexes. With Alice's birth, the feminine principle achieves temporary dominance. The male residents of the house feel ousted and supplanted: 'They had a fear that the child would destroy the world they had made around them' (p. 39).

The disruptive effects of Alice's birth are represented metaphorically by the fantastic antics performed by the woollen ball hanging at the end of her cot. It undergoes a series of surreal transformations, becoming alternately the orb of the sun, the globe of the world and even the atom bomb, 'a new ball of destruction' (p. 43). In the pre-oedipal stage of Alice's existence, Mrs Paxton reigns unchallenged. A queen with a sceptre of feathers, she harnesses the natural forces of wood and river to help her with her domestic chores. Engaging in an orgy of cosmic spring-cleaning, she turns the house into a round 'nest', 'a round ball, suffocating as a ball of wool' (p. 49). Her reign is, however, short-lived. When Alice grows older, the mother's power declines and male dominance reasserts itself. Although in the novel historical changes are described as taking place, ideals of the British Empire giving way to a new focus on technology and social equality, the male supremacist order remains as strong as ever. On reaching womanhood, Alice runs away from the country to London. Whether or not she achieves any form of liberation is open to question since she moves from the care of her father to the more brutal control of her boyfriend Joe. As is generally the case with Tennant, the disruptive effects of femininity appear ephemeral. Though momentarily disturbing, they are unorganized and thus easily contained or reversed.

A striking feature of the novel is Tennant's inventive re-working of a number of concepts from Lacanian psychoanalytic theory and feminist reinterpretations. The distinction between the biological father and the 'symbolic father' is registered by the division of the male interest in the novel into two separate characters – Mr Paxton and the Old Man. The various stages of Alice's psychological development, including the mirror stage and the anal stage, are vividly described. The novel also contains a brilliantly effective representation of the concept of the phallic mother; to quote Tennant, 'Alice's mouth still gaped open at the mother standing there: at the power of the woman with the phallus of the sun between her legs' (p. 64).

Readers like me who find Weldon's and Tennant's idealized accounts of motherhood and woman's relegation to the domestic domain sentimental and politically regressive, will turn with relief to Atwood's *The Handmaid's Tale*. Atwood exposes the identification of women with nature, the body and the domestic sphere of life as by no means natural but as constructs created and enforced by a patriarchal culture. She also emphasizes more forcefully than any other contemporary writer the horrific degree of exploitation, degradation and suffering to which they can give rise.

While the choice of utopian fiction for the representation of the political aspects of sexual reproduction is relatively common among writers,[21] the dystopian format which Atwood selects is considerably less so. She makes, in fact, admirable use of it. The account she gives of the totalitarian political regime of Gilead and its oppressive treatment of women has been aptly described by one reviewer as 'the ultimate feminist nightmare'.[22] Offred, the central character and eponymous handmaid, has been forcibly separated from her family and lives as a slave in a Gilead household. Deprived of independence and with her womb regarded as a 'national resource',[23] she exists merely for the purpose of breeding children. She is thoroughly dehumanized – reduced, in her own words, to the status of 'a womb on legs'. The only moments of pleasure she enjoys lie in memories of the past. Despite the process of brainwashing to which she has been subjected, she is capable of remembering details of her life with her mother, husband and (the most poignant memories of all) her young daughter.

Atwood's *The Handmaid's Tale* is, in fact, one of the few novels which succeeds in bringing together the two contrary attitudes to motherhood and sexual reproduction found in feminist theory and women's fiction. These are the negative view of women's reproductive capacities as making her vulnerable to male manipulation and control, and the positive view of them as a source of personal pleasure and fulfilment. Juxtaposing these contrary perspectives, Atwood manages to balance the two opposing aspects of motherhood defined by Rich – thus oppressive facets of the patriarchal 'institution' against the pleasures of the 'experience'. To achieve this, she constructs a delicately contrived discontinuous narrative interweaving scenes from Offred's past and present life. Episodes depicting Offred's relations with her mother and daughter, set in the past and presenting motherhood in a pleasurable light, are interspersed with episodes set in the present and focusing on the horrors of her life as a slave, 'a womb on legs'. Atwood's treatment of the latter episodes reveals many points of affinity with theoretical analyses of the oppressive circumstances of women under patriarchy. The women in Gilead, deprived of economic independence and the right to participate in paid work, are separated into the categories of Marthas, Econowives, Handmaids and Nonwomen. The categorization of infertile women as 'Nonwomen' recalls Rich's observation that 'historically, cross-culturally, a woman's status as childbearer has been the test of her womanhood', a test which gives rise to the divisive categories of 'mother, matron, spinster, barren, old maid'.[24]

As in her earlier works, Atwood continues to explore the position assigned to woman in a phallocratic culture as the *other* of man. Whereas Rennie in *Bodily Harm* comes to perceive herself as 'raw material', the ground for men's experiments in sex and violence, Offred finds herself internalizing male-defined myths of feminine evil and pollution. She starts to accept men's view of women as responsible for the current wave of infertility, and thus deserving the pains of childbirth. Atwood's analysis of the contradictory stereotypes in which women are trapped reveals interesting similarities to Irigaray's. Irigaray points out that a male-defined culture defines woman, on the one hand, in terms of privation; she is 'a void' and 'empty receptacle'. Yet, on the other hand, it perceives her simultaneously as possessing a 'potency' for evil which makes her a positive threat.[25] Offred and her female companions emerge as trapped in a similar double-bind.

The Handmaid's Tale, as well as interweaving contrary attitudes to motherhood and reproduction, also succeeds in bringing together two perspectives which – as I observed in Chapter 1 – generally prove incompatible in theory and fiction. Atwood, in fact, achieves the rare feat of combining a psychoanalytical perspective with an overtly political one. The novel, while organized around the motif of the fractured self, simultaneously prioritizes the theme of collective feminist struggle. The strategy she uses to combine these two apparent opposites is to structure the text around *two* female characters. Offred, the narrator whose subjectivity is fully delineated, is the focus of personal, psychological interest. The subordinate figure Moira, a lesbian feminist who spearheads the feminist resistance against the Gilead regime, is the focus of the political interest. This division does give rise, however, to certain problems. Moira emerges as a stereotype rather than a convincingly drawn character. Her courage and political commitment are excessively idealized. She is, in fact, an extreme example of 'the lesbian as superwoman'. This is a species we have already encountered in Toder's novel *Choices*.

In treating the theme of sexual reproduction, Atwood also investigates certain other related issues. Which kind of society proves most oppressive to women, one with libertarian attitudes which encourages them to be sexy, and makes them the object of pornographic representation (as in *Bodily Harm*), or one which denies them sexual pleasure and forces them to conceal their bodies beneath heavy robes (as in *The Handmaid's Tale*)? Another topic Atwood touches on is changing fashions in feminism. Offred is portrayed as reacting against her mother's radical feminist principles and adopting a liberal stance. The mother, however, sticks to her convictions. 'You're just a backlash. Flash in the pan,' she tells Offred teasingly. 'History will absolve me!' (p. 131). In the light of the horrific acts of oppression the novel recounts, ones which possess a basis in fact, it certainly does![26]

Lesbian motherhood

My decision to devote part of this chapter to a discussion of the theme of lesbian motherhood in novels and short stories, as well as reflecting my own personal interest in this topic, is motivated by the impressive amount of fiction which it has generated. This, of course, illustrates its importance to contemporary feminism in practical and theoretical terms. At a practical level, many lesbian feminists are themselves mothers. Some of them, with the aim of establishing support networks and campaigning to improve their situation regarding child custody, have succeeded in setting up local groups and organizing regional and national conferences. The topic has also received theoretical analysis in a number of studies and essays. The political implications which it possesses make it an appropriate sequel to the discussion of *The Politics of Reproduction* in which I have just engaged.

Lesbian motherhood relates to the realm of sexual politics in a variety of different ways. There is, for example, the matter of the prejudice and discrimination which, in present society, are levelled against women who raise children outside the patriarchal family unit. This prejudice, especially in the period prior to the 1970s when lesbian relations tended to be erased from discourse, commonly takes the form of public ignorance. As Jackie Forster and Gillian Hanscombe point out in their study, the fallacious notion that lesbians are 'mannish' and invariably hate men, combined with people's failure to distinguish female sexual pleasure from the process of reproductive sex, has promoted the erroneous view that they are incapable of conceiving and bearing children.[27] If, by some quirk of fate, they do happen to bear them, then it is assumed that they will be 'unfit' mothers, unable to care for their children effectively. So strongly entrenched is the idea that lesbian motherhood is a contradiction in terms that lesbians themselves sometimes internalize and endorse it. Jill Johnston, in what must be one of the earliest analyses of the political implications of lesbian motherhood, opens her account of a lesbian feminist conference she attended with the disarmingly honest confession, 'I had had a hazy idea we would all be getting together to celebrate the *end* of motherhood or something'. Acknowledging her mistake, she draws the reader's attention to the number of mothers and would-be mothers who attended the event. Johnston explains her negative view of motherhood by reference to the restrictive, glamorized stereotypes of the figure of the mother current in the 1950s and 60s. Like many of us, she was unable to identify with the image of the mother then in fashion, one which she humorously describes as 'a soft fuzzy-edge tinted photo of the young ageless beautiful cosmically fulfilled mother with her cooing dentine baby on the cover of one-a-them ladies' magazines ...'[28]

The mistaken idea that lesbian motherhood is somehow an anomaly continues to trouble women. Jill Brown, in a fascinating account of her experience of pregnancy and maternity, admits that, on account of the prejudiced attitudes she inherited, 'lesbian pregnancy felt like a contradiction'. Like Johnston, she attributes this feeling to conflicts stemming from the restrictive stereotypes and prohibitions surrounding motherhood in contemporary society: 'I was struggling with the conflict between motherhood and myself as a sexual being and with my internalised lesbian oppression which wrongly teaches us that we are not allowed to become mothers.'[29]

As well as having to cope with oppression in its internalized form, lesbian mothers also, of course, have to struggle with its external, social manifestations. These are especially apparent in the case of child custody. Lesbians are frequently categorized in the law courts – along with prostitutes, criminals and the insane – as 'unfit' mothers, incapable of caring for their children. Discrimination against lesbian mothers is by no means a thing of the past but is, in the UK, even more vicious today than in previous years. The notorious Clause 28 (now Section 28 of the Local Government Act) poses a new and serious threat. It effectively gives discrimination against them legal sanction by describing their family units as 'pretended'. And, as Eleanor Stephens observes, while, from the bigoted point of view of the patriarchal establishment, any lesbian is morally dangerous, 'a lesbian with openly feminist ideas poses a double threat. She is seen as a direct challenge to family life and the traditional sexual roles which the courts uphold.'[30] This quotation illustrates another way the topic of lesbian motherhood relates to the domain of sexual politics. It constitutes, many feminists claim, a challenge to the patriarchal family unit and the asymmetrical gender socialization which it promotes. Whether or not this challenge is effective is an issue of debate in the Women's Movement. To what degree can the individual mother, in bringing up her children, counteract the stereotypes of masculinity and femininity encouraged by the media and society in general? What kind of problems do women face bringing up children alone? What are the merits and demerits of the alternative methods of childcare in a lesbian feminist communal household? These questions, as well as receiving discussion in theoretical works, are the focus of enquiry in the novels and short stories presented for discussion below.

A writer who has made an especially valuable contribution to the fictional representaiton of lesbian motherhood, exploring its complexities in lively humorous prose, is the New York figure Jan Clausen. Her short story 'Daddy' has already been mentioned in connection with the topic of patriarchal relations. This and other of Clausen's stories, collected under the title *Mother, Sister, Daughter, Lover* (1960), focus attention on the situation of the lesbian mother bringing up a daughter. Clausen avoids idealizing or sentimentalizing the mother; she refuses to depict her in either a heroic light or as the helpless victim of social stigma. And, by concentrating on those aspects of her situation shared by all women bringing up children alone, Clausen makes her portrayal relevant not only to lesbians but to women in general.

'Today is the first Day of the Rest of Your Life' is typical of Clausen's focus. The story takes as its theme the relationship between Alice and Jackie, a mother and daughter living in New York. While asserting the strength of the attachment between the two, Clausen also foregrounds the contradictions and problems of Alice's position. Though relieved to be separated from her ex-husband and enjoying her newly acquired independence, Alice misses the financial benefits of his salary – and finds herself surreptitiously envying his new wife her affluent circumstances! While committed in principle to the lesbian feminist community and its campaigning activities, she resents the demands they make on her time, objecting to the intrusion of politics on her personal life. And, though generally she finds caring for one child more than enough to cope with, she occasionally contemplates having another one. The story, in fact, opens with her pondering the different means available to her to become pregnant. Humour is a device which Clausen uses to good effect. Jackie, the daughter, is at the stage of wanting to establish her own identity. She complains disconsolately of being 'nothing', in contrast to her class-mates at school who identify as Italian or Jewish or Puerto Rican, and her mother who enjoys the distinction of 'being with women'![31] In episodes describing Jackie's relations with her class-mates, the language of prejudice is a theme Clausen explores. The children bandy the epithets 'white bitch', 'fucking Jew' and 'dyke'. This is another pressure with which mother and daughter have to contend.

In her novel *Sinking, Stealing* (1985) Clausen treats yet another aspect of lesbian motherhood; the situation of the non-biological mother. Clausen explores the predicament of the woman who, on the death of her partner, discovers to her distress that she is denied custody rights and even right of access to the child whom she has co-parented. After the tragic death of her partner Rhea in a car crash, Josie, the central character, makes an effort to maintain a relationship with ten-year-old Ericka, Rhea's daughter. Daniel, Ericka's father, however disapproves of Josie's feminist attitudes and does his best to break their relationship. He unexpectedly announces that he is leaving New York to live in Cleveland – and intends to take Ericka with him. When Josie objects that the move will prevent Ericka and herself from meeting, he ridicules her protests as naive:

> 'Come on, Josie, you can't seriously mean that you expect an entire family to base its choice of residence on proximity to the husband's ex-wife's former lesbian lover! The sixties are over, remember?'[32]

As usual in contemporary society, conventional family ties claim precedence over ones originating in a lesbian partnership.

The story, however, does not end here. Josie and Ericka actively resist Daniel's efforts to separate them. They resort to drastic measures. They run away together and, assuming false names, travel round the USA by Greyhound bus. *En route* they experience a number of adventures, some frightening, others predominantly funny. In these particular episodes Clausen succeeds in combining a critique of the rigidities of patriarchal bourgeois methods of child-care with a humorous exposé of the follies and excesses of cultural feminist ones. Bringing up children on a diet of millet stew and dogmatically insisting on 'natural childbirth' even if it endangers the baby's life are, she illustrates, neither practical nor humane.

The themes which Clausen explores in *Sinking, Stealing* are of interest to the feminist reader on a number of different counts. For a start, she successfully champions the rights of the non-biological mother, drawing attention to her lack of legal status and social recognition. Ericka and Josie invent a new term to denote the non-biological mother – *flommy!* 'Do you think someday *flommy* will be in the dictionary?', Ericka asks hopefully and, when Josie expresses scepticism, she staunchly replies, 'It's not fair. You ought to have a title' (p. 255). Clausen simultaneously exposes the injustices carried out in the name of father-right, a concept which has received a considerable amount of publicity in recent years. The theorists Selma Sevenhuijsen and Petra de Vries point out that the anti-feminist backlash taking place in the 1980s has caused women's rights to custody and access to be increasingly eroded. They observe, 'Now that divorce legislation is being reviewed we see a boomerang effect. Men try to use the proposed new legal provisions to limit women's rights.'[33] It is this kind of 'boomerang effect' which Clausen both illustrates and challenges in the novel.

Problems relating to custody and access encountered by lesbian mothers are a theme treated, of course, by other writers besides Clausen. An early representation occurs in Piercy's *Small Changes* (1972), while Roberts also focuses attention on it in *A Piece of the Night* (1978). The latter novel will be discussed in the following section in connection with the motif of relations between mothers and daughters.

Whereas Clausen and Roberts concentrate on describing the mother bringing up a daughter, other writers focus attention on her relations with her sons – and the conflicts it can involve. Alther treats the topic humorously. Caroline, the central character of *Other Women*, does her best to inculcate in her sons principles of harmony and cooperation – with notably little success! A more serious treatment of the topic occurs in Caeia March's two short stories 'The Survivors' and 'Photographs'.[34] March contrasts the pleasure the mother takes in her boys' vitality and infant eroticism with her feelings of distress at the brutal models of masculine behaviour presented to them by the media, and the conduct of the children they mix with at school.

Representations of lesbian motherhood in fiction include not only women who are raising children but also ones who are eager to do so. In *Peeling* (1986) by Grace Bartram the protagonist Jane is portrayed as confronting the dilemma many lesbians face: 'She did want a baby, wanted it desperately, passionately, insanely . ... And how was she to going to have one, when she didn't want a man to give it to her?'[35] The solution she adopts to the problem and the conflicting responses it provokes from her mother, Ally, constitute a dominant strand in the narrative. The novel will be discussed in more detail in the subsequent section.

Sara Maitland in her short story 'After the Ball Was Over' (*Tales I Tell My Mother*, 1978) contrasts the support and approval which society gives the woman who conceives a child within marriage with the stigma attached to the one who conceives it in the context of a lesbian relationship. Everyone – friends, acquaintances, doctors – do their best to persuade Kelly, living with her lover Ann, to reconsider her decision to have a baby and terminate the pregnancy. The story, one which leaves the reader with a distinctly bitter taste, illustrates very forcefully indeed the strength of patriarchal ideals of motherhood. As Rich cogently reminds us, 'Motherhood is "sacred" so long as its offspring are "legitimate" – that is, as long as the child bears the name of a father who legally controls the mother.'[36]

Relations between mothers and daughters

In choosing to devote the final section of this chapter to an analysis of relations between mothers and daughters, rather than concentrating on relations between mothers and sons, I am influenced by the importance the former topic assumes in works of fiction today. Mother–daughter involvements and their ambiguous pains and pleasures are, in fact, a focus of immense interest among contemporary women writers. This makes a welcome contrast to the neglect they have suffered in the past. Writing in 1976, Rich observed that, while examples of classical drama such as *Oedipus*, *Hamlet* and *Lear* contain detailed, often celebratory, accounts of attachments between mothers and sons, and fathers and daughters, 'there is no presently enduring recognition of mother–daughter passion and rapture'.[37] That this omission is starting to be remedied and the mother–daughter bond is achieving re-evaluation is due largely to the writing of Rich and other theorists, and the stimulating effect it has had on fiction.

Relations between mothers and daughters in contemporary women's fiction make, in fact, a fascinating object of study. The approaches writers take to the topic have not remained static but reflect a number of significant shifts. As I pointed out in the introductory section of this chapter, feminists writing in the early years of the Women's Movement took a distinctly unsympathetic view of the figure of the mother. Their antagonistic attitudes constitute in part a continuation of what Daly calls 'the blaming the mother'[38] school of thought promoted by psychiatrists in the 1950s and 1960s. One of the chief contributors towards this was, of course, R. D. Laing. Laing constructed the portrait of 'the unhappy, insecure, cold, but possessive mother'[39] whose smothering attentions are regarded as responsible for the daughter's failure to achieve maturity and autonomy. In 1960s' culture, as Segal observes, the mother featured as a 'target of ambivalent aggression'. She was the symbolic representative of 'the home, the family and the straight world', institutions which children of both sexes sought to reject. As well as inheriting these hostile attitudes, feminists writing in the 1960s and 1970s also had their own particular axe to grind. They attacked the mother as the tool of patriarchy, accusing her of socializing the daughter into a subordinate role. To quote Orbach's summary: 'To prepare her daughter for a life of inequality, the mother tries to hold back her child's desires to be a powerful, autonomous self-directed, energetic and productive human being.'[40]

Feminist hostility towards the mother in her role of socializer and upholder of the patriarchal status quo has interesting, though unpleasant repercussions, in certain works of fiction written in the 1970s. Lessing's *The Memoirs of a Survivor* (1974), Atwood's *Lady Oracle* (1976) and Piercy's *The High Cost of Living* (1978) all introduce caricatured portrayals of the mother drawn from the daughter's resentful viewpoint. Distinctive features the portrayals display are one-sidedness, exaggeration – and an element of cruel caricature. All are variations on the theme of the mother as monster. The prejudiced stereotypes on which they draw include: the vampirish mother who drains the daughter's vitality constructed by psychoanalysts, Laing's neurotic smotherer, and the inculcator of restrictive codes of femininity from feminist theory. The most grotesque and horrific is undoubtedly Mrs Foster, the mother of the narrator Joan, in Atwood's *Lady Oracle*. Seeing an image of her mother in a dream sprouting three heads, Joan concludes, 'it seemed merely a confirmation of something I'd always known ... the secret that I alone knew: my mother was a monster.'[41] In a subsequent episode Mrs Foster lives up to her monstrous reputation: she sticks a knife in her daughter's arm!

It is important to emphasize that these caricatured portrayals represent only one facet of the three writers' depiction of the mother. Complex and sympathetically drawn descriptions, emphasizing her subjectivity, are to be found in other of their novels.[42]

That relations between mother and daughter have eventually achieved reappraisal depends on the work of a number of theorists. Rich, Chodorow and Irigaray are three of the most significant names. Although their approaches to the topic differ, all three place emphasis on the pre-oedipal attachment between mother and daughter. Certain key features of their analyses are particularly relevant to the works of fiction discussed below. One is the contrasting constructs of masculinity and femininity to which, as Chodorow illustrates, the asymmetrical childcare arrangements in contemporary society give rise. She points out that the mother, while treating her son as an autonomous individual from a relatively early age, tends to cultivate a symbiotic bond with her daughter since she seeks unconsciously to re-create the intimate bond she enjoyed with her own mother. The consequence is that boys grow up possessing a strong sense of autonomy, whereas girls are likely to feel a greater sense of interdependence and connection with other people. Debate exists among feminists about whether these typical feminine attributes are beneficial or disadvantageous. Judith Kegan Gardiner summarizes the contrary viewpoints as follows:

> Dinnerstein, Chodorow and Rich describe gender differences in terms that imply women are nicer than men. Empathy, responsibility and interdependence seem preferable to defensive aggression, destructive rage against women and nature and a compulsion for control. However, other feminists evaluate the same characteristics in terms of female disadvantage. For Jane Flax and Jessica Benjamin, women's fluid ego boundaries are a weakness. They see women's chief problems as achieving independence, separation from others and autonomous individual identities.[43]

Writers of fiction, we shall see, regard the bond between mother and daughter and the feminine attributes which it produces in a similarly ambiguous light.

Another point which is relevant to the works of fiction under review in this section is the problematization of heterosexual relations which occurs, with differing degrees of radicalism, in the works of Rich, Chodorow and Irigaray. Joanna Ryan correctly remarks that 'a strength of most psychoanalytic accounts is that they do not see a girl's pathway to heterosexuality as either straightforward or inevitable.' Commenting on Chodorow's description of woman's sexual development, she observes, 'We are left with a view of women as pushed and pulled out of their original homosexual intimacy [with the mother] into an ambivalent and very incomplete heterosexuality, where men may be the exclusive and primary erotic objects but are for the most part emotionally secondary to women.'[44]

Psychoanalytic theorists, as well as formulating a number of key ideas significant to works of fiction, also bring into prominence certain images representing different facets of the mother–daughter bond. The images which form the basis of Irigaray's essay 'And the one doesn't stir without the other' are especially pertinent. There is Irigaray's description of the mother constituting, paradoxically, both 'the feeder' and 'the food' of the daughter, with the effect of emotional suffocation, paralysis and loss of identity boundaries in which it results. The daughter tells her mother, 'You put yourself in my mouth, and I suffocate.'[45] Another image Irigaray uses is the representation of mother and daughter as two 'living mirrors', each reflecting the other. A third is the depiction of the mother 'haemorrhaging blood', introduced to describe the syndrome of maternal self-sacrifice. These images are archetypal. They recur, as we shall see, in a number of novels.

The four novels I have chosen to illustrate the current interest in the theme of mothering make reference to three and in some cases four generations of mother–daughter relations. Alther's *Kinflicks* (1976) and Roberts's *A Piece of the Night* (1978), though written prior to the publication of Chodorow's significant study, treat the phenomenon which today we call 'the reproduction of mothering'. They also investigate some of the stratagems available to women to resist and elude the pressures of the traditional maternal role. Eva Figes's *Days* (1974) and Bartram's *Peeling* (1986) explore, each in a different way, incidents of breakdown of communication between mother and daughter, and the problems to which they give rise.

Alther's *Kinflicks* and Roberts's *A Piece of the Night*, the two novels I propose to discuss first, will no doubt strike the reader as an unlikely duo to select for comparison. The authors differ as regards nationality, ideological attitudes and narrative style. Alther adopts a libertarian stance. Representing her hero Ginny as engaging in a quest for fulfilment which is purely personal, she foregrounds the typical 1960s themes of hedonistic experimentation with different lifestyles, sex and drugs. Roberts, in contrast, takes a radical feminist position. Her hero Julie, identifying as lesbian feminist, discovers the value of women's community and ideals of collectivity. Despite these pronounced differences, the two novels do possess notable similarities. Both are versions of the female quest for self-discovery, a theme which – as Elizabeth Wilson points out – was extremely popular with women writing in the 1970s.[46] Moreover, Alther and Roberts both take as their hero a college-educated woman in her mid-twenties who, having separated from her husband, is in the process of rethinking and coming to terms with her past. They juxtapose scenes describing her attendance at the sick-bed of her mother who is critically ill, with episodes from her past life illustrating her development and quest for identity. Whereas *Kinflicks* concludes with the mother's death, *A Piece of the Night* concludes with an event which, though less drastic, none the less has implications which are terminal and disruptive. Julie's mother Claire makes up her mind to sell the family home in Normandy and move to Switzerland to live with her son. The decision is one which causes Julie great distress.

The *topos* of the maternal death-bed in women's fiction, which is central to both novels, has received critical attention from Gardiner. She sees the fictional representation of the mother's illness and death as representing a desire on the daughter's part (and also the author's) to reject the oppressive aspects of the maternal role and the mother's influence. She claims, very feasibly, that 'dying mothers [in fiction] thus embody both the stultifying roles and the negative personal traits that the daughters want to bury'.[47] However, there is more to Alther's and Roberts's treatments of the *topos* than Gardiner's analysis suggests. A striking feature of both is the fact that they explore the mother's subjectivity in some detail, focusing attention on her own perspective on her illness, as well as her daughter's. And the daughters, in rejecting the maternal role in its traditional form, are described as experiencing a strong degree of conflict and guilt – emotions which Gardiner's analysis tends to underemphasize.

The blurb on the cover of the Penguin edition of *Kinflicks* entices the (presumably male) reader to buy the book with spicy references to 'teenage sex-freaks, lesbian hippies' and 'thwarted suburban mothers'. It makes no allusion to what is, in fact, the dominant theme of the novel – Ginny's relationship with her dying mother, Mrs Babcock. Alther is a writer who specializes in producing works informed by an element of ideological contradiction and inconsistency. *Kinflicks*, her first publication, certainly sets the trend in this respect. While the humorous account she gives of Ginny's youthful escapades with a series of lovers emerges today as sexist and dated, her serious depiction of Ginny's relations with her mother is both moving and, in terms of the early date of the novel, remarkably radical. Two of the images Alther introduces to describe the traditional aspects of the maternal role merit comment. The syndrome of maternal self-sacrifice in which Mrs Babcock is trapped and which Ginny herself determines to reject is represented by the bloodclotting haemorrhaging disorder from which the former suffers. This symbolizes, as Alther remarks, the 'bleeding herself dry, as it were, for the children' in which mothers frequently engage.[48] Another dominant image in the text is the clutch of fledgling birds which Ginny rescues and attempts to feed. The parent birds have deserted them, a fact which illustrates Alther's point that maternal self-sacrifice, far from being 'natural', is, on the contrary, a cultural construct. The fledglings are also used by Alther to ridicule playfully contradictions of human response and the entrenched quality of the ideology of motherhood. Ginny, quite forgetting that she has deserted her own daughter, in a fit of temper rebukes the mother-bird for neglecting its young, calling it a 'goddam bastard' (p. 169)!

These images and motifs prepare the reader for the climactic event of the novel – the episode in which Ginny, with her mother's help and 'permission', succeeds in breaking free from what Alther aptly calls 'the generational spell' of the reproduction of mothering (p. 474). She liberates herself, temporarily at least, from feelings of guilt at rejecting the maternal role, and starts to lead her own life.

As mentioned above, Alther's treatment of the mother–daughter bond contains a number of radical perceptions. For example, she contrasts the enjoyment mother and daughter take in physical contact with one another in the latter's infant years with the sense of mutual embarrassment it causes them when the daughter reaches puberty. Certain omissions in the novel may come as a surprise to the present-day reader. For example, Alther makes little if any connection between the lesbian attachment Ginny forms with her college-friend Eddie and the theme of pre-oedipal relations between mother and daughter, a topic the novel also treats. Her failure to make the link between the two areas, one which would no doubt occur in a work of fiction written today, indicates the novel's relatively early date of publication (1976). It reminds us of the radical developments in feminist psychoanalytic theory which have taken place in the past decade or so.

Unlike Ginny, who, in order to liberate herself from the 'reproduction of mothering', leaves her daughter in the care of her husband and travels alone, Julie Fanchot, the hero of Roberts's *A Piece of the Night*, takes a less drastic course. She challenges the patriarchal constructs of motherhood and childcare by bringing up her daughter Bertha in a lesbian feminist communal household. Roberts' description of the commune is by no means idealized. Insecure living conditions, financial difficulties and precarious relationships are a source of frequent worry to the women. None the less, their life together does possess a number of advantages. The sharing of childcare activities enables mothers and co-mothers to enjoy a degree of freedom and privacy. They also have access to emotional nurturance and practical support which, as Rich and Chodorow agree, they are unlikely to find in the context of the nuclear family. One of the points Roberts makes in the novel is that the edifice of patriarchal culture is built on the disruption of attachments between both mothers and daughters, and women in general. The text includes numerous examples of what Rich describes as 'the societal forces which wrench women's emotional and erotic energies away from themselves and other women and from woman-identified values'.[49]

In relation to this topic, Roberts highlights the destructive pressure which the practice and expectations of family life exert on the mother–daughter dyad. The demands made on the mother's nurturing abilities by the male members of the family (both son and father), combined with the expectation that the daughter will eventually renounce her bond with her mother to form a relationship with a man, are two examples she explores. A concept at the hub of her text is the recognition that not only does the family fail to provide the mother with nurturance, but it also actively 'devours' her energy and wellbeing. As Julie herself bitterly comments, 'My being a mother cancels out most possibilities of my being taken care of, my needs drown in the claims made on me by other people.'[50] The dream she experiences when she sees her mother lying on the table, with the other members of the family greedily attacking her body with knives and forks while she herself fastens her mouth on her breast, symbolically represents this idea. Julie's distress at the dream resembles the request the daughter sadly voices to the mother at the end of Irigaray's essay, 'And what I wanted from you, Mother, was this: that in giving me life, you still remain alive.'[51]

A Piece of the Night is, in structural and stylistic terms, very ambitious, interweaving a number of different narrative strands. The interplay of these strands sometimes appears over-contrived. However, the merging of past and present, and of different subjectivities, which Roberts achieves is admirably suited to the theme of female interdependence and the symbiotic mother–daughter attachment which the novel treats.

As the theorist Judith Arcana notes, one of the effects of the pressures of a phallocratic culture and the primacy it gives to male interests, is to promote patterns of deceit and breakdown of communication between mother and daughter.[52] While these themes are touched on in the novels discussed above, they lie at the very heart of Figes's *Days* and Bartram's *Peeling*. The two writers treat them in a very different manner. Figes uses modernist narrative methods to explore syndromes of deceit and their destructive effect on the female psyche. Bartram, in contrast, writing in realist mode, focuses in more cheerful vein on the healing of such psychic wounds.

Figes's *Days* is structured on the image of paralysis, both literal and psychic. The image represents, as in Irigaray's essay, the immobilizing effect to which the destructive aspects of the mother–daughter bond can give rise. The novel opens with the nameless narrator lying helpless in a hospital bed. Only in the final pages is her paralysed condition revealed to be the consequence and symbolic expression of the mesh of deceit and non-communication in which she and her mother have become trapped. This has its roots in a specific event in the past. The narrator remembers how, when she was a teenager, her father deserted the family. Her mother, who was in hospital at the time, failed to face up to the situation. The result was, the narrator was burdened with the responsibility, one often imposed on daughters, of stifling her own anger at the event and smoothing over the crisis in the home. She recollects:

I poured syrup on my brother's food, and honeyed words on everything, trying to mellow the situation. I tried to mellow my hate, I spun a cocoon round the stone that dug a pain between my ribs so I would not feel it, because if I had not done so everything would have come to a stop. We continued this way for years. I twisted my body to accommodate the lies, the new shape that the house had taken now, since my mother came home. She has never fully accepted the truth. We contoured ourselves to the lies ...[53]

It is this deceit which is the source of the narrator's paralysed state. As she admits, 'the lump of stone with its grey cocoon has become part of my anatomy.... Eventually it was necessary to lie still, to discontinue all movement, so as to avoid agony.' The novel concludes, it is important to emphasize, on a positive note. Having mentally relived her previous life, she succeeds in liberating herself from her past self and starts to walk again.

The novel contains a powerful indictment of male irresponsibility and abuses of power, along with women's willingness to collude with them. Figes illustrates how, when men tire of family life and walk out, they leave women – teenage daughters included – to bear the brunt. Women meanwhile, rather than striving to achieve independence, further their own oppression by supporting traditional notions of male privilege. The narrator's mother, while spending money and effort on her own son's education to give him a successful future, pays no attention to her daughter's. The consequence is that history repeats itself. The daughter takes up a dead-end secretarial post, becomes pregnant, gives birth to a girl and is deserted by the father. As is apparent from my analysis, Figes in no way idealizes either mother–daughter relations or the bearing of children. She suggests, in common with a number of theorists, that many women become mothers not from positive choice but due to the pressures of convention and the lack of any satisfying alternative.

Days is brilliantly written. A striking feature of the novel is the strategies Figes utilizes to represent the merging of the identities of mother and daughter, along with the symbiotic bond linking generation upon generation of women. As in Irigaray's essay, mother and daughter are portrayed as 'living mirrors'. The narrator, describing her daughter visiting her in hospital, remarks: 'She leaned down towards my head and I saw a tiny woman's head, white, distant, repeated twice over in the two pupils before she came closer and out of focus' (p. 104). The younger generation are depicted as repeating not only the behaviour-patterns but also the physical poses of the older. In hospital the narrator thinks wearily, 'I sit up in bed now as my mother once sat' (p. 87). Another device Figes adopts is deliberately to blur the distinction between mother and daughter, allowing their identities to merge. The reader is thus at times uncertain which particular generation is the focus of the narrative. Is the woman whom the narrator sees lying on the bed in the final pages of the novel herself, her mother or – possibly – both? Figes is to be congratulated on creating a profoundly compelling representation of the problematic aspect of mother–daughter relations in contemporary society.

Bartram in *Peeling* also takes as her theme a woman's struggle to liberate herself from the psychic and social patterns of the past. She describes the struggle waged by fifty-four-year-old Ally to survive emotionally and regain her self-respect after her marriage has broken up, her husband Rowley having left her for another woman. After an initial period of distress when she takes refuge in binges of overeating and comes close to a breakdown, Ally succeeds in accepting the changes in her situation. She slowly manages to achieve independence, eventually making for herself what she describes as 'daring, new, exciting life'.[54]

An important feature of the 'new life' which Ally forges is that it takes her outside the private sphere of the home. The result is that the theme of relations between mother and daughter forms only one strand in the novel's narrative design. A major part of the text is devoted to a study of women's community and the destructive effects of male violence, both of which Ally encounters when she takes up a job at the local Women's Refuge. None the less, mother–daughter involvements certainly do play a significant part in the novel. The breakdown of communication which occurs between Ally and her daughter Jane again has its roots in past events. As a result of certain traumatic experiences each has suffered, mother and daughter possess a similar inability to express feelings of grief. Problems stemming from this are exacerbated by Ally's inability to accept – initially at least – the fact that Jane is involved in a lesbian relationship. Despite a number of setbacks, reference to which prevents the mood of the novel from appearing over-optimistic, relations between the two women do start to improve. In describing this process, Bartram successfully brings together the motif of relations between mothers and daughters, and the theme of women's community. The skills of sympathetic listening and counselling which Ally learns in the course of her work at the Refuge are shown to have personal as well as social value, helping her to solve her own problems. They enable her to relax and, as the title of the novel implies, to start to 'peel off' her various defensive layers. She ceases, in her own words, to be a mere 'onlooker' on life and becomes instead a 'participant'. These beneficial changes which take place enable her to make contact not only with her daughter Jane but also with certain friends with whom she has been experiencing difficulties of communication. As my account of the novel indicates, *Peeling* is unusual in the range of different areas it brings together. Bartram successfully correlates the theme of mother-daughter relations with the wider one of women's community.

Conclusion

Motherhood and mothering are topics which are multifaceted, and in this study I have unfortunately had space to consider only a few of their varied aspects. One serious omission from my discussion is the treatment of the theme of childbirth in novels and short stories. This possesses, of course, major relevance to the realm of sexual politics. A number of contemporary writers examine the control the medical profession exerts on childbirth and women's reproductive processes, along with the attempt it makes to pathologize pregnancy and birth.[55] Writers also explore the efforts women make to challenge these pressures. Another topic they treat is the way women's experiences of childbirth differ according to their social background and to the historical era in which they live.[56]

Among the insights this study has yielded one of the most significant is the kind of themes which writers choose to treat. These, as the reader will have noticed, are on the whole radical feminist as opposed to socialist feminist in nature. This is especially apparent in the case of childcare. Despite the recommendations made by Dinnerstein and Chodorow that, in order to break down rigid gender constructs and liberate women from the domestic domain, women should share childcare practices with men, the topic seldom makes an appearance in works of fiction. A number of factors help to account for this. Judging from recent research on the topic, the sharing of childcare with men, with the latter making an equal or major contribution to the process, exists at the moment more as an ideal than an actual practice.[57] Moreover, there are indications that, even if it were feasible, a number of women would not favour it. They doubt if at present men possess the skills to raise children. They also understandably fear that the surrender of childcare practices to men will deprive them of the one area of power and authority which they do possess, without necessarily giving them full access to the public world of paid professional work and political decision-making. The recognition of the male capacity for violence, manifested in the home in acts of battery and incest (a topic much in the news at the moment), further increases their doubts. In fact, rather than seeking to share childcare with men, many women, as Pauline Bart points out, are taking up the option which Arcana and Rich recommend and adopting 'women bonding as the solution to the oppressive nature of motherhood as an institution'.[58] These radical feminist perferences have made, as we have seen, a pronounced impact on women's fiction. They are discernible, for example, in the focus on co-parenting and lesbian motherhood in Clausen's stories and Roberts's *A Piece of the Night*.

There is yet another feature of the treatment of motherhood and mothering in contemporary women's fiction which is worth commenting on. This is the increasing tendency of writers, taking their cue from psychoanalytic theory, to link the theme of relations between mothers and daughters to that of women's community and to attachments, both erotic and non-erotic, between women in general. Reference to such links makes an apt conclusion to this chapter. It creates a vital bridge with the topic of Sisterhood, relations between women, and women's community which is the focus of discussion in the subsequent one.

Notes

1. *A Piece of the Night* (Women's Press, 1978), p. 91.
2. Hester Eisenstein, *Contemporary Feminist Thought* (Unwin, 1984), p. 69. An excellent account of the Women's Movement's contrary attitudes to motherhood exists in Selma Sevenhuijsen and Petra de Vries, 'The Women's Movement and Motherhood', *A Creative Tension: explorations in socialist feminism*, ed. Anja Meulenbelt et al., trans. Della Couling (Pluto, 1984), pp. 9-25.
3. Eisenstein, op. cit., pp. 69-70.
4. 'Why men don't rear children: a power analysis', *Mothering: Essays in Feminist Theory*, ed. Joyce Treblicot (Rowman and Allanheld, 1984), p. 35.
5. *Of Woman Born* (Virago, 1977), p. 14.
6. Toril Moi, *Sexual/Textual Politics* (Methuen, 1985), pp. 113-19.
7. Ibid., pp. 167-8. See also Julia Kristeva, *Desire in Language: a semiotic approach to literature and art*, ed. Leon S. Roudiez, trans. Thomas Gora et al. (Basil Blackwell, 1981), pp. 192-5, 224, 242.
8. Piri Marcus, 'Motherhood: a letter', *Sweeping Statements: writings from the Women's Liberation Movement 1981-83* (Women's Press, 1984), p. 296.
9. *Breaching the Peace*, ed. cit., p. 27.
10. 'Women's retreat into motherhood: back to the nursery', *New Statesman*, 113, no. 2910 (2 January 1987), p. 17.
11. 'Husband-right and father-right', *On Lies, Secrets, and Silence: selected prose 1966-1978* (Virago, 1980), p. 216.
12. *Subject Women* (Martin Robertson, 1981), p. 206.
13. 'The contemporary emergency and the quantum leap', *On Lies, Secrets, and Silence*, ed. cit., pp. 263-4. The contrary facets of motherhood receive

attention not only in feminist theory and fiction but also in painting. This is illustrated by the works of the British artist Amanda Faulkner (Exhibition at the Angela Flowers Gallery, Jan.-Feb. 1985).

14. See the essays in Joyce Treblicot (ed.), *Mothering: essays in feminist theory* (Rowman and Allanheld, 1984).
15. Janine Chasseguet-Smirgel, *Female Sexuality: new psychoanalytic views* (Virago, 1981), p. 26.
16. 'Alice Walker: the black woman artist as wayward', *Black Women Writers*, ed. Marie Evans (Pluto, 1985), p. 465.
17. *Meridian* (Women's Press, 1982), p. 40. Subsequent references are to this edition and are in the text.
18. *Down Among the Women* (Penguin, 1973), p. 20. Subsequent references are to this edition and are in the text.
19. *Puffball* (Coronet, 1981), p. 109. Subsequent references are to this edition and are in the text.
20. *Alice Fell* (Picador, 1982), p. 14. Subsequent references are to this edition and are in the text.
21. See Charlotte Perkins Gilman, *Herland* (1915); and Marge Piercy, *Woman on the Edge of Time* (1976).
22. Maureen Freely, *Observer*, 10145 (16 March 1986), p. 25.
23. *The Handmaid's Tale* (Jonathan Cape, 1986), p. 75. Subsequent references are to this edition and are in the text.
24. 'The contemporary emergency and the quantum leap', *On Lies, Secrets, and Silence*, ed. cit., p. 261.
25. *Speculum*, ed. cit., pp. 165-6.
26. The erosion of women's liberties described in the novel bears close resemblance to contemporary events in Iran.
27. *Rocking the Cradle - Lesbian Mothers: a challenge in family living* (Peter Owen, 1981), pp. 1-38.
28. 'Return of the Amazon Mother' (1972), *Amazon Expedition: a lesbian anthology*, ed. Phyllis Birkby et al. (Times Change Press, 1973), p. 67.
29. Jo Chambers and Jill Brown, 'Two personal experiences', *Sex and Love*, ed. cit., pp. 81-2.
30. 'Out of the closet into the courts', *Spare Rib*, 50 (September 1976), p. 6. Other studies of the topic include Forster and Hanscombe, op. cit.; and Rights of Women Lesbian Custody Group, *Lesbian Mothers' Legal Handbook* (Women's Press, 1986). For reference to the implications of Clause 28, see *Spare Rib*, no. 188 (March, 1988), p. 16.
31. *Mother, Sister, Daughter, Lover: Stories* (Women's Press, 1985), p. 80.
32. *Sinking, Stealing* (Women's Press, 1981), p. 82. Subsequent references are to this edition and are in the text.
33. Op. cit., p. 21.
34. *The Reach and Other Stories: lesbian feminist fiction*, ed. Lillian Mohin et al. (Onlywomen Press, 1984), pp. 95-101; *Girls Next Door*, ed. cit., pp. 26-32.
35. *Peeling* (Women's Press, 1986), p. 35.
36. *Of Woman Born*, ed. cit., p. 42.
37. Ibid., p. 237.
38. *Gyn/Ecology*, ed. cit., p. 265.
39. Lynne Segal, '"Smash the family?" recalling the 1960s', *What is to be done about the Family?*, ed. cit., p. 36.
40. Op. cit., p. 27.
41. *Lady Oracle*, ed. cit., p. 67.

42. See Atwood, *Surfacing* (1972); Piercy, *Fly Away Home* (1984); and Lessing, *The Summer before the Dark* (1973).
43. 'Mind mother: psychoanalysis and feminism', *Making a Difference*, ed. cit., pp. 134-5.
44. 'Psychoanalysis and women loving women', *Sex and Love*, ed. cit., p. 206.
45. Op. cit., trans. Helene Vivienne Wenzel, *Signs*, 7, no. 1 (Autumn 1981), p. 61.
46. 'I'll climb the stairway to Heaven: lesbianism in the seventies', *Sex and Love*, ed. cit., p. 192.
47. 'A wake for mother: the maternal deathbed in women's fiction', *Feminist Studies*, 4, no. 2 (1978), p. 148. Gardiner discusses *Kinflicks* but not *A Piece of the Night*.
48. *Kinflicks* (Penguin, 1977), p. 289. Subsequent references are to this edition and are in the text.
49. *Compulsory Heterosexuality and Lesbian Existence*, ed. cit., pp. 9-10.
50. *A Piece of the Night* (Women's Press, 1978), p. 16.
51. 'And the one doesn't stir ...', ed. cit., p. 67.
52. *Our Mothers' Daughters* (Women's Press, 1981), pp. 40-9.
53. *Days* (Bloodaxe Books, 1983), p. 118. Subsequent references are to this edition and are in the text.
54. *Peeling* (Women's Press, 1983), p. 93.
55. Caroline Bowder, *Birth Rites* (Harvester Press, 1983); Nicole Ward Jouve, 'Forceps Birth', *Shades of Grey* (Virago, 1981), pp. 9-38.
56. Atwood, 'Giving birth', *Dancing Girls*, ed. cit., pp. 225-40; Maitland, 'Forceps Delivery', *Weddings and Funerals* by Maitland and La Tourette (Brilliance Books, 1984), pp. 103-13.
57. Charlie Lewis and Margaret O'Brien (eds), *Reassessing Fatherhood: observations on fathers and the modern family* (Sage Publications, 1987).
58. 'Review of Chodorow's *The Reproduction of Mothering*', Treblicot, ed. cit., p. 149. See also Sevenhuijsen and de Vries, op. cit.

Chapter Six

Sisterhood, Relations between Women, and Women's Community

Crones know who we are. The time has come for rekindling the Fire of
Female Friendship.
Mary Daly, Gyn/Ecology: *The Mataethics of Radical Feminism*
p. 365

Tell me again because I need to hear ...
how sister gazed at sister
reaching through mirrored pupils
back to the mother
Adrienne Rich, 'Sibling Mysteries', *The Dream of a Common
Language: Poems 1974–1977*, p. 50.

Introduction: Changing attitudes to sisterhood and female relations

There are two reasons which prompt me to place the discussion of
themes of sisterhood and relations between women towards the end
of this study. First, the discussion recapitulates, as we shall see,
certain of the ideas and issues which we have encountered previously. The political significance of women's community explored in
the chapters relating to sexual politics and patriarchal relations, and
the psychoanalytic theme of women's capacity for symbiotic bonding mentioned in connection with motherhood and mothering, are
two topics which will receive further attention here. Secondly, sisterhood and women's community may be described, with justification,
as constituting the very heart and centre of contemporary feminism.
The separatist nature of the present Women's Movement along with
its decision openly to promote, in the face of controversy and

hostility, ideas of woman-identification and the political importance of lesbianism, serve to distinguish it from earlier Movements focusing on women's rights. These features give it, to a degree, its distinctive tone and character. It is appropriate that the discussion of themes relating to these matters occupy a prominent position. Approaches to sisterhood in feminist theory, far from remaining static, have undergone over the past twenty years a series of dramatic changes. The most notable of these I shall now summarize.

Sisterhood and women's community are generally regarded by feminists as providing both a refuge *from* and a challenge *to* the oppressive facets of a patriarchal society. These ideas formed, of course, the foundation of the radical feminist movement of the early 1970s. To heal the rifts which a patriarchal culture forges between women, feminists strove to achieve political solidarity by focusing on the common aspects of female experience. Consciousness-raising in the small group, as Eisenstein explains, was instrumental to achieving this goal:

> Through consciousness-raising women sought (not always with success) to identify and to develop the qualities that united them, across the boundaries set by social categories: mothers with nonmothers; heterosexual women with lesbians; white women with women of color; and privileged women with poor women. Ultimately, it was thought, the condition and experience of being female would prove to be more important in defining women than the specifics of our differences from one another.[1]

The sentiments expressed above, though continuing to form the basis of feminist commitment and work-projects, are likely to sound somewhat naive and idealistic today. The reason is that in the late 1970s and 1980s the concept of sisterhood has met with a series of challenges, both intellectual and practical. One challenge stems – ironically – from the successful establishment of Women's Studies programmes in colleges and universities. The setting up of these programmes, initially inspired by a belief in the common nature of female experience and the specificity of women as a gendered group, has led paradoxically to the problematization of these ideas. The scrutinizing of women's individual circumstances, which is a key feature of these courses, has led to an increasing recognition of differences of class, race and sexual orientation. The consequence is that ideas of female commonality and specificity are now often criticized on the grounds of false universalism.[2]

Another challenge to ideas of sisterhood and ideas of female solidarity comes from psychoanalytic critiques of 'the unitary self'. If, as the Lacanian theory of the fractured self suggests, no such thing as a 'unitary woman' exists, then women's community is destabilized and ceases to provide an obvious basis for political organization and struggle.[3] Although the average feminist may dismiss these critiques as esoteric and politically spurious, they have undoubtedly had the effect of weakening a commitment to ideas of sisterhood – in academic circles at least.

Another factor relevant to both the development and the problematization of sisterhood is the growth of lesbian feminism as a force within the Women's Movement. The effect of this phenomenon is, one has to admit, decidedly double-edged. From a positive point of view, it is women who identify as lesbian like the American group Radicalesbians and the theorist and poet Adrienne Rich who have made the strongest contribution to promoting and popularizing ideas of women's community and woman-identification. From a negative one, however, the extreme separatist stance adopted by groups such as Political Lesbians has been a source of disunity in the Movement. It has antagonized many women, causing rifts between hetero and lesbian feminists. Moreover, the sexual aspect of lesbian relationships, while having a vitalizing effect on feminist community and increasing its appeal and aura of glamour, has simultaneously proved to be a disruptive influence. It has made visible the existence of divisive emotions of passion and jealousy in an area which was previously regarded (incorrectly, no doubt!) as free from them. Frankie Rickford sums up extremely well the ambiguities of the situation. Describing the remarkable expansion in sexual awareness which has occurred among women in recent years, she points out that 'in the context of the women's movement the boundaries between the erotic and the non-erotic shifted: we were able to perceive our pleasure in each other as desire and pursue it.' However, as she goes on to observe, women often paid a heavy price for the pleasures and positive aspects of lesbian involvements: 'Sometimes the disappointment of discovering that lesbianism, which was and is seen by many feminists as a political solution to the problem of men, could be just as bitter and painful and debilitating as heterosexuality, was devastating.'[4] The breakdown of personal relationships and the re-entry into heterosexuality in the 1980s of women who in the previous decade chose to identify as lesbian has involved many of us in episodes of distress and crisis. Events such as these, as well as being a source of conflict, have understandably disillusioned many women, deflecting their energies from feminist struggle.

The varied trends and currents outlined above all play a part in the works of fiction discussed in this chapter. Notable dissimilarities of attitude and outlook between writers are discernible. Authors writing in the 1970s or early 1980s such as Oosthuizen, Piercy and Barbara

Wilson, while affirming the ideal of sisterhood, describe with remarkable honesty, the difficulties women experience in achieving it.
In their novels differences between women are presented as a source
of enrichment as well as a cause of discord and division. The mid-
1980s, in contrast, have seen the growth of a new and disturbing kind
of fiction which, deliberately interrogating 1970s concepts of sisterhood, concentrates attention on female antagonism and acts of
betrayal. Dworkin's novel *Ice and Fire* (1986) and the collection of
short stories gloomily entitled *The Things That Divide Us* (1985) are
two examples. At the moment ideas of sisterhood are in a stage of
transition. Contrary approaches exist side by side. In the same years
as the revolutionary feminist Dworkin problematizes complacent
assumptions of women's community, Atwood and Carter, whose
outlook is less radical, are just starting to recognize that sisterhood
exists and to introduce positive representations of it into their novels![5]

   The depressing aspect of feminist approaches to sisterhood, illustrated by the current emphasis in fiction on rifts and divisions, are
amply offset, of course, by the successes which the Women's Movement has achieved in the area. Again, to quote Rickford:

> Contemporary feminism has propelled thousands of women of one
> generation to make an irreversible commitment to womankind and
> radically reform their relationships with other women on the basis of
> solidarity and pride rather than competitiveness and shame . . . Not
> only do we take each other more seriously, we have also discovered *en
> masse* the delights of women's company. . . [6]

The magnitude of the achievement described above appears all the
more impressive when contrasted with the negative situation existing previously. In the first half of this century relations between
women suffered a quite appalling degree of marginalization and
trivialization in both art and life. Pratt observes that, on account of the
lesbian stigma, 'after 1920 it became far less acceptable for women
authors to exhibit strong feelings between their heroes than during
the previous era'.[7] The Sexual Revolution of the 1960s, with its
fiercely heterosexist bias, accelerated this trend, exacerbating its
effects. Juliet Mitchell, drawing on personal experience, describes
the pressures put on women to prevent them from conversing with
one another and forming friendships – and her astonishment when
the advent of the Women's Movement started to reverse this trend
and to make contact possible:

> I do remember being surprised that it was 'all right' talking just to
> women. Many of us came out of predominantly male political move-
> ments, girl-friends belonged to childhood, women's coffee parties
> were not for us. . . seriousness was men. I can remember a male

comrade asking me who I'd lunched with and when I mentioned a woman's name, saying 'I hate women who have other women for friends'. I can remember the men I worked with at my job and the men I worked with politically saying complacently of me, 'Oh, she likes being the only woman'. How could I not have been flattered by my position? And I suppose I was.[8]

Mitchell, it is important to note, is writing here about the stigmatization not of intimate attachments between women but of mere acts of verbal communication. This illustrates with painful vividness the brutally misogynistic climate prevalent in the period.

Mitchell continues her account of the stigmatization of female friendships in the 1960s by pointing out that the identification of men with seriousness and women with triviality effectively discouraged the latter from communicating since 'as women, could we afford to like each other without trivializing ourselves?' The destructive combination of self-contempt and scorn for members of one's own sex which characterized women's attitudes at that time is aptly summed up by Rich by the term 'horizontal hostility'. She defines this as 'the fear and mistrust of other women, because other women are ourselves'.[9]

The emergence of the Women's Movement in the early 1970s did not, of course, result in the disappearance of attitudes of 'horizontal hostility' overnight. Their legacy is apparent in certain novels written in the period. A tendency to ignore or trivialize female friendships is reflected in textual omissions and absences, as well as in contradictions of authorial attitude and stance. Bryant's novel *Ella Price's Journal* (1972), along with Friedan's theoretical work *The Feminine Mystique* (1963) with which it shares several common themes, provide illustrations of both phenomena. Bryant and Friedan both take as their theme the situation of the married woman who is expected by society to sacrifice self-fulfilment and intellectual ambitions on the altar of motherhood and domesticity. The two writers, one notes, fail to refer to the supportive or pleasurable aspects of female relationships. Bryant, on the few occasions when she does mention her hero Ella's relations with women friends, presents them in a totally utilitarian light. She ignores their potential for emotional warmth and enjoyment. Ella and her fellow student Laura, lonely misfits whose marriages have broken up, are portrayed as cultivating one another's company unwillingly. They regard one another with pity and suspicion as outcasts from the world of marriage and heterosexual love-affairs which for them, as for the reader built into the text, clearly constitutes the only available reality.

Omissions and contradictions of a similar kind are apparent in Atwood's early novels *The Edible Woman* (1969) and *Surfacing* (1972). As I have illustrated elsewhere, they are also a feature of Carter's *The Magic Toyshop* (1967) and *Heroes and Villains* (1969).[10]

A perplexing feature of these novels by Bryant, Atwood and Carter is that in many cases the reader is uncertain whether it is the author, the characters she creates or possibly both whose attitudes to female friendships and women's community are dismissive, contradictory and confused. Ambiguities of this kind and the impression of authorial unease which they convey reflect, no doubt, the cultural climate of the period in which the novels were written. All three authors, it is interesting to note, create positive representations of female friendships and involvements in the novels which they published subsequently.

Today, on account of the influence of feminism, relations between women are no longer ignored but enjoy a central place in fiction. The varied treatment they receive will become apparent in the following pages. Before proceeding, however, to examine a selection of fictional texts, I need to say something about the way I have chosen to organize my discussion of material and ideas in this chapter. The reader may wonder why I have not taken what appears, at first sight, the simplest course available and divided representations of female relationships in works of fiction into the contrasting categories of 'non-erotic friendships' and 'lesbian relations'. However, a cursory acquaintance with feminist and psychoanalytic theory indicates why I rejected this particular course, dismissing it as invalid and impractical. For a start, since all relationships exist in a state of flux and may be described as to a degree sexual in basis, the categories of the 'erotic' and the 'non-erotic' frequently overlap. The distinction between them is in many cases minimal or extremely difficult to gauge. Several of the writers whose novels I discuss in this chapter (for example Oosthuizen and La Tourette) do, in fact, make this point. Further, the definition of the term lesbian is at the moment an issue of controversy. Debate exists about whether its connotations are primarily political or erotic. Thus, rather than work with these problematic categories, I have chosen headings which more accurately reflect the true interests of writers and theorists. These are: Political approaches to relations between women, Psychoanalytic approaches, Lesbian continuum, and Community and collectivity. The two former headings are of major importance and deserve a word of explanation. They represent, in fact, yet another version of an ideological division which we have already encountered in this study. This is the division between the radical feminist focus on collective organization and political struggle, on the one hand, and the apolitical concern with the personal history of the individual female subject associated with psychoanalysis, on the other. A brief description of these two kinds of fiction highlights how extreme and artificial this division is.

Writers who take a political approach to sisterhood in novels generally reproduce radical feminist ideas of women's community as a basis for feminist organization and acts of resistance to patriarchy. Treating the category 'women' as unproblematic, they present it as providing a stable basis for political organization and action. The goal of the protagonists in their novels is generally the achievement of a unified identity and integration within feminist community. When representing lesbianism, the writers present it in terms of woman-bonding and acts of cooperation. They pay little attention to its sexual and emotional complexities. In keeping with the emphasis they place on the value of a unified identity, they tend to depict bisexuality as morally suspect. The bisexual appears as an unreliable, transgressive figure whose shifting allegiances and desires have a disruptive effect on women's community and feminist projects.

Writers who adopt a psychoanalytical approach, on the contrary, pay little if any attention to the collective, political aspects of relations between women. Instead, they concentrate on exploring their personal, psychological nuances, highlighting their problematic as well as their positive features. Their avoidance of themes of collectivity is, of course, understandable. The focus they place on the motif of the fractured self and on the shifting meanings of the sign 'woman' leads them inevitably to problematize, overtly or by implication, the concept of 'women' and 'women's community'. When representing lesbianism, the writers focus attention on its erotic aspects. They ignore or underemphasize its political value as the basis for feminist struggle. They tend to envisage women's liberation more in terms of the subject's free play of multiple identities and heterogeneous desires than in social or economic terms. In consonance with this, they present bisexuality in an attractive, sympathetic light even though acknowledging its disruptive, transgressive aspects.

The bifurcation of fictional representations of sisterhood and relations between women into 'political' and 'psychoanalytic' categories is, of course, by no means satisfactory. It promotes an unreal divorce between two areas which, as we know from our own lives, are interrelated and interdependent. The division, though regrettable, is however easy to account for. It reproduces a rift between personal/political, and private/public realms which is ingrained in British fiction. The rift is discernible, as Janet Todd illustrates, in eighteenth- and nineteenth-century novels in the contrast between 'sentimental', 'social' and 'erotic' friendships between women on the one hand, and 'political' friendships on the other.[11] While the former are described as providing a source of mere personal fulfilment, the latter have public import since they constitute a challenge to patriarchal attitudes. The division recurs, this time in a more extreme form, in novels written in the first half of this century in the contrast between the representation of the collective struggle waged by the suffragettes, and the totally different depiction of sexual relations between women in the works of Djuna Barnes and other novelists. The friendships of the suffragettes are recognized as possessing political value, since they confront and challenge patriarchal structures. Lesbian involvements, on the contrary, are depicted as amoral and transgressive. Ostracized by mainstream society, lesbians are portrayed as existing in an isolated, private space devoted to the pursuit of personal pleasure and cut off from the public world of social relations and politics.[12]

The division of the fictional representation of female relations into 'politics' and 'psychoanalysis', while having its roots in the cultural rifts described above, is exacerbated by certain trends in contemporary feminism. One of these relates to perspectives on lesbianism. A major achievement of the Women's Movement has been to recognize and foreground the political implications of lesbianism. As a result, however, its erotic aspects are often ignored or marginalized.[13] Many of us validly believe that it involves both areas. We regard our lesbian identity in both political and personal terms. This point of view, however, is unfortunately seldom represented in works of fiction. Influenced by the traditional rift between 'public' and 'private' realms, and by the divorce between 'politics' and 'psychoanalysis' which continues to dog and burden feminism, writers – as we shall see – tend to portray lesbianism in terms of either exclusively politics or sex.

Political approaches to relations between women

A concept which has been instrumental in fostering and promoting the political implications of sisterhood is woman-identification. Radicalesbians explain it as follows:

> Only women can give to each other a new sense of self. That identity we have to develop with reference to ourselves, and not in relation to men.... For this we must be available and supportive to one another, give our commitment and our love, give the emotional support necessary to sustain this Movement. Our energies must flow toward our sisters, not backward toward our oppressors.[14]

The idea of feminist community as a source of solidarity and confidence, and the problems women encounter in implementing this goal, are themes central to the novels by Piercy, Barbara Wilson and Oosthuizen discussed below. In consonance with feminist principles of collectivity, all three writers structure their texts around projects and activities of a communal kind. Their representation of the development of female friendships and involvement in the context of these projects agrees with Rich's comments: 'More and more women are creating community, sharing work, and discovering that in the sharing of work our relationships with each other become larger and more serious'.[15] Making reference to feminist work-projects also gives the writers the opportunity to introduce a varied cast of female characters. It enables them to bring together within a single text women with different ideological attitudes, and hetero and lesbian figures. In Wilson's and Oosthuizen's novels, indeed, certain of the characters move from one identification to another, discovering their capacity for lesbian relations *en route*.

The three writers focus attention on a variety of different activities and organizations. Piercy in *Small Changes* (1973) explores the setting up of women's communal houses and, in *The High Cost of Living* (1978), the running of a rape-crisis line and a refuge for battered women. Her treatment of these projects is far from idealized. *The High Cost of Living* in particular emphasizes the precariousness and problematic aspects of feminist social structures. Antagonisms stemming from differences of economic position between women have such a disruptive effect on the feminist community that they undermine the hero Leslie's faith in the possibility of sisterhood. She remarks unhappily, 'We're all supposed to be sisters, but they [privileged women with private means] have more money and more control and more options, and they decide things to suit themselves.'[16] The Women's Movement is also depicted as weakened by ideological and intellectual rifts. Women who live on a pittance and work without pay for feminist organizations are understandably hostile to others such as Leslie who, attaching themselves to the male-dominated institution of the university, look forward to obtaining a well-paid academic post. Leslie, on the other hand, upholding academic standards of scholarship, feels equally unsympathetic to those women who, in their eagerness to promote the new feminist culture, dismiss such standards as phallocratic and outdated. These rifts and antagonisms are used by Piercy as a foil to highlight the acts of selfless commitment performed by certain figures in the novel. Mary and Liz continue to give refuge to battered women, despite lack of support from their more affluent sisters. Tasha, bravely surmounting problems of apathy and lack of helpers, remains staunchly committed to the work of the rape-crisis line and the women's education collective.

Wilson's *Ambitious Women* (1982) places a similarly strong emphasis on feminist work-projects. The quotation from a poem by Piercy which heads the novel indicates the possible influence of her ideas. The feminist organizations on which Wilson focuses attention are a print-shop run by the two central characters Allison and Holly, and a shelter for battered women where Allison works as a volunteer. The design of the novel foregrounds, in a somewhat schematic manner, both the *value* and the *precariousness* of sisterhood and women's community. The novel is divided into three sections and each, in fact, centres on an act of female support or betrayal. In the first section Allison makes the dangerous decision to let a woman terrorist stay in her own home instead of housing her in the Women's Shelter. She does this to avoid putting the Shelter in jeopardy with the police. The second, concentrating on Holly's experiences, describes her betrayal by Magda, the colourfully portrayed bisexual journalist with whom she has a brief affair. In the third section, with Allison absent in jail because of her involvement with the terrorist, Holly struggles to run the print-shop on her own. She receives assistance from Denver, a lesbian feminist who subsequently becomes her lover. She also staunchly withstands the pressure put on her by Allison's ex-husband Tom to withdraw her allegiance from the shop and let it collapse. Her analysis of the meaning of this event spells out to the reader the affirmation of the value of sisterhood which is the chief message of the novel:

> I took the bus back to the shop, refusing his ride, thinking of the word 'loyalty' in a spirit of triumph. I felt as if I had found the one word that expressed it all, that gave a meaning to the most disparate things: Allison's going to jail to protect the shelter; Magda's betrayal; the shop and all it stood for. It was the loyalty of friends, it was women's loyalty, maybe all we have. ... Loyalty is the only thing we can do for each other. The only thing women can do for each other.[17]

The novel provides an intriguing insight into the kind of value-scheme adopted by writers who take a political approach to the theme of sisterhood. A contrast is drawn between the hetero feminist Allison who is 'ambitious' to create feminist community and make a success of the print-shop on a cooperative basis, and the bisexual Magda who, in keeping with the libertarian values she espouses, is ambitious to achieve personal pleasure, power and success. A puritanical ethos is at times discernible. Attributes prized by the author are hard work, loyalty, independence and the development by the female subject of a strong identity with which to confront the oppressive aspects of patriarchy. The pursuit of pleasure and personal success, one notes, are associated with Magda, the self-centred, unreliable bisexual. Lesbian relationships, illustrated by Holly's and Denver's involvement, are treated in terms not of eroticism but cooperative acts and woman-bonding. The disruptive aspects of sexual desire are associated with the bisexual Magda.

Another writer who treats relations between women in the context of feminist groups and work-projects is Oosthuizen. The dominant theme of her novel *Loneliness and other Lovers* (1981) is, in fact, woman-identification. The interest of the novel lies in its detailed, carefully documented account of the reasons which prompt women to cease making men the focus of their lives and, instead, transfer their allegiance and love to women. By making her hero Jean a woman in her mid-forties, recently separated from her husband, Oosthuizen emphasizes the way the advent of the Women's Movement has enabled many older women to overcome social and economic difficulties and make a fresh start in life. The novel opens with Jean leaving her middle-class home in the provinces and, acting on information supplied by her teenage son, moving into a squat in the London borough of Camden. Here she meets Sara, a woman who, younger than herself, is unmarried and familiar with independence and city life. At the start of the novel the two identify as heterosexual. However, though economic pressures and social convention encourage them to relate to men, their growing affection and mutual trust steer them gradually towards involvement with one another. Their friendship, based on reciprocal acts of cooperation and support, is strengthened by their recognition of the links they possess in common. Here the theme of the commonality of female experience is important. Both women have personal knowledge of male exploitation. They encounter sexist treatment, Oosthuizen points out, not only from men with traditional 'family' values but also from the pseudo-liberated men they meet at the squat. The feminist events and activities taking place in the area encourage their friendship to flourish. They visit women's bookshops together, attend a feminist conference and become involved in running a group for young women. In a key episode in the novel Sara articulates the contradiction she feels in continuing to relate sexually to men while devoting her political, practical and emotional energies to women. She remarks that, while the outer circle of her life is filled with activities 'mostly with women, the trouble is that the small space is often filled by a man – and somehow the two can't coexist. You have to choose, one or the other.'[18] The concluding pages of the novel indicate that she and Jean choose to give priority to women.

Oosthuizen introduces pastoral imagery, cultural feminist in tone, to represent the allure of the woman-identified values and emotions which lie submerged beneath the phallocratic attitudes of contemporary society. Picking flowers with Sara on the river-bank, Jean thinks, 'the names were nothing like the tamer names of garden flowers: they seemed magical, as if they were part of some ancient hidden knowledge that Sara was passing on to her' (p. 68). When Sara effectively supports her through the crisis of her mother's death, Jean finally perceives that it is she, as opposed to her neglectful boyfriend Clive, who merits her love and commitment. She thinks wistfully, 'O Sara, it should be you and me. You're the one I'm closest to, who won't let me down' (p. 151). Judging from signs such as this, the novel concludes with the two women on the verge of becoming lovers. In terms of the theme of woman-bonding which Oosthuizen treats, her decision to terminate the narrative at this point is perfectly appropriate since it presents the relationship as open-ended, a continuing process. From an ideological point of view, however, it can be seen as being a cop-out. It enables her to avoid describing the sexual and erotic facets of lesbian love. As is often the case with writers who appoach female relations in terms of sexual politics, this dimension of lesbian involvements is avoided.

The political and social aspects of sisterhood and relations between women also, of course, play a significant role in a number of short stories. Notable examples are Barbara Burford's 'The Pinstripe Summer' (*The Threshing Floor*, 1986), Anna Wilson's 'The Reach' (*The Reach*, 1984) and Jean Thompson's 'The People of Color' (*Love Stories by New Women*, 1978). The latter culminates in an episode in which two women, confronted with an incident of male violence, discover that their allegiance to one another transcends marital loyalties and colour differences. Anira Rowanchild's 'A Bit of Help' (*Girls Next Door*, 1985) also merits attention. The narrative strategies which Rowanchild utilizes depend for their effectiveness on the reader's familiarity with concepts of sisterhood and woman-identification. The fact that these concepts are considerably better known to readers than they were fifteen years ago allows Rowanchild to signal their significance, relieving her from the cumbersome process of giving them detailed definition. She does not spell out to the reader the precise kind of 'help' which the gypsy woman Zinnia, a visitor from the past, intends to give Linda Evans, an over-worked widow burdened with children and domestic chores. She has no need to do so. In the lesbian-feminist context of the volume in which the story appears, we recognize it as a sisterly combination of domestic, social and erotic elements.

Psychoanalytic approaches to relations between women

In striking contrast to the novels and short stories reviewed above, which explore the social and political significance of female relations, are a number of other works which investigate their psychological and personal attributes. This latter kind of fiction complements, to a degree, the former. Many of the emotional complexities of relations between women which texts taking a political perspective tend to ignore receive detailed treatment in ones which adopt a psychoanalytic approach. These include, shifting power-relations between friends and partners, as well as problems arising from feelings of possessiveness, over-dependence and the confusion of individual ego boundaries. Problems of this type, as the reader will no doubt recall, are very similar to those which writers describe as characterizing relations between mothers and daughters. The two areas, as we shall see, have a considerable amount in common.

Other differences also exist between works of fiction adopting a political approach and ones whose perspectives are chiefly psychoanalytic. While the former generally attribute discords and misunderstandings between women to the intervention of individual men or male institutions, the latter, in contrast, tend to explain them in terms of 'the infant origin of adult emotion'[19] and 'the Law of the Father' which, informing the structures of family life, is internalized by the female subject.

The novels discussed in this section make remarkably adventurous use of both ideas from psychoanalytic theory and avant-garde strategies of writing, utilizing techniques of intertextuality and discontinuous narrative. However, as the comments I've made above suggest, they frequently reveal marked social and political limitations. While concentrating, sometimes with claustrophobic intensity, on the emotional life of the female protagonist or pair of characters they ignore women's involvement in both feminist community and the public domain of paid work. They may also in some cases be justly accused of perpetuating the traditional view of woman as an irrational, emotional creature who finds fulfilment solely in the private sphere of feeling and sexuality. Certain lesbian texts (for example Millett's *Sita*) may also be accused of perpetuating the ideology of romantic love, transferring its codes unchanged and unchallenged from hetero love affairs to affairs between women. The attitudes revealed by the writers towards issues of class are also decidedly limited. By presenting the central characters as having nothing more pressing to do with their time than explore nuances of love and friendship, they give the impression of woman as a leisured, privileged being who leads a life insulated from economic and political realities. This is not the kind of existence, I need scarcely mention, the majority of us lead!

A motif which unites several of the novels considered in this section, albeit the treatment of it differs considerably, is the analysis of female relations in the context of the pre-oedipal mother-daughter bond. In representing friendships and involvements between women as reproducing facets of this bond, the writers agree with the findings of feminist poets and theorists who have investigated the area. Rich, for example, in her famous poem 'Sibling Mysteries', introducing the 'mirroring-mothering' image which is a conventional feature of the *topos*,[20] poignantly describes 'how sister gazed at sister/ reaching through mirrored pupils/back to the mother'.[21] Rich herself, Elizabeth Abel, Jane Flax[22] and Joanna Ryan have all contributed to the theoretical exploration of the topic. Excerpts from Ryan's essay make an informative introduction to its treatment in works of fiction. She points out that women are often understandably unwilling to see their relations with one another interpreted in terms of the mother-daughter bond on account of the prejudiced and pathologizing use frequently made of the idea. She cites as an example the crude and reductive description of lesbian relations as 'incest with the mother'. As she observes, this description is totally unjustified: 'the imposition of heterosexuality is seen at its starkest: what men are allowed in terms of suitably displaced union with the mother is disallowed to women and made taboo.'[23] It is vital, she insists, that women feel free to analyse their relations with one another in terms of the mother-daughter attachment without regarding it as in any way invalidating. One of the achievements of the writers discussed here is that they succeed in doing this. The one exception is Tennant who, as I shall subsequently argue, in her novel *The Bad Sister* (1978) unfortunately *does* give a prejudiced and unfair view of lesbian relationships.

Millett's *Sita* (1976), illustrates in an extreme manner many of the attributes I have cited as typifying the psychoanalytic approach to relations between women. Bringing together fiction and autobiography, the novel illustrates the experimentation with genre which was a feature of many feminist texts written in the early 1970s. Writing in the first person, Millett recounts the turbulent and distressing closing stages of her relationship with her Italian lover Sita. Sita is the older of the two women and has led a more cosmopolitan life than Kate. Ironically, the very qualities which attract Kate to Sita – Sita's bisexuality, her multifaceted personality and her rich experience of life, including marriage, child-bearing and numerous love affairs – contribute to the demise of the relationship. They cause Sita to tire of Kate's company long before Kate tires of hers.

The novel has received, on the whole, very unfavourable reviews. It has been damningly described as 'the most awful book', possessing the appeal of 'a soap opera'.[24] There are several explanations for this. To start with, feminists find sexuality – especially the kind of self-revelatory account in which Millett engages – a topic notoriously difficult to cope with. Attacking the puritanism of the Women's Movement, Dorothy Allison complains:

> Instead of speaking out in favour of sex, most feminists seem to avoid this discussion in any way possible. It is too dangerous, too painful, too hopeless – like racism, class, anti-semitism, and all the important issues that require so much of us. Everyone is afraid of what might be revealed about our personal fears and desires.[25]

To go on with, critics have failed to comprehend the complexities of the analysis of power relations between women which is Millett's central theme.

One feature of the novel which has puzzled critics is the state of abject passivity and lack of autonomy to which Kate is reduced in the final throes of the love affair. She becomes, under the dominance of Sita's spell, totally submissive and lacking in will-power – this despite the fact that she has achieved the status of successful writer and sculptor. These aspects of her situation, however, appear both intelligible and skilfully depicted if they are interpreted in the way which, to judge from her allusions to the Persephone–Demeter myth, Millett intends us to read them.[26] This is as an unconscious re-enactment of the early relationship between daughter and mother. Recognizing that Sita is on the verge of leaving her, Kate projects onto her the image not of the benevolent mother-figure but of the cruel, witch-like mother. The latter figure, according to Dinnerstein, is characterized by her abuse of power and the capricious way she gives and withholds nurture and affection. Sita is portrayed as behaving in a similarly capricious manner. She comes and goes without explanation, with the result that Kate feels she has no control over her appearances and absences. Images of paralysis, suffocation and imprisonment, used by Irigaray to describe the oppressive aspects of mother–daughter relations, are interwoven in the text. Kate feels 'afraid, forbidden to stir. A prisoner' (p. 211). She experiences 'a paralyzing, humiliating dependence' on Sita (p. 136). She feels that the boundaries between her own identity and her lover's are about to collapse. At night she longs for Sita to join her in bed but, when Sita does so, experiences her presence as stifling. Waiting in vain for Sita to make love to her, she thinks 'the suffocation, the rigid waiting. And something new: my fists double up, a convulsion all through the body. Anger' (p. 211). Here Kate appears to have regressed to the position of the frustrated child, angry at being denied maternal nurturance. Her description of Sita's face 'looming over her' also vividly evokes the image of the all-powerful mother seen from the child's point of view.

Kate confesses on occasion that, in her present abject state, the act of writing serves as a means to preserve some remnants of sanity and identity. This also agrees with psychoanalytic interpretations of mother–daughter relations. Jane Gallop comments that 'according to Julia Kristeva, woman needs language, the paternal, symbolic order, to protect her from the lack of distinction from the mother'.[27] This is certainly true of Kate's involvement with Sita. The novel, far from being 'awful', emerges, on the contrary, as very daring. Millett courageously explores destructive aspects of lesbian love, including imbalances of power and sado-masochistic emotions, the discussion of which is often taboo among feminists even today.[28]

A much more cheerful and balanced account of love between women is provided by La Tourette's *Nuns and Mothers* (1984). The novel is an exceptionally complex one and deserves to be more widely known. Breaking new ground, La Tourette gives a detailed description of the construction of a lesbian relationship. She treats the topic with wit and perception, concentrating on the interaction between social, psychological and erotic planes. The relationship exists between her two central characters Helena and Georgia. La Tourette is unusual among the writers discussed in this section in focusing attention on the pressure exerted by economic and social factors. Lack of financial security and social recognition are shown to have a predictably disruptive effect on the relationship.

The novel is structured on the motif of the quest. This possesses both geographical and psychological implications. With her husband and children absent in England, Helena embarks with Georgia on a brief tour of the USA. Her situation, which is typical of the bisexual, is, she admits, unstable and precarious in the extreme: 'One foot on either side of the Atlantic, with the ground constantly turning soggy under my feet. One foot in straight domesticity and motherhood and one in wild wanton lesbian love with Georgia.'[29] The tour of the USA represents, to quote her words, 'an odyssey back into the past' which gives the two women the opportunity to visit people and places influential to their development. These include certain of Helena's relatives and the Convent of the Assumption where the two studied as children. The women's relationship is described as reproducing facets of the mother–daughter bond and other familial ties. Helena mentally explores her attachment to her mother Marguerite and to certain deceased members of the family such as her grandmother and her beloved father Wall. In semi-humorous mood she pictures herself confessing to her mother, 'Yes, Marguerite,... I was in love with Wall. And with you...' She is uncertain if her mother would be 'flattered or insulted' (p. 208). The reunion between mother and daughter which occurs in the final pages makes an appropriate ending to the novel. Similarities and differences between the two are both acknowledged: '"*We look terrific*," I say as we stand in front of her mirror, and it's the truth. Not only terrific, but alike. So alike. And so different' (p. 211).

The institutions of the family and the Roman Catholic Church provide La Tourette with a fruitful context for investigating the subordinate position which society assigns to women. Nuns and mothers, though unsympathetic to one another's attitudes, are discovered to possess a great deal in common. Both are expected to display qualities of self-sacrifice and a capacity for caring. Both moreover inhabit institutions which, ruled by the Law of the Father, marginalize relations between women, treating them as inauthentic. A central theme in the novel is, in fact, the pressures patriarchal society exerts to separate women, preventing them from becoming too closely involved.

Despite their marginalized status, however, female ties and attachments are shown by La Tourette to have a distinctly subversive effect on patriarchal values and culture. This is illustrated by the witty manner she subverts Christian imagery, using it to describe lesbian sexual practice. Helena admits that in loving Georgia, instead of the Trinity of 'Father, Son and Holy Ghost, I find Mother, Daughter and Dark Lord or Lady' (p. 148). Kissing her between the thighs and savouring the 'glistening clitoral pearl', she thinks, 'Worship and receive this communion on my outstretched tongue' (p. 65). The mingling of sacred and profane imagery in the novel, apparent in these quotations, continues a tradition which has been employed with transgressive effect by writers as different as John Donne, Djuna Barnes and James Kirkup. La Tourette makes an important contribution to the vitality and development of this tradition.

Another topic La Tourette successfully explores is the shifting positions of masculine and feminine adopted by the women in their relationship. An element of role-play, far from being condemned as politically unsound, functions as a source of carnivalesque pleasure and frivolity. Helena appropriately spends some of her money which she inherits from her grandmother on treating Georgia to an expensive meal in a restaurant, pretending the two are celebrating their engagement. The event highlights, by way of contrast, the lack of financial independence which women generally possess. Helena, summing up the links between economics and patriarchal power, ruefully observes, 'If you're a mother, your husband pays if you've got one. If you're a nun, the church pays.... Either way, he who pays the piper, calls the tune' (p. 104)!

Another writer who gives her central character a Roman Catholic upbringing, portrays her rejecting Catholicism and also uses Christian iconography to represent the complexities of female relations, is

Michèle Roberts. The theme of her novel *The Visitation* (1983) is, however, not lesbian love but non-erotic friendship between women. Although, as I pointed out in Chapter 2 where I discussed the novel in terms of sexual politics, the friendship between Beth and Helen forms only one strand in the narrative, it certainly assumes an important place. It is women who assist and support Helen in her attempts to achieve independence and to become a creative writer. Here Roberts agrees with the comment voiced by the theorist Flax that 'only through relationships with other women can women heal the hurts suffered during their psychological development'.[30]

Roberts delineates not only the positive aspects of female friendship but also the problematic ones. Helen's unsatisfactory relationship with her mother, whom she feels favours her twin brother, combined with the dismissive view of female relations prevalent in contemporary society, cause her to have little faith in women. Roberts comments: 'The last thing she dared hope for was female companionship on her journey, a woman walking with her and watching over her. She didn't know that women liked and trusted one another.'[31] The friendship which Helen forms with Beth encourages her to overcome these prejudices. It is described as reproducing certain positive attributes of the mother–daughter bond, including nurturance and encouragement. In a passage of symbolic narrative towards the end of the novel, Beth is represented as spiritually 'rebirthing' Helen, enabling her successfully to achieve autonomy.

The friendship between Helen and Beth, though sensitively depicted, does have certain limitations, ones of which the author appears unaware. Students with whom I have discussed the novel pointed out that the friendship emerges as curiously one-sided and lacking in reciprocity. Whereas Beth takes a sympathetic interest in Helen's situation, supporting her in various difficulties, Helen shows very little interest in Beth's. Roberts presents an alternative and more balanced view of friendship between women, it is interesting to note, in her poem 'Magnificat'.[32]

The most eccentric and perplexing of the texts I have chosen to consider in this section is Tennant's *The Bad Sister* (1978). The novel is riddled with contradictions and arouses in me conflicting responses. I find it a difficult work to discuss fairly, and here have space only to pinpoint certain of its problematic aspects and the issues they raise.

In terms of genre the novel, treating events set in Scotland and London, represents a highly individualistic version of Gothic fantasy. Its central focus is the relationship between Jane, the illegitimate daughter of a member of the aristocracy, and her legitimate half-sister Ishbel. Jane feels intense envy and hatred for Ishbel because of her privileged position, and in the course of the narrative attempts to murder her. She is encouraged and assisted by Meg, the mysterious, witch-like leader of a radical feminist commune. The problematic aspects of the novel hinge on Tennant's representation of feminist community and female relations. She describes them as essentially destructive and transgressive. They are depicted as constituting a kind of terrorist subculture which undermines and disrupts, often by violent means, the logocentric, rationalistic domain of patriarchal society. Her treatment of women's community and lesbian relations contains elements which are downright prejudiced and offensive. She sensationalizes them, identifying them with a lurid world of witchcraft, violence, drugs and sado-masochism. In this respect, she does contemporary feminism a disservice, reproducing the misogynistic stereotypes of femininity popularized by a phallocratic culture. The novel illustrates, very disturbingly, that the association of lesbianism with vampirism and violence, which is a feature of certain nineteenth- and twentieth-century novels,[33] continues to flourish not only in the popular medium of the horror film but also in serious fiction.

The version of sexual politics which Tennant presents in the novel is, as is often the case in her works, a 'manichean' one. She identifies women with a transgressive, intuitive energy and passion. Men, in contrast, are portrayed as inferior, imperceptive creatures who achieve power primarily by preying on female vitality. Trapped in the pseudo-rational attitudes they themselves have created, they live on a shallow plane, out of touch with the deeper reaches of the psyche. This perspective appears to reflect a distorted version of the cultural feminist ideas of writers such as Daly. Unlike Daly, however, it is women, not men, whom Tennant associates with violence. And far from celebrating women's community, she describes it as characterized by intrigue and lust for power. An element of homophobia also mars the novel.

Yet, despite Tennant's prejudiced view of lesbian relationships, *The Bad Sister* is a very accomplished work in terms of design and style, and makes stimulating reading. One of Tennant's achievements is to interrogate the terms sisterhood and sister, revealing them to be the site of conflicting discourses and meanings. Her dialogic approach questions unitary ways of seeing, enabling us to read the relationship between the two sisters, which is the hub of the novel, in several different ways. On a literal level, Jane's obsessive hatred for her half-sister and her attempt to murder her are motivated by envy of her social and economic privileges. Simultaneously, however, the introduction of the motif of the double and of Jungian ideas of androgyny encourages the reader to interpret the relationship in a psychoanalytic light. On this level, Jane's attempt to kill Ishbel represents, symbolically, an attempt to rid herself of the 'feminine' component of her psyche – the component which is subservient, obedient and conformist.[34] Yet a third reading of sisterhood is built into the text. This is feminist sisterhood. Tennant treats this theme, as I have illustrated above, with distinct prejudice.

Ideas of lesbian continuum

A concept which helps us interpret representations of relations between women in works of fiction by certain contemporary American and British writers is 'lesbian continuum'. Formulated by Rich in an essay published in 1980,[35] it emphasizes the political aspects of lesbianism rather than the erotic. It has thus aroused a degree of controversy. Features of Rich's discussion relevant to the novels by May Sarton and Anna Wilson which I review in this section are summarized below.

Rich opens her essay by making the point that heterosexuality, rather than being 'natural' and 'innate', is a construct – an 'institution', as she puts it – into which women are coerced and recruited by a variety of different means. The effect of the pressure of 'compulsory heterosexuality' is, she illustrates, to marginalize lesbian experience and make it appear deviant. In extreme cases, it becomes culturally invisible. She subsequently introduces the term 'lesbian continuum', defining it as follows:

> I mean the term *lesbian continuum* to include a range – through each women's life and throughout history – of woman-identified experience; not simply the fact that a woman has had or consciously desired genital sexual experience with another woman. If we expand it to embrace many more forms of primary intensity between and among women, including the sharing of a rich inner life, the bonding against male tyranny, the giving and receiving of practical and political support. (p. 20)

As Rich explains, she deliberately uses the term 'lesbian continuum', as opposed to *lesbian*, to avoid the clinical and narrowly sexual associations of the latter. She seeks to signify by the term ideas of female friendship and political comradeship, as well as sexual involvement between women.

The points which Rich makes in her essay have proved contentious. Critics argue that by describing heterosexuality as *compulsory*, she ignores the pleasurable aspects of relations with men. They also suggest that by describing it 'as the key mechanism of male domination'[36] she underestimates the importance of other kinds of patriarchal control, including the economic and social. The concept of 'lesbian continuum' has also met with criticism. Critics have attacked it as 'ahistorical', pointing out that, since the lesbian identity as we know it today is a twentieth century construct, to place women living in earlier eras on a 'lesbian continuum' is to attribute to them a sexual identification which they did not possess and would not recognize. The concept has also been criticized as reductionist. It has been accused of blurring the distinction between the terms *lesbianism*, *feminism* and *femaleness*, collapsing the three together.[37]

Other feminists, myself included, have welcomed the concept of the 'lesbian continuum', regarding it as a vital tool of feminist strategy. As well as rescuing lesbians living in earlier centuries from oblivion, it affirms the political value of lesbianism, acknowledging it as 'part of a politics of woman-centred resistance'.[38] And by defining lesbianism in terms of woman-identified experience rather than from a narrowly sexual point of view, it foregrounds the multi-faceted nature of lesbian relations. It also makes connections between lesbian and hetero feminists, helping to heal the rifts which have developed between them.

The connection and comparisons which Rich makes between different kinds of woman-identified experience (emotional, political and erotic) and between women from different historical periods, shed light on and enable us to appreciate similar kinds of links made by writers of fiction. May Sarton in *A Reckoning* (1978) organizes her text around the consciousness of a single character, exploring the different forms of woman-bonding she has encountered in her life. Anna Wilson in *Cactus* (1980), in contrast, examines changing constructs of lesbian identity, investigating affinities and discrepancies between women of different generations and age-groups.

Rich's discussion of the concept of 'lesbian continuum' includes a strikingly moving passage in which she brings together the contraries of youth and age, life and death. The concept, she observes, allows us to connect images as apparently disparate as 'the infant suckling her mother's breast, to the grown woman experiencing orgasmic sensations while suckling her own child ... to the woman dying at ninety, touched and handled by women' (p. 23). Sarton's *A Reckoning* is structured around a similar combination of contraries. The central character Laura, on being informed by her doctor that she is dying of cancer, rejects the attention and care proffered by her immediate family. She insists, instead, on making what she calls 'a final reckoning'.[39] This takes the form of affirming the value of 'the real connections' in her life. These 'connections', it quickly becomes apparent to the reader, all involve experiences of woman-bonding and woman-identification. Laura explores in her memory the frustrated lesbian relationship which her sister Jo experienced and, more important from a personal point of view, the intense emotional attachment which she herself formed with her college friend Ella. She affectionately describes Ella as ' a kind of spiritual twin' (p. 12). As Laura admits to Harriet, the young lesbian writer whom she meets in the course of her job with a publishing firm:

'I had to face the fact that for me myself one of the real connections, one of the deepest and most nourishing, in some ways more than my marriage, good as that was, had been a passionate friendship with a woman.' (p. 243)

Laura's son Ben is involved in a homosexual relationship. This is another example of same-sex attachments which impinge on Laura's consciousness in the final weeks of her life.

The pressures which 'compulsory heterosexuality' exerts on women's lives is also a dominant theme in the novel. Laura recognizes that it was her marriage which fractured her friendship with Ella. Parental intervention similarly destroys and terminates Jo's relationship with her woman lover. Laura gradually comes to perceive the patriarchal source of these disruptions. She remarks thoughtfully, 'women have been in a queer way locked away from one another in a man's world'. She perceives that with the rebirth of feminism 'all that is changing', expressing the hope that now 'perhaps women will be able to give one another a great deal more than ever before' (p. 192).

Certain episodes in *A Reckoning* reveal interesting affinities with Virginia Woolf's novel *Mrs Dalloway*. Laura's re-creation, in her memory, of the close attachment she formed with Ella and the destructive effect on it of her marriage, resembles Clarissa Dalloway's memories of her relationship with Sally Seton. Like Clarissa, moreover, she remembers with pleasure the 'ravishing kisses' she and her friend enjoyed. Unfortunately for Sarton, the comparisons with Woolf serve merely to highlight the limitations of *A Reckoning*. The novel lacks the fierce indictment of patriarchal power which gives Woolf's work vigour and fire. Its mood, totally lacking in anger, is one of tepid resignation and sentimental nostalgia. Certain facets of the novel, moreover, are notably unsuccessful. The reader, though obviously expected to sympathize with the dying Laura, finds her elitist attitudes and interference in other people's lives irritating and manipulative.

Unlike Sarton, who structures her text around the consciousness of a single individual, Wilson in *Cactus* chooses to share the narrative interest between four female characters. The novel, an exceptionally fine one which deserves a wider readership, is appropriately published by the radical feminist Onlywomen Press. It responds to a reading which prioritizes the historical aspects of 'lesbian continuum'. Wilson contrasts the attitudes and experiences of Eleanor and Bea, an isolated lesbian couple living in the pre-feminist period of the 1940s and 1950s, with those of Dee and Ann, a couple living in the 1970s who enjoy the support of the burgeoning lesbian feminist movement.

Wilson's description of the oppressive facets of heterosexual culture and her representation of lesbian existence as constituting a challenge to patriarchal value-schemes, reveal pronounced affinities with Rich's ideas. Other features of the novel, however, such as her exploration of the way constructs of lesbian identity alter from age to age and the emphasis she places on issues of class, have more in common with those of Rich's critics. The novel achieves, in fact, an admirable fusion of radical and socialist feminist perspectives. Wilson is as acutely aware of the pressures which social and economic factors exert on women's lives, as she is of the significance of sexual orientation.

The novel opens with a description of Eleanor and Bea, who are holidaying together at a seaside resort, walking along the beach. The passage, typifying the austere clarity and functionality of Wilson's style, possesses symbolic implications and is worth quoting:

> They walked in single file along the beach at the tide's edge, the sands long and faintly glimmering, the two women strung out apart. Eleanor felt the thread of connection cast between them, binding them across the sand.[40]

The images which Wilson introduces predict the break which will occur in the couple's relationship, as well as the emotional tie which continues to link them. The pressures of 'compulsory heterosexuality' prove too strong for Bea, with her middle-class background, driving her to marry. The consequence is that the two women are forced to separate and, like many of their peers in the hostile climate of the 1940s and 1950s, live their lives 'strung out apart'. None the less, a 'thread of connection' continues to bind them, leading them to seek out and achieve a brief reunion in later years.

An admirable feature of the novel is Wilson's perceptive description of the intangible cultural forces which bring about the breakdown of the relationship between the two women. Using phrases necessarily verging on paradox and contradiction, she presents lesbian involvement and identity as the 'absence' at the centre of the male supremacist culture. Before leaving Bea, Eleanor struggles painfully to explain to her the total impracticality of their relationship, given the pressures of hetero convention:

> There's no place for it.... You can't live a secret, because out in the open you find you're living something else. It's odd that, isn't it – the secrecy is so exciting in a way, having something that you can't begin to explain

to anyone else; and then you realise that there really is no way of explaining it – that it's so totally inexplicable to the rest of the world that it doesn't exist. You can't live it. Everything we do out there denies it. Everything. (p. 7)

The accumulation of negative constructions presses home the point which Wilson is making. Lesbian identity and relationships are social entities and require social recognition in order to survive. In a culture which refuses to credit their reality and allows them no space, they can scarcely be said to exist.

Unlike Bea, who marries, Eleanor chooses to keep the thread of woman-identification intact, preserving her integrity at a heavy cost. Relying on 'cactus skills' of survival, she leads the lonely, financially deprived life of a working-class spinster, engaging (to quote Rich) in 'marriage resistance'. Her very existence, Wilson suggests, constitutes a mute challenge to conventions of femininity, the ideology of romance and family life:

> She had worked in offices, silent behind her typewriter as others spoke of their dresses, their conquests, their families. She had sat in cafés as families had spilled themselves onto her table, throwing their quarrels down among the sugar cube wrappings. She had visited old friends, and they had unburdened themselves to her. She saw them as if to the bone and said little. (p. 33)

Wilson's portrayal of Eleanor and Bea, confined in the culturally prescribed roles of spinster and wife, is extremely poignant. It recalls Rich's reference to the way both 'the lesbian trapped in the "closet"', the woman imprisoned in prescriptive ideas of the "normal", share the pain of blocked options, broken connections, lost access to self-definition freely and powerfully assumed' (p. 29).

The two older women, living in the period before the rebirth of feminism, see lesbianism solely as a matter of personal preference. Dee and Ann, on the contrary, living in the 1970s, regard it in political terms as an act of commitment to women and a challenge to patriarchal values. Wilson convincingly represents the situation and points of view of both couples. She succeeds in achieving a delicately poised balance of sympathy.

Community and collectivity

The effect of feminist principles of community and collectivity on the narrative strategies adopted by contemporary writers has on occasion been exaggerated by critics. Nina Auerbach, for example, writing in the 1970s, regretfully claims that the authors' preoccupation with these ideas results in the protagonists they create 'losing their life as characters'.[41] Patricia Stubbs, commenting on the fact that in

certain novels 'notions of individual experience and private moral-
ity have disappeared altogether', suggests that 'this perhaps indicates the direction in which fiction will move'.[42] However, contrary
to Stubbs's view, and as is illustrated by the works discussed in this
chapter, a focus on 'character' and 'individual experience' has not
disappeared but continues to flourish. Monique Witting's *Les
Guérillères* (1969), one of the novels which aroused the critics' cries of
alarm, has proved, in fact, exceptional in the emphasis it places on
collectivity.

The disintegration and modification of the concept of 'character'
which has taken place in certain modernist novels is attributable, in
my opinion, less to the influence of feminism than to structuralist and
post-structuralist trends. The psychoanalytic interest in the concept
of the 'fractured self' which has accompanied them is an important
contributory factor. Feminist theorists have, of course, elaborated
these ideas, using them as the basis for formulating textual strategies
whereby women writers can subvert and disrupt the dominant
phallocratic culture. Cixous, in her essay 'The Character of "Character"' challenges the concept of the unitary self. In her analysis of the
concept of *écriture féminine* she focuses attention on a mode of
writing which has its source in the pre-oedipal resonance of the
mother's voice. Kristeva's account of the semiotic *chora*, a provisional articulation which, echoing the pulsations of the pre-oedipal,
undermines and disrupts symbolic language, similarly foregrounds
strategies of non-rational discourse, textual omissions and absences.[43]

The majority of works of fiction by Anglo-American women
writers, however, rather than rejecting ideas of individual experience and character outright, tend to maintain a tension between the
interests of the individual and those of the group. This is the case with
French's *The Women's Room* (1977) and Weldon's *Down Among the
Women* (1971). The two novels make inventive use of strategies and
techniques highlighting ideas of collectivity and community.

Several features of *The Women's Room* indicate French's desire to
achieve a 'compromise' between the *individual*, on the one hand, and
the *group*, on the other. While structuring the text around the consciousness of a single female narrator, she simultaneously dimin-
ishes her individuality by concealing her name and identity. Although the reader may guess that the narrator is Mira, only in the
concluding episode of the novel are her suspicions confirmed. Another
strategy which French employs to diminish Mira's individuality is to
transform her, at certain key points, into a mouthpiece for the voices
of other characters. Mira comments:

> I hear Martha's voice often as I walk along the beach. And others' too
> – Lily, Val, Kyla. I sometimes think I've swallowed every woman I ever

knew. My head is full of voices.... I feel as if I were a medium and a whole host of departed spirits has descended on me clamouring to be let out.... I am going to try to let the voices out. (p. 17)

The construction of an interplay of different voices to foreground ideas of community and collectivity is a device recommended by the Marxist critic Mikhail Bakhtin, and is put into practice by certain British writers of socialist fiction.[44] Contemporary women writers make effective use of it for similar purposes.

The Women's Room incorporates the motif of the group into its design in other ways. The novel is modelled to a degree on the processes of a feminist consciousness-raising group. The aim of the C R group is to share and analyse personal experience in order to perceive its communal, political significance. Mira's experience of marriage – both her own to Norm and the marriages of her friends and neighbours which she has witnessed – provide her and her fellow students at Harvard with material for making just such an analysis. Mira, with some prompting from her radical friend Val, comes to recognize that the domestic and sexual exploitation she and her friends suffer reflects common factors of female experience. Analytical comments interspersed in the text – 'It seems more a general than an individual problem' (p. 270) and 'Women's problems *do* all spring from the same root ... an education in the suppression of the self' (p. 79) – nudge the reader (somewhat heavily!) towards this perception. Although the claim 'This novel changes lives' on the cover of the Sphere edition may be an exaggeration, the text is certainly organized to raise the reader's consciousness!

The interplay of voices which Weldon creates in *Down Among the Women* is more genuinely dialogic than French's. The tone of authorial address Weldon adopts also differs. The reader, instead of being subjected to Mira's rather hectoring tones, is entertained by a series of witty comments satirically exposing women's abject and exploited plight. The phrase 'Down among the women', reiterated at intervals, assumes the insistent note of a refrain. Repeated references to certain stereotypical female situations and occupations (pregnancy, childcare, housework, exploitative encounters with men) and certain drab locations associated with women (the home, the hospital ward, the park) emphasize the monotony and dreariness of the characters' lives. The common aspect of the daily routines and psychological syndromes in which Jocelyn, Scarlet and the other female characters are trapped is emphasized by authorial comments. Weldon's use of the pronoun 'we', moreover, has the effect of mischievously undermining the female reader's pretensions to superiority. It pulls her down to the ignominious level of the characters, forcing her to identify with their subordinate state. Brilliantly parodying women's willingness to act as skivvies to men and massage the male ego, Weldon remarks, '"Yes, God," we say, "here's your slippers and your nice hot dinner. In the meantime, just feed us, keep us, fetch the coal and say something nice while you're about it"' (p. 83). And, highlighting women's masochistic capacity for self-sacrifice and over-work, 'Down among the women, we don't like chaos. We will crawl from our sickbeds to tidy and define. We live at floor level, washing and wiping. ... We have only ourselves to blame' (p. 83).

In *Down Among the Women*, as in her subsequent novel *Female Friends*, Weldon describes female identity in terms not only of biology (menstruation, childbirth, choices of contraceptive) but also of certain cultural factors. The latter include financial deprivation, domestic servitude and an uncritical acceptance of male supremacy and the ideology of romantic love. Women are represented, in a manner which looks forward to the ideas of the theorist Baker Miller, as possessing a number of disadvantageous attributes which unite them in a 'subordinate group'. A capacity for self-hatred, guilt and over-work, combined with a crippling fear of success, are the most prominent. It is ironic that French's novel, with its celebratory affirmation of ideals of sisterhood, should conclude with a pessimistic description of Mira walking alone and disillusioned on the beach, while Weldon's satiric exposé of women's oppression and self-oppression ends with the cheerfully positive comment: 'We are the last of the women.' The word 'women' here carries ironic resonances. Weldon uses it as a synonym for a group of downtrodden underlings.

In *Down Among the Women* and more especially in *Female Friends* (1975), Weldon places considerable emphasis on antagonisms and rivalries among women. The latter novel contains numerous examples of discords erupting between married and unmarried women, women with children and women who are child-free. These, as Rich and other theorists point out, constitute typical sources of antagonism in a phallocratic culture. The focus which Weldon adopts looks forward to the preoccupation with female differences and divisions which, as I pointed out in the introductory section, is a feature of feminist culture in the 1980s. As the theorist Barbara Sinclair Deckard observes, 'Women, even Movement women are not yet all sisters. Class and race divide us.'[45] In consonance with this trend, novels such as March's *Three Ply Yarn* (1986) and Fairbairns's *Closing* (1987), while introducing acts of cooperation between women, also explore divisions stemming from differences of race, class, age, sexual orientation and ideology.

March and Fairbairns in the novels mentioned above present

differences between women as a source of enrichment as well as of discord. They also succeed in achieving a balance between themes of cooperation and antagonism, communality and division. Fairbairns's *Closing*, in particular, while showing with depressing accuracy the way divisions between women make the Women's Movement vulnerable to exploitation and appropriation by the forces of patriarchy and capitalism, simultaneously highlights the value of female acts of cooperation. In contrast, other novelists writing in the 1980s choose to focus exclusive attention on breakdown of communication and acts of rivalry and betrayal. An important exponent of this trend is Andrea Dworkin. In her theoretical work *Right Wing Women* (1978) she investigates from a revolutionary feminist point of view ideological antagonisms between women. Many women, she convincingly illustrates, deliberately adopt an anti-feminist position and collaborate with men in order to survive. In her novel *Ice and Fire* (1986) she treats similar themes in fictional form, exploring the psychological and cultural roots of individual acts of treachery, cruelty and neglect.[46] The novel analyses, often in a very disturbing manner, the reasons which prompt women to bully, exploit and even torture one another. They engage in such acts, Dworkin suggests, both for survival and to enjoy a gratuitous sense of pleasure and power. A pivotal phrase in the novel, voiced by the narrator and functioning as a kind of refrain, is 'I was the deserter'. It is a confession of woman's capacity to hurt and betray her sisters. *Ice and Fire* is, in many respects, a brilliant piece of fiction. Dworkin, as well as excelling in the description of the brutal facets of city life, achieves an atmospheric distillation of the cultural movements of the 1960s and 1970s. She is acutely aware of ideological perspectives, moving from an interrogation of the values of liberal individualism to a strongly feminist analysis of patriarchal power and woman's position as object of exchange. She is a talented writer of fiction, and it is to be hoped that she will publish more in this area in the future.

An aspect of collectivity of particular interest to women writers, one which has received little if any attention from critics, is the processes involved in the production of a feminist publication. The topic concerns writers on both a practical and a theoretical level. As well as participating in such projects, they also on occasion introduce representations of them into their fiction. Zoë Fairbairns's work furnishes examples of both. In her Introduction to the volume of short stories *Tales I Tell My Mother* (1978), produced cooperatively by herself and four other writers, she succinctly sums up the pros and cons of collectivity. The passage is worth quoting since it is relevant not only to women's fiction but also to other feminist activities such as the setting up of Women's Studies courses and the running of rape-crisis centres and lesbian help-lines:

Collectivity is a word that is bandied about a lot in the women's movement. Sometimes 'collective' is just a trendy euphemism for the same old committee. Sometimes it's an excuse for not doing anything. At its best though – and it has been good for us – it really can mean a group of equals, united by a genuine determination to get on with the job, and disciplined (in the sense of feeling strong obligation to do what you said you would do) by the simple realisation that, busy though I am, and valuable as my other work may be, it is no more so than hers: and I have no right to waste her time by deeming my time to have priority. The word is respect. It's not a thing women are generally taught to have for each other. But it's basic if a collective is to function.[47]

Whereas in the Introduction to *Tales I Tell My Mother* Fairbairns records her own experiences of a collective publishing venture, in her novel *Closing* (1987) she treats the topic in fictional terms. Here I need to point out that she is one of the few writers to show a consistent interest in a topic sadly neglected in contemporary fiction – the situation of women in paid professional work. The context of the action of *Closing* is, in fact, the ruthlessly competitive, professional world of selling and business deals. The three leading characters in the novel initially encounter one another on a sales trainirg course. Here the indefatigable Daphne Barclay instructs them in the complexities of buying, selling and closing deals. One of the three is Teresa Beal. The product which she seeks to market differs radically from the more tangible products of her colleagues. It is the feminist magazine *Atlanta*. Teresa both owns the magazine and is a key member of the collective which produces it. The magazine is in dire financial straits, and the question exercising her thoughts is:

Could a radical magazine, an ideology, a moral system, be sold in the same way as an insurance policy, a home-made toy or a time-share villa in Lanzarote? For the rest of this week she was suspending her scepticism and believing that it could.[48]

The quotation signals one of the dominant themes of the novel. This is the contradictions and compromises between feminist principles of collectivity and equal opportunity, on the one hand, and capitalist principles of competition, commercialism and individual enterprise on the other. The chief message to emerge from *Closing* – a depressing one – is the vulnerability of feminist projects and enterprises to appropriation by the forces of patriarchy and capitalism. *Closing* is Fairbairns's most skilfully written and satisfying novel to date. It is also, I emphasize, essential reading for people interested in the state of the Women's Movement in the 1980s and the problems feminists face today.

Fairbairns is not the only writer to treat in fictional form the production of a feminist magazine. An episode in Miner's *Bloodsisters* (1981) describes the controversies which the collective discussion necessary to the project can arouse.

The treatment of the topic of collectivity in the fiction of the 1980s resembles in many respects that of sisterhood. Writers are more likely to criticize and interrogate than to celebrate it. The content of their critiques, however, is by no means new. From the early years of the Movement dissenting voices, contradicting the enthusiastic endorsement of principles of non-hierarchy, decentralization and collectivity, have been audible. Joreen's famous essay 'The Tyranny of Structurelessness' (1972) remains even today one of the most intelligent and incisive critiques.[49] Joreen correctly predicts that, since the Movement possesses no overt structures and rules and no officially elected leaders, it will speedily develop covert and unofficial ones. These, she suggests, will prove to be more insidiously oppressive and difficult to dislodge than the traditional patriarchal kind. She also warns women that, while the Movement's decentralized methods of working and use of the small group are admirably suited to certain feminist activities, they are cumbersome and inefficient in the case of long-term projects and campaigns on a national scale. Jo Freeman's subsequently published analysis of the Movement's structures, one which is superbly comprehensive, supports and elaborates many of the points Joreen makes.[50]

In works of fiction, critiques of the Movement's organizational practices and structures are often introduced at a subordinate level, serving to underpin the main narrative line. Writers investigate the difficulties women encounter in trying to work together on a collective basis. They explore the divisive effects of jealousy and rivalry, examining the abuses of the 'star system'. They also investigate the way women with money, power or a strong personality tend to dominate Movement activities. They discuss the disputes and antagonisms which, as many of us know from painful experience, weaken the Movement's efficiency, causing feminist groups and projects to either collapse or stagnate. Burford, Fairbairns, Piercy, Oosthuizen and Barbara Wilson all concentrate in different ways on these topics. A recent contributor to their analysis is Elizabeth Wilson. In her novel *Prisons of Glass* (1986) she traces the growth of feminism since the period of the 1960s, highlighting some of the disadvantageous side-effects of principles of collectivity and non-hierarchy.

Conclusion

Feminist attitudes to relations between women and the concept of sisterhood, as I mentioned earlier, are in a state of flux. The idealistic belief in sisterhood which formed the basis of the feminism of the early 1970s has recently given place to a more clear-sighted appreciation of social, radical and ideological differences between women. Writers vary as to the precise emphasis they place on these developments. None the less, though I find it difficult to generalize about their treatment of the topic, from the discussion of texts which has taken place in this chapter certain points of interest undoubtedly do emerge. Superficially it appears that the wheel has come full circle. Antagonisms, rivalry and incidents of breakdown of communication between women once again furnish themes for novels and short stories, in the way they did in the pre-feminist era of the 1950s and the 1960s. In fact, however, the attitudes expressed in the fiction of the two periods possess very little in common. Novels published in the 1980s do not ignore or trivialize female friendships and relationships or reveal a confused approach towards them, as was the case in the 1960s. On the contrary, they give them a central place, treating them very seriously. The stance they adopt is often highly analytical, revealing a detailed knowledge of theoretical perspectives. Dworkin's representation of female acts of neglect and betrayal in *Ice and Fire*, for example, involves a close investigation of the roles of 'subordinate' and 'object of exchange' which a phallocratic culture assigns to woman. Moreover, although in some novels differences between women are depicted as resulting in antagonism, in others they are celebrated as a source of welcome variety.

In discussing representations of relations between women in novels and short stories in this chapter, I have used as section headings the categories 'political' and 'psychoanalytic' as these accurately sum up the two contrasting approaches to the topic which writers frequently adopt. However, as I emphasized in the introductory section, I strongly regret the fact that writers find it necessary to separate the two main areas in such a rigid manner and to create what is, in reality, an artificial rift between them. This rift, and the divisions which it involves, are, in my opinion, one of the chief problems facing writers of fiction at the moment. The two approaches to female relations are, as we have seen, very different and, in their approach to women's community, contradict one another. Fiction which takes a political approach, appropriating ideas from radical feminist theory, presents women's community as a valuable base for feminist work-projects and political struggle. Fiction which takes a psychoanalytic one, on the contrary, re-working the motif of the fractured self and foregrounding the personal life of the female subject, tends to problematize, either deliberately or by implication, the terms 'women' and 'women's community'. A touchstone of the divergence between the two modes is the contrary attitudes writers take ⌐

bisexuality. The bisexual emerges – very intriguingly – as the hub of conflicting ideological discourses and points of view. She is either portrayed unsympathetically as a disruptive presence, a source of problems and discord for the group as a whole, or she is presented in an attractive light as a symbol of the free play of multiple identities and heterogeneous desires.[51] This depends on whether the writer's position is predominantly 'radical feminist' or 'psychoanalytic'.

The perennial conflict between 'politics' and 'psychoanalysis', and between the group and the individual female subject, which the divisions between the two kinds of fiction reflect, make their different themes and interests very difficult indeed to reconcile or even link. It is possible however that a writer, by adopting a dialogic stance, might succeed in exploring the discrepancies and interplay between the two. Certain writers, in fact, have made a start at bridging the gulf, though not in this particular way. La Tourette in *Nuns and Mothers* manages to bring together the interests of the individual and the group. While tracing the psychological construction of a lesbian relationship, she simultaneously investigates the political implications of the two contrasting female categories, patriarchal by definition, of 'nuns' and 'mothers'. Representations of relations between women in Atwood's recently published novels also bring together the different domains of 'politics' and 'psychoanalysis'. The relationship between Rennie and Lora in the concluding section of *Bodily Harm* functions on a political level as a depiction of the ambiguities of comradeship/hostility between two women of different races. It can also be read, however, on a psychoanalytic level as a study of the interaction between ego and alter-ego. This is, of course, one of Atwood's favourite themes in her fiction. No doubt in the future writers will develop other strategies and methods to link these two contrary areas.

Notes

1. *The Future of Difference*, ed. Hester Eisenstein and Alice Jardine (G.K. Hall, 1980), p. xvii.
2. Hester Eisenstein, *Contemporary Feminist Thought* (Unwin, 1984), p. 141.
3. See Denise Riley, 'Does sex have a history? "Women" and feminism', *new formations*, 1 (Spring 1987), pp. 35-45.
4. Op. cit., pp. 144-5. Accounts of the development of lesbian feminism as a force within the Women's Movement and the rebuffs experienced by lesbians in the early stages are to be found in Freeman, op. cit.; Charlotte Bunch and Nancy Myron (eds), *Lesbianism in the Women's Movement* (Diana Press, 1975); and Judith Hole and Ellen Levine, *Rebirth of Feminism* (Quadrangle, 1971).
5. See Margeret Atwood's *The Handmaid's Tale* (1986), and Angela Carter's

Nights at the Circus (1984).
6. Op. cit., pp. 143-4. The current interest in female friendship is illustrated by the popularity of works such as Janice G. Raymond's *A Passion for Friends: towards a philosophy of female affection* (Women's Press, 1986).
7. Op. cit., p. 96.
8. *Women's Estate* (Penguin, 1971), p. 57.
9. 'Anne Sexton: 1928-1974', *On Lies, Secrets, and Silence*, ed. cit., p. 122.
10. See my essay on Carter's fiction in *Women Reading Women's writing* (Harvester Press, 1987).
11. *Women's Friendship in Literature* (Columbia University Press, 1980).
12. See Lillian Faderman, *Surpassing the Love of Men: romantic friendship and love between women from the Renaissance to the present* (Junction Books, 1981); Jane Rule, *Lesbian Images* (Doubleday, 1975); and Dale Spender (ed.), *Feminist Theorists* (Women's Press, 1983).
13. See Elizabeth Wilson, 'The Context of "Between pleasure and danger": The Barnard conference on sexuality', *Feminist Review*, 13 (1983), p. 37.
14. 'The woman identified woman', *Radical Feminism*, ed. cit., p. 245.
15. 'Conditions for work', *On Lies, Secrets, and Silence*, ed. cit., p. 208. See also Alexa Freeman and Jackie MacMillan, 'Building feminist organisations', *Building Feminist Theory*, ed. cit., pp. 260-7. Organizations and groups which form the hub of the radical feminist movement include rape-crisis lines, women's refuges and lesbian help-lines. An example of the latter is CLL, the East Anglian help-line to which I belong.
16. *The High Cost of Living* (Harper and Row, 1978), p. 123.
17. *Ambitious Women* (Women's Press, 1983), pp. 191-2.
18. *Loneliness and Other Lovers* (Sheba, 1981). References are to this edition and are in the text.
19. Kegan Gardiner, 'Mind mother: psychoanalysis and feminism', *Making a Difference*, ed. cit., p.113.
20. See Ronnie Sharfman, 'Mirroring and Mothering in Simone Schwarz-Bart and Jean Rhys', *Yale French Studies*, 62 (1981), pp. 88-106.
21. *The Dream of a Common Language: Poems 1974-1977* (W.W. Norton, 1978), p. 50.
22. Rich, *Of Woman Born*, ed. cit.; Abel, '(E)Merging identities: the dynamics of female friendship in contemporary fiction by women', *Signs*, 6, no. 3 (Spring 1981), pp. 413-35; Flax, 'The conflict between nurturance and autonomy in mother-daughter relationships and within feminism', *Feminist Studies*, 4, no. 2 (June 1978), pp. 171-99.
23. 'Psychoanalysis and women loving women', *Sex and Love*, ed. cit., p. 208.
24. Review, *New York Times* (29 May 1977), p. 13. See also Ann Barr Snitow's crass and imperceptive discussion of the novel in 'The front line: notes on sex in novels by women, 1969-1979', *Women: sex and sexuality*, ed. C.R. Stimpson and E. Spector Person (University of Chicago Press, 1980), p. 166.
25. 'Public silence, private terror', *Pleasure and Danger: exploring female sexuality*, ed. Carole S. Vance (Routledge and Kegan Paul, 1984), p. 113.
26. *Sita* (Virago, 1977), p. 268. References are to this edition and are in the text.
27. *Feminism and Psychoanalysis: the daughter's seduction* (Macmillan, 1982), p. 115.
28. See Susan Ardill and Sue O'Sullivan, 'Upsetting an applecart: difference, desire and lesbian sadomasochism', *Feminist Review*, 23 (Summer 1986), pp. 31-7.
29. *Nuns and Mothers* (Virago, 1984), p. 16.

30. Op. cit., p. 179.
31. *The Visitation*, ed. cit., p. 169.
32. *Touchpapers*, ed. Judith Kazantzis et al. (Alison and Busby, 1982), p. 46.
33. See Faderman, op. cit., pp. 276-94, 341-50.
34. See *The Bad Sister* (Picador, 1979), p. 63; and 'John Hafenden talks to Emma Tennant', *The Literary Review*, 66 (December 1983), p. 39.
35. *Compulsory Heterosexuality and Lesbian Existence* (Onlywomen Press, 1981) (first published in *Signs*, 5, no. 4, 1980). References are to the Onlywomen Press edition and are in the text.
36. Ann Ferguson, 'Patriarchy, sexual identity, and the sexual revolution', *Feminist Theory: a critique of ideology*, ed. Nannerl O. Keohane et al. (Harvester Press, 1982), p. 160.
37. Elizabeth Wilson, 'I'll climb the staircase to Heaven ...', *Sex and Love*, ed. cit., p. 187.
38. Jacquelyn N. Zita, 'Historical amnesia and the lesbian continuum', *Feminist theory: a critique of ideology*, ed. cit., p. 170.
39. *A Reckoning* (Women's Press, 1984), p. 143. References are to this edition and are in the text.
40. *Cactus* (Onlywomen Press, 1980), p. 1. References are to this edition and are in the text. As well as relating to Rich's ideas, the novel also has connections with Sheila Jeffreys, *The Spinster and her Enemies: feminism and sexuality 1880-1930* (Pandora, 1985).
41. *Communities of Women: an idea in fiction* (Harvard University Press, 1978), p. 191.
42. *Women and Fiction: feminism and the novel 1880-1920* (Methuen, 1981), p. xvi.
43. See Hélène Cixous, 'The character of "Character"', trans. Keith Cohen, *New Literary History*, 5, no. 2 (Winter 1974), pp. 383-402; and Toril Moi, op. cit., pp. 108-10, 161-6.
44. See H. Gustav Klaus (ed.), *The Socialist Novel in Britain: towards the recovery of a tradition* (Harvester Press, 1982).
45. *The Women's Movement: political, socioeconomic, and psychological issues* (Harper and Row, 1975), p. 436.
46. Some of the stories in *Girls Next Door*, ed. cit., also focus on antagonisms, misunderstandings and breakdown in communications between women.
47. *Tales I Tell My Mother: a collection of feminist short stories*, ed. Fairbairns et al. (Journeyman Press, 1978), p. 3.
48. *Closing* (Methuen, 1987), p. 57.
49. *Radical Feminism*, ed. cit., pp. 285-99.
50. *The Politics of Women's Liberation*, ed. cit.
51. A focus on the celebration of the free play of identities is found in Cixous's statement: 'Men or women, complex, mobile, open beings. Admitting the component of the other sex makes them at once much richer, plural, strong, and to the extent of this mobility, very fragile' ('Sorties', *New French Feminisms*, ed. cit., p. 97). It appears relevant to the position of the bisexual.

Chapter Seven

Conclusion

This study, while having as its primary aim the correlation of works of fiction with feminist theory, also succeeds – I hope – in drawing attention to the variety of women's fiction today. Certain interesting conclusions, ones relevant to feminist politics as well as to contemporary narrative, emerge from the analysis of works of fiction I have carried out.

Many of the novels and short stories which I have presented for review in the previous pages will no doubt be unfamiliar to the reader. This fact highlights more effectively than any commentary could do the tendency on the part of critics to neglect contemporary women's fiction – especially the kind of fiction which appropriates and reinterprets feminist ideas. Contrary to the views expressed by students of literature, it is not only novels written by women in earlier periods which are in need of discovery and evalution.[1] Those published in the past fifteen years, such as Anna Wilson's *Cactus*, Bartram's *Peeling* and La Tourette's *Nuns and Mothers*, can also be described, with justification, as in a similar position. Though available in print and possessing a large following of non-academic readers, they are on the whole unknown to staff and students in colleges and universities. The writers' ingenious re-working of ideas from feminist theory along with the strategies they utilize to treat the themes of feminist struggle, women's community and female relations which form their focus, constitute, as I have illustrated, a fascinating topic for research projects and critical analysis. However, because of the failure of academic critics and teaching staff to engage intellectually with fiction of this kind, they do not receive the attention they merit. This results in the neglect of an important area of female creativity. It also reinforces the marginalization of themes and ideas which are of major significance to women.

As I pointed out in Chapter 1, a number of reasons help to explain the failure of critics to engage with fiction which incorporates and reinterprets feminist ideas. There is the aggressively male bias of academic criticism, one which no doubt reflects the male-dominated composition of departments of English Studies in colleges and universities. There is also the discrepancy between the interests and perspectives of feminist critics, on the one hand, and those of writers of fiction, on the other. There is, of course, nothing unusual in the views of critics and writers being at odds, and this is an especially interesting example. Many of the themes which fiction writers are intent on exploring at present are, as we have seen, radical feminist in tenor. Feminist critics, in contrast, the majority of whom are based in academia, tend to hold perspectives which are socialist feminist or psychoanalytic. The work of Cora Kaplan, one of the most prominent feminist critics writing at the moment, illustrates this point. In a recently published essay she argues persuasively for bringing together socialist feminist and psychoanalytic critical approaches in the analysis of fiction.[2] However, as is typical of feminist critics writing in the UK, she makes no reference to *radical feminist critical approaches*, and the concern with themes of woman-identification, feminist community, lesbian relations and relations between mothers and daughters which distinguish them. This omission is regrettable and needs to be remedied. I should like to add to the two types of feminist criticism which Kaplan mentions a strong plea for the integration of a radical feminist approach to literature.

As well as highlighting the failure of critics to engage with contemporary women's fiction, the discussion of texts carried out in this study also serves to disprove certain misconceptions and fallacies which critics express about its character. The unfounded generalizations they sometimes make and the false limitations they attribute to such fiction suggest that, in some cases, their actual acquaintance with it is perfunctory and slight. Ann Rosalind Jones, for example, in an essay on the romance, contrasts the 'happy endings' of Mills and Boon novels with the pessimistic or uncertain endings on the note of 'slammed doors, or doors opened tentatively onto uncertain futures' which she sees (erroneously) as typifying feminist fiction. She asks, 'Is a more utopian mode imaginable in 1986?... How successful might a hybrid novel combining feminist depth of analysis with a plausibly positive ending be? Is such a hybrid possible?'[3] In taking this line, Jones betrays her ignorance of the fact that, since writers of feminist fiction have already appropriated the structures and ending of the romance, the kind of 'hybrid novel' she describes does, indeed, exist. The endings of contemporary novels are, in fact, immensely varied. Whereas some novels such as French's *The Women's Room* and Oosthuizen's *Loneliness and Other Lovers* conclude on the pessimistic or tentative note which Jones mentions, others such as Barbara

Wilson's *Ambitious Women* and Hanscombe's *Between Friends* make very effective use of the device of the happy ending. *Ambitious Women* concludes on a note which is positively euphoric. Allison is about to be released from gaol, the print shop survives and, to complete the mood of happiness, Holly even makes a reconciliatory phone call to the bisexual Magda and forgives her for her previous act of betrayal. As for the ending of *Between Friends*, it is structured on the model of the romance. The love-affair between Meg and Jane and their decision to live together despite their earlier disagreements, demonstrate to the reader's satisfaction the power of true love to overcome differences of ideological attitude. In the public realm harmony also reigns supreme. Lesbian and hetero feminists succeed in burying their differences, uniting in a political campaign to affirm the value of a woman-defined sexuality and acts of marriage-resistance. And what, I ask cynically, could be more utopian than this? It is an event which has not occurred in real life – and, in the present fragmented state of the Women's Movement shows no sign of doing so! *Ambitious Women* and *Between Friends* are, in fact, excellent examples of the kind of hybrid novel which Jones recommends feminist authors to write. They successfully combine 'feminist depth of analysis with a plausibly positive ending'. There are other novels which appropriate the structures of the romance in different ways. French's The *Bleeding Heart*, which I described in a previous chapter as 'a feminist version of the romance', is an interesting, if not altogether successful, example.

It is ironic to note that, whereas Jones advises feminist writers to make more pronounced use of 'utopian' structures and endings, other critics recommend an opposite course. Elizabeth Wilson, for example, in an essay satirically entitled 'I'll Climb the Stairway to Heaven: lesbianism in the seventies', criticizes fiction writers for creating excessively idealized representations of relationships beween women.[4] Whichever choice writers adopt, critics find fault with their novels. As is usually the case, they just can't win!

Another misconception about contemporary women's fiction which this study disproves, one which has been challenged by other critics, is the idea that the 'modernist' or anti-realist text, organized around the concept of the fractured self and making use of non-linear methods of narrative, is necessarily more 'revolutionary' or politically radical than any other. This idea, associated with the French theorist Kristeva and the concept of the semiotic *chora* she defines, has been interrogated by Toril Moi. Moi asks the pertinent question:

> Who or what is acting in Kristeva's subversive schemes? In a political context her emphasis on the semiotic as an unconscious force pre-

cludes any analysis of the conscious decision-making processes that must be part of any *collective* revolutionary project.[5]

Moi goes on to express agreement with the Marxist-Feminist Literature Collective who criticize Kristeva's poetic as 'politically unsatisfactory' and with Allon White who describes her politics as 'purified anarchism in a perpetual state of self-dispersal'.

The analysis of works of fiction carried out in this study certainly supports the conclusion arrived at by Moi and the critics she cites. Texts which focus on the fractured self or are in some way 'decentred' such as Figes's *Days* and Tennant's *Alice Fell* provide, as we have seen, illuminating analyses of the situation of the female subject trapped in the phallocratic structures of family life and society. However, they make little if any attempt to portray her engaging in deliberate acts of resistance at a collective level. On the contrary, they paint a depressing picture of her as isolated from her female peers and vulnerable to the pressures of psychological and cultural forces beyond her control. In order to find representations of woman as active agent, striving to exert control over her own life and joining with other women to challenge manifestations of patriarchal power, we need to turn to another kind of text. This is, of course, the so-called 'realist' text. On account of its appropriation of feminist ideas and the explicitly ideological appeal which it makes to the reader, I have re-termed it 'fiction of ideas'. Though giving a less sensitive and convincing depiction of female subjectivity than its 'modernist' counterpart and making use of the unfashionable concept of 'the unitary self', it is a valuable and understandably popular form of fiction. It possesses the advantage of being extremely versatile. It lends itself, as we saw in Chapter 3, to the debate and problematization of aspects of feminist practice and theory, as well as to their affirmatory delineation. All in all, it provides a very effective vehicle for the representation of themes which are overtly social and political.

To see the two narrative modes described above as totally separate is, of course, something of a simplification. Writers do experience, however, considerable difficulty in reconciling and uniting their respective themes and interests. The rift between 'psychoanalysis' and 'politics', as theorists point out, is one of the chief problems confronting feminism at the moment, one which shows little sign of achieving a satisfactory solution.[6] It also has a restricting and generally adverse effect on works of fiction. It is rare to find a writer who succeeds in combining a focus on the psychological complexities of female subjectivity with the overtly political themes of collective feminist struggle and women's community. One of the few writers who does achieve this, as we have seen, is Atwood in her novel *The Handmaid's Tale*. The novel is, in fact, remarkable for its successful reconciliation of thematic and stylistic opposites. The rift between psychoanalytical and political areas of experience is, we discovered in Chapter 6, most clearly in evidence in fiction which treats the topic of relations between women. Here the challenge issued by psychoanalysis to the concept of the 'unitary woman' and, by implication, to ideas of sisterhood and women's community, has maximum effect. One the one hand, there are novels which focus on the personal and often problematic aspects of female relations. On the other, there are ones which represent, often in an idealizing manner, collective feminist struggle and women's community. It is to be hoped that in the future writers will manage to contrive strategies to bring together these two different realms, if not in harmony at least in creative tension. Again, Atwood shows signs in her recently published novels of achieving this, or at any rate, of moving towards it. While I have no wish to create an alternative 'feminist' canon or to encourage the cult of the individual author, I feel I need to emphasize once again the exceptional brilliance and daring of Atwood's fiction. Her writing is consistently experimental and she bravely confronts challenges in the field of narrative which other writers are too timid to take on.

It is tempting to conclude this study on a complacent note by drawing attention again to the flourishing state of women's fiction today. However, the situation is problematic and complicated. I thus intend to conclude in a more uncomfortable manner by alerting the reader's attention to certain anomalies and contradictions existing between contemporary women's fiction and feminist politics. Critics and reviewers understandably present the success encountered by the feminist publishing houses and the lively state of women's fiction at the moment in a positive light as illustrating women's ability to find a voice and play an active role in social and cultural realms. Interpretations of a more pessimistic kind are, however, also valid. The vitality of women's fiction may well indicate, as Freeman implies in her comments on feminist publications, the decline of the Women's Movement from a political organization which seeks to improve women's social and material circumstances to one which is predominantly cultural in nature. Women's feelings of disquiet and anxiety at this decline are reflected, in fact, in works of fiction published in the 1980s. One gains the impression from certain novels that the author, rather than writing out of anger at patriarchal oppression and injustice and with the hope of promoting political change as tended to be the case in the 1970s, is, on the contrary, motivated by feelings of frustration and irritation at the ineffectualness and fragmentation of *the Women's Movement itself*. Fairbairns's *Closing* (1987) provides an interesting illustration. The novels exudes, in fact, a very strong sense of frustration and concern at the rivalries and antagonisms dividing women, and the vulnerability of the Movement to exploitation and appropriation by the forces of capitalism and patriarchy which this promotes. Fairbairns aims in the novel, it appears, to make an intervention in feminist politics, alerting women to the existence of these dangers and threats.

Other contradictions between fiction and feminist politics are also discernible. An intellectual and economic climate sympathetic to the production and publication of women's fiction is not necessarily conducive to other kinds of feminist activity. It is likely that, as Liz Kelly claims, the rifts in the Women's Movement have been exaggerated to a degree and, in the UK, are more a feature of London life than of the provinces.[7] None the less, the present state of the Movement is certainly not one of unity. Its disintegration into a number of divergent feminisms serves to bestow, as Weldon humorously suggests, increased prominence on the writer's role by giving women the opportunity to produce publications which 'currently hold the Movement together'.[8] The situation is, however, by no means a welcome one. Controversy and disputes, though creating a lively context for the production of fiction, and giving writers ideas to debate in their novels, do not provide a stable base for social activity and political struggle. In a case such as this, fiction appears to flourish in opposition to, or even perhaps at the expense of, effective political action in the social and material areas of life. This is especially deplorable at a time when, in the UK, women's rights are under attack and suffering increasing erosion. One can cite numerous examples. Three of the most serious are: the abolition of the universal maternity grant (replaced by a means-tested payment); the (unsuccessful) anti-abortion bill introduced by David Alton; and Clause 28 of the Local Government Act which, effectively making discrimination against lesbians and homosexuals legal, seeks to prevent the public funding of their organizations, thus endangering the survival of the lesbian help-lines and support groups on which many of us depend.[9] We have to counter these kinds of attacks with every means available – social, political and cultural. The problematic question of how writers can create a form of fiction which makes an intervention in the political arena instead of merely reproducing existing conditions or deflecting attention from them is clearly as urgent today as it was in earlier periods.

Representations of motherhood in works of fiction give rise, as we saw in Chapter 5, to another important set of problems. Celebratory accounts of the pre-oedipal bond between mother and child or the processes of pregnancy and birth, as in Tennant's *Alice Fell* or Weldon's *Puffball*, may be praised for focusing attention on aspects of women's life which are generally taken for granted or devalued. However, they are also open to criticism on the grounds that, by presenting motherhood in an over-glamorous light, they have the politically regressive effect of reconciling women to their isolated and oppressed position in the nuclear family. They serve, in fact, to deflect the reader's attention from the burdensome and humdrum aspects of the maternal role.

The contradictions beween women's fiction and feminist politics I have mentioned above and the complex issues which they raise have received, on the whole, very little discussion from critics. They are of vital importance to feminist writers, readers and women in general. It is to be hoped that they will receive a greater degree of analysis and investigation in the future.

Notes

1. See Sydney Janet Kaplan, 'Varieties of feminist criticism', *Making a Difference*, ed. cit., pp. 37-58.
2. 'Pandora's Box: subjectivity, class and sexuality in socialist feminist criticism', *Sea Changes: culture and feminism* (Verso, 1986), pp. 147-76.
3. 'Mills and Boon meets feminism', *The Progress of Romance: the politics of popular fiction*, ed. Jean Radford (Routledge and Kegan Paul, 1986), p. 215.
4. *Sex and Love*, ed. cit., pp. 180-95.
5. Toril Moi, *Sexual/Textual Politics* (Methuen, 1985), p. 170.
6. See Lynne Segal, *Is the Future Female?* (Virago, 1987), pp. 126-34.
7. 'The New Defeatism', *Trouble and Strife*, 11 (Summer 1987), pp. 23-8.
8. *New Society*, 68, no. 1123 (31 May 1984), p. 354.
9. For information about these matters, see *The Guardian*, 6 April 1987, p. 10; 27 October 1987, p. 24; and 9 December 1987, p. 3.

Select Glossary

Details of the texts cited here are to be found in the Bibliography unless otherwise stated.

Different feminist discourses

The reader needs to remember that these discourses are less distinct in practice than they are in theory. Features of them merge and overlap. Works which give useful definitions include Hester Eisenstein, *Contemporary Feminist Thought* (London, Unwin, 1984) and Cheris Kramarae and Paula A. Treichler, *A Feminist Dictionary* (London, Pandora, 1985).

Academic feminism This kind of feminism flourishes in colleges and universities. Female academics, while participating in Women's Studies courses and writing books and dissertations on topics relating to women, generally show little interest in the more radical aspects of feminism, such as women's community, sexual politics and political campaigns. Since their attitudes tend to be individualist and elitist, they often regard other women primarily as rivals and competitors. Adrienne Rich analyses the problem and proposes a solution in 'Toward a Woman-Centred University' (*Lies, Secrets and Silence: Collected Prose 1966–1978*, pp. 125–55).

Cultural feminism 'The belief that women will be freed via an alternative women's culture.' (Brooke, 'The Chador of Women's Liberation: Cultural Feminism and the Movement Press', *Heresies*, 3:1, Issue 9 (1980), p. 70. Quoted by Kramarae and Treichler in *A Feminist Dictionary*, ed. cit., p. 112). The emphasis placed by cultural feminism on 'an alternative women's culture' results in it being associated with the therapy movement, meditation, woman-bonding, cults of matriarchy, goddess worship, and the study of women in literature and art. An important manifestation of cultural feminism is the Women's Peace Movement, exemplified by the Greenham Common Peace Camp. Exponents of cultural feminism are often criticized by radical and socialist feminists for being inward looking and 'contemplating their navels'. They are accused of concentrating excessively on achieving spiritual and psychological liberation and pursuing personal cultural goals, when they should be engaging in political campaigns and struggling to transform society. They are also criticized for perpetuating phallocratic stereotypes of femininity by focusing on topics traditionally associated with women, such as spirituality, healing, nature, the maternal and peace.

Lesbian feminism Women who identify as lesbian have made, of course, a major contribution to the contemporary women's movement, especially the radical feminist aspect, both practically and theoretically. Theories which lesbians have produced include: the concept of 'woman identification' (Radicalesbians, 'The Woman Identified Woman', 1970, 1973); the idea that lesbian feminist analyses of male power and women's community from the basis of women's liberation in general (Charlotte Bunch, 'Not for Lesbians Only', 1975, 1981); Political Lesbianism; and ideas of 'lesbian continuum' and 'compulsory heterosexuality' (*Rich, Compulsory Heterosexuality and Lesbian Existence*, 1980, 1981).

Liberal feminism Liberal feminists agree with the aim of equal job opportunities and equal pay for women. They believe that this goal can be achieved without fundamentally changing the existing structures of society. They are in general opposed to strategies of positive discrimination. They tend to be uninterested in the more radical aspects of the Women's Movement, such as critiques of male power and a focus on sexual politics and women's community.

Psychoanalytic feminism This refers to the attempts made by feminist theorists to appropriate and reinterpret the ideas of Sigmund Freud, Jacques Lacan and other authorities in the field of psychoanalysis. The interests and viewpoints of these theorists differ considerably. Some, like Nancy Chodorow and Joanna Ryan, develop aspects of object-relations theory, while others, such as Hélène Cixous, Luce Irigaray and Juliet Mitchell, reinterpret the ideas of Freud and Lacan. Key themes which they treat include: the construction of femininity and masculinity, relations between mother and daughter in the pre-oedipal stage, patriarchal relations, and female sexuality. They are sometimes criticized by radical and socialist feminists for failing to place sufficient emphasis on class and on the economic base of society, and for pessimistically implying that gender positions and psychological structures are too deeply entrenched to achieve transformation.

Political lesbianism The ideas of the Political Lesbian Movement, based on the Radicalesbians' paper 'The Woman Identified Woman' (1970, 1973), were formulated by the Furies Collective (Washington DC) and the Leeds Revolutionary Feminist Group (UK). Hilary Allen defines them as follows: 'Political Lesbians argue, that in order for women to overcome male supremacy they must first withdraw from the system of privileges derived from men. To this end, Political Lesbians advocate the cessation of all commitments to men, and as far as possible a withdrawal from the economy of male power and privilege, enacted both materially and psychologically'. The innovatory feature of this perspective, as Allen points out, is that 'Heterosexuality is not to be read, in this analysis, in terms of sexual pleasure (which is assumed to be dependent on false consciousness) but in terms of the maintenance of power: symbolically and materially the penis colonises the female body'. ('Political Lesbianism and Feminism – space for a sexual politics?', *m/f*, no. 7, (1982), pp. 19, 20). The demand voiced by Political Lesbians that women cease consorting with men and become either celibate or lesbian promoted a rift between lesbian and heterosexual feminists in the seventies. This, however, has been partially healed by the cultural feminist emphasis on woman-bonding and by Adrienne Rich's concept of 'lesbian continuum'.

Radical feminism This term has at least two different meanings, as follows. 1. It was first used in the USA in the 1960s to describe those women in the New Left who become feminists. It differentiated their views, on the one hand, from New Left Politics and, on the other, from liberal feminism, represented by women such as Betty Friedan. The term 'The Radical Feminist Movement' is thus sometimes used to signify the contemporary Women's Movement in general, highlighting its radical emphasis on sexual politics. It differentiates the contemporary Women's Movement from earlier ones such as the Suffragette Movement which were concerned merely with equal rights. 2. Used more specifically, the term 'radical feminism' denotes the particular branch of contemporary feminism which prioritizes concepts of sexual politics and the dialectic of sex. Liz Kelly describes its interests as follows:

> Radical feminism is for me a theoretical position which argues that men, collectively and as individuals, have an interest in maintaining women's oppression. It contains within it a call to action to change the world. It is also premised on the pro-woman line – that our feminist energies are for ourselves and other women. Beyond these basic premises there are considerable differences within radical feminist theory and practice. . . ('The New Defeatism', *Trouble and Strife*, 11 (Summer 1987), p. 24)

Topics which radical feminist theorists explore include: gender–role stereotyping, women's oppressed position in the family and workplace; the political significance of lesbianism; critiques of male violence in terms of power (rape, battery, pornography, etc.). The concept of patriarchy, though controversial and admittedly imprecise, is a useful tool in their political analysis since it brings to the foreground the significance of male dominance and the dialectic of sex in every area of life. The Radical Feminist Movement posits an integral link between practice and theory. It has thus initiated a number of political campaigns and service-groups. These include: Rape Crisis Centres, Lesbian Help-Lines, Women's Refuges, Incest Survivor Groups, Reclaim the Night Marches, WAVAW Groups (Women Against Violence Against Women). In the 1980s it is increasingly focusing attention on issues of race and physical disability. Radical feminists are sometimes accused by socialist and psychoanalytic feminists of regarding gender as biologically determined. This accusation is, on the whole, false. As Kelly points out, 'Theoretical analyses which are based on the assertion that gender is biologically determined are as unacceptable to most radical feminists as they are to most socialist feminists. This is precisely one of the things we have in common'. (Op. cit., p. 27.)

Revolutionary feminism This is an offshoot of radical feminism and is, in fact, difficult to distinguish from it. The two terms are, I believe, interchangeable.

Socialist feminism Socialist feminists attempt to combine a 'socialist' analysis of society with a 'feminist' one, exploring the interaction between the dialectic of class and that of sex. The alliance between the two is, on the whole, uneasy. As Heidi Hartmann wittily observes, 'The 'marriage' of marxism and feminism has been like the marriage of husband and wife depicted in English common law; marxism and feminism are one, and that one is marxism'. (The Unhappy Marriage of Marxism and Feminism:

Towards a more progressive union', p. 2.) Topics which socialist feminists discuss include: the status of domestic labour, a feminist definition of class, women's position in the family and the labour force, issues of equal pay, etc. Socialist feminists make a practical contribution to politics. They often work in mixed groups, joining with men in Trade Union work, and in city and parliamentary politics. They also organize campaigns for state-run crèches.

Literary and psychoanalytic terms

Useful glossaries of psychoanalytic terms include Janine Chasseguet-Smirgel, *Female Sexuality: New psychoanalytic views* (London, Virago, 1981, p. xvii) and J. Laplanche and J.B. Pontalis, *The Language of Psycho-analysis* (London, Hogarth Press, 1973).

Anti-realism Anti-realist fiction makes use of devices and strategies which advertise the fictionality and artifice of the text. Textual fragmentation, internal monologue and a focus on the fractured self have the effect of disorientating the reader, preventing her from identifying with the characters in the text. An analysis of inner consciousness and an interplay between past and present, influenced in general terms by psychoanalysis, are characteristics of this kind of fiction.

Fetishism This signifies from a psychoanalytic point of view 'A perversion of the sexual instinct whereby sexual desire is stimulated by, or has as its goal, some kind of inanimate object... or a particular non-sexual part of the body (feet, hair, etc.) or the performance of certain non sexual actions' (*Oxford English Dictionary*). The term is used loosely to denote the concentrating of sexual attention upon an object or upon one particular feature of the person (breasts, hair, etc.).

Intertextuality The emphasis on deconstruction in contemporary criticism foregrounds the heterogeneity of the text, representing it as an amalgam of 'grafts' in which one discourse is inserted into another. Jonathan Culler points out that 'In recent critical analyses, the celebration of heterogeneity, the description of texts as grafts or intertextual constructs, the interest in teasing out incompatible strands of argument or logics of signification, and the linking of a text's power to its self-deconstructive efficacy have all worked to deny the notion of organic unity its former role as the unquestioned telos of critical interpretation'. He quotes Barthes's statement that 'the text is not a line of words releasing a single 'theological' meaning (the 'message' of an Author-God) but a multi-dimensional space in which a variety of writings, none of them original, blend and clash'. (*On Deconstruction: Theory and Criticism after Structuralism* (London, Routledge and Kegan Paul, 1983), pp. 199–200, 32–3.)

Logos This is a term used by Greek philosophers signifying 'reason' and 'word'. In Christianity it has religious connotations, since it is used in the *New Testament* as a designation for Christ. The platonic antithesis logos (masculinity)/matter (femininity), as Irigaray illustrates in *Speculum of the Other Woman*, functions to the detriment of woman since it portrays her as representing the material base upon which man builds his intellectual and cultural constructs.

Narcissism This is 'the ego's direction of love and libidinal cathexes [psychical energy] towards itself'. (Chasseguet-Smirgel, op. cit., p. xvii.)

Phallocratic A phallocratic literature or culture is one which is structured symbolically around the phallus, the traditional signifier of masculinity. Mary Daly describes feminists as engaged in 'an active struggle to overcome and transcend phallocracy, the social, political, ideological system that spawns racism and genocide as well as rapism and genocide'. (*Pure Lust: Elemental Feminist Philosophy* (Boston, Massachusetts, Beacon Press, 1984), 5n.)

Realism Realist fiction gives a convincing illusion of life as we experience it. It offers the reader pleasures of identification and involvement with the characters in the text. The term 'realism' is, however, problematic. Novels such as George Eliot's *Middlemarch* and the works of Jane Austen, often cited by critics as examples of realism, diverge in many ways from our expectations of real life and contain features which advertise the fictionality of the text.

Specular fiction This is fiction of a visionary nature in which the author creates a speculative representation of the future or of a fantasy world. Utopian fiction, science fiction and fantasy are examples.

Scopic economy This is the organization (system) of the visual.

Sujet en procès This is the representation of the human subject or consciousness as fractured, heterogeneous and in a state of flux (process). Associated with Freudian and Lacanian psychoanalytic theory, it is a typical feature of modernist and antirealist fiction.

Symbolic narrative This is narrative which functions indirectly on a symbolic plane. The reader infers the meaning by interpreting symbols, images and their associations.

Bibliography

Novels and short stories

Alther, Lisa, *Kinflicks* (New York, Knopf, 1976; Harmondsworth, Penguin, 1977).

Alther, Lisa, *Other Women* (New York, Knopf, 1984; Harmondsworth, Penguin, 1985).

Atwood, Margaret, *Bodily Harm* (Toronto, McClelland and Stewart, 1981; London, Virago, 1983).

Atwood, Margaret, *The Edible Woman* (Toronto, McClelland and Stewart, 1969; London, Virago, 1980).

Atwood, Margaret, *The Handmaid's Tale* (Toronto, McClelland and Stewart, 1985; London, Virago, 1986).

Atwood, Margaret, *Lady Oracle* (Toronto, McClelland and Stewart, 1976; London, Virago, 1982).

Atwood, Margaret, *Surfacing* (Toronto, McClelland and Stewart, 1972; London, Virago, 1979).

Atwood, Margaret, 'Giving Birth' and 'Polarities', in *Dancing Girls and Other Stories* (Toronto, McClelland and Stewart, 1977; London, Virago, 1984), pp. 225-40, 51-75.

Bambera, Toni Cade, 'Raymond's Run' and 'Talkin Bout Sonny', in *Gorilla, My Love* (New York, Random House, 1972; London, Women's Press, 1984), pp. 21-32, 77-84.

Barfoot, Joan, *Gaining Ground* (London, Women's Press, 1980). First published as *Abra* (Ryerson, Toronto, McGraw-Hill, 1978).

Bargate, Verity, *No Mama No* (London, Jonathan Cape, 1978; London, Fontana, 1979).

Barker, Pat, *Blow Your House Down* (London, Virago, 1984).

Barker, Pat, *Union Street* (London, Virago, 1982).

Bartram, Grace, *Peeling* (London, Women's Press, 1986).

Boucher, Sandy, 'The Cutting Room', in *Mae West is Dead: recent lesbian and gay fiction*, ed. Adam Mars-Jones (London, Faber, 1983), pp. 182-94.

Bowder, Caroline, *Birthrites* (Brighton, Harvester Press, 1983).

Bradshaw, Jan, and Hemming, Mary (eds), *Girls Next Door: lesbian feminist stories*, introd. Alison Hennegan (London, Women's Press, 1985).

Brown, Rebecca, 'The Joy of Marriage', in *The Evolution of Darkness and Other Stories* (London, Brilliance Books, 1984), pp. 19-26.

Bryant, Dorothy, *Ella Price's Journal* (Berkeley, California, Ata, 1972).

Bryant, Dorothy, *Miss Giardino* (Berkeley, California, Ata, 1978).

Bulkin, Elly (ed.),*Lesbian Fiction: An Anthology*. (Watertown, Mass., Persephone, 1981)

Burford, Barbara, 'Coming of Age', 'Dreaming the Sky Down' and 'Miss Jessie', in *The Threshing Floor* (London, Sheba, 1986), pp. 51-7, 1-12, 43-9.

Carter, Angela, *The Bloody Chamber and Other Stories* (London, Gollancz, 1979; Harmondsworth, Penguin, 1981).

Carter, Angela, *Heroes and Villains* (London, Heinemann, 1969; Harmondsworth, Penguin, 1981).

Carter, Angela, *The Infernal Desire Machines of Dr Hoffman* (London, Hart-Davis, 1972; Harmondsworth, Penguin, 1972).

Carter, Angela, *The Magic Toyshop* (London, Heinemann, 1967; London, Virago, 1981).

Carter, Angela, *The Passion of New Eve* (London, Gollancz, 1977; London, Virago, 1982).

Carter, Angela, *Nights at the Circus* (London, Chatto and Windus, 1984).

Clausen, Jan, 'Daddy' and 'Today is the First Day of the Rest of Your Life', in *Mother, Sister, Daughter, Lover: Stories* (Trumansberg, Crossing Press, 1980; London, Women's Press, 1981), pp. 16-21, 60-101.

Clausen, Jan, *Sinking Stealing*. (London, Women's Press, 1985).

Conlon, Faith, da Silva, Rachel, and Wilson, Barbara (eds), *The Things that Divide Us* (Seattle, Seal Press, 1985; London, Sheba, 1986).

Dorcey, Mary, 'A Country Dance', in *Girls Next Door*, ed. Jan Bradshaw and Mary Hemming (London, Women's Press, 1985), pp. 159-75.

Duff, Moira, *The Vocation of Pearl Duncan* (London, Women's Press, 1982).

Dworkin, Andrea, *Ice and Fire* (London, Secker and Warburg, 1986).

Edwards, Nicky, *Mud* (London, Women's Press, 1986).

Fairbairns, Zoë, *Benefits* (London, Virago, 1979).

Fairbairns, Zoë, *Closing* (London, Methuen, 1987).

Fairbairns, Zoë, *Here Today* (London, Methuen, 1984).

Fairbairns, Zoë, Maitland, Sara, Miner, Valerie, Roberts, Michèle, and Wandor, Michelene, *Tales I Tell My Mother: a collection of feminist short stories* (London, Journeyman, 1978).

Figes, Eva, *Days* (London, Faber, 1974; Newcastle upon Tyne, Bloodaxe, 1983).

French, Marilyn, *The Bleeding Heart* (London, Andre Deutsche, 1980; London, Sphere, 1980).

French, Marilyn, *The Women's Room* (New York, Summit, 1977; London, Sphere, 1978).

Hanscombe, Gillian, *Between Friends* (Boston, Mass., Alyson, 1982; London, Sheba, 1983).

Lessing, Doris, *The Memoirs of a Survivor* (London, Octagon, 1974; London, Picador, 1976).

Lessing, Doris, *The Summer before the Dark* (London, Cape, 1973; Harmondsworth, Penguin, 1975).

Maitland, Sara, *Virgin Territory* (London, Michael Joseph, 1984).

Maitland, Sara, 'After the Ball was Over', in *Tales I Tell My Mother: a collection of feminist short stories*, ed. Zoë Fairbairns et al. (London, Journeyman, 1978), pp. 64-70.

Maitland, Sara, 'Forceps Delivery' in *Weddings and Funerals* by Sara Maitland and Aileen La Tourette (London, Brilliance, 1984), pp. 103-13.

Maitland, Sara, 'The Loveliness of the Long-Distance Runner', *Mae West is Dead: recent lesbian and gay fiction*, ed. Adam Mars-Jones (London, Faber, 1983), pp. 217-26.

March, Caeia, 'Photographs', in *Girls Next Door: Lesbian feminist stories*, ed. Jan Bradshaw and Mary Hemming (London, Women's Press, 1985), pp. 26-32.

March, Caeia, 'The Survivors', *The Reach and Other Stories: lesbian feminist fiction*, ed. Lilian Mohin and Sheila Shulman (London, Onlywomen Press, 1984), pp. 95-101.

March, Caeia, *Three Ply Yarn* (London, Women's Press, 1986).

Mars-Jones, Adam (ed.), *Mae West is Dead: recent lesbian and gay fiction* (London, Faber, 1983).

Millett, Kate, *Sita* (New York, Farrar, Strauss and Giroux, 1977; London, Virago, 1977).

Miner, Valerie, *Blood Sisters: an examination of conscience* (London, Women's Press, 1981).

Miner, Valerie, *Movement: a novel in stories* (Trumansberg, Crossing Press, 1982; London, Methuen, 1985).

Mohin, Lilian, and Shulman, Sheila (eds), *The Reach and Other Stories: lesbian feminist fiction*, (London, Onlywomen Press, 1984).

Oosthuizen, Ann, *Loneliness and other Lovers* (London, Sheba, 1981).

Page, Kathy, *Back in the First Person*, (London, Virago, 1986).

Piercy, Marge, *Braided Lives* (New York, Summit, 1982; Harmondsworth, Penguin, 1983).

Piercy, Marge, *Fly Away Home* (London, Chatto and Windus, 1984).

Piercy, Marge, *The High Cost of Living* (New York, Harper and Row, 1978; London, Women's Press, 1979).

Piercy, Marge, *Small Changes* (New York, Doubleday, 1973; New York, Fawcett, 1974).

Piercy, Marge, *Woman on the Edge of Time* (New York, Knopf, 1976; London, Women's Press, 1979).

Prager, Emily, 'Agoraphobia', in *A Visit from the Footbinder and Other Stories* (London, Chatto and Windus, Hogarth, 1983), pp. 112-22.

Riley, Joan, *The Unbelonging* (London, Women's Press, 1985).

Roberts, Michèle, *A Piece of the Night*, (London, Women's Press, 1978).

Roberts, Michèle, *The Visitation* (London, Women's Press, 1983).

Roe, Sue, *Estella, Her Expectations* (Brighton, Harvester Press, 1982).

Rowanchild, Anira, 'A Bit of Help', in *Girls Next Door: lesbian feminist stories*, ed. Jan Bradshaw and Mary Hemming (London, Women's Press, 1985), pp. 101-4.

Sarton, May, *A Reckoning* (New York, W.W. Norton, 1978; London, Women's Press, 1984).

Swansea, Charleen, and Campbell, Barbara (eds), *Love Stories by New Women* (North Carolina, Red Clay Books, 1978; London, Women's Press, 1979).

Tennant, Emma, *Alice Fell* (London, Jonathan Cape, 1980; London, Picador, 1982).

Tennant, Emma, *The Bad Sister* (London, Gollancz, 1978; London, Picador, 1979).

Tennant, Emma, *Hotel de Dream* (London, Gollancz, 1976; London, Picador, 1983).

Thompson, Jean, 'The People of Color', *Love Stories by New Women*, ed. Charleen Swansea and Barbara Campbell (North Carolina, Red Clay Books, 1978), pp. 9-23.

Toder, Nancy, *Choices* (Watertown, Mass., Persephone Press, 1980).

Tomasetti, Glen, *Man of Letters: a romance* (Melbourne: McPhee Gribble, 1981; Brighton, Harvester Press, 1983).

Tourette, Aileen La, *Nuns and Mothers* (London, Virago, 1984).

Tourette, Aileen La, 'Passing', *Mae West is Dead: recent lesbian and gay fiction*, ed. Adam Mars-Jones (London, Faber, 1983), pp. 178-81.

Walker, Alice, *The Color Purple* (New York, Harcourt Brace Jovanovitch, 1982; London, Women's Press, 1983).

Walker, Alice, *Meridian* (New York, Harcourt Brace Jovanovitch, 1976; London, Women's Press, 1982).

Walker, Alice, 'Porn' in *You Can't Keep a Good Woman Down* (New York, Harcourt Brace Jovanovitch, 1971; London, Women's Press, 1982), pp. 77-84.

Ward Jouve, Nicole, 'Forceps Birth', in *Shades of Grey* (London, Virago, 1981), pp. 9-38. Originally published as *Le Spectre du Gris* (Paris, Editions des femmes, 1977).

Weldon, Fay, *Down Among the Women* (London, Heinemann, 1971; Harmondsworth, Penguin, 1973).

Weldon, Fay, *The Fat Woman's Joke* (London, McGibbon, 1967; London, Coronet, 1982).

Weldon, Fay, *Female Friends* (London, Heinemann, 1975; London, Pan, 1981).

Weldon, Fay, *The Life and Loves of a She-Devil* (London, Hodder and Stoughton, 1983; London, Coronet, 1984).

Weldon, Fay, *The President's Child* (London, Hodder and Stoughton, 1982; London, Coronet, 1983).

Weldon, Fay, *Puffball* (London, Hodder and Stoughton, 1980; London, Coronet, 1981).

Wilson, Anna, *Cactus* (London, Onlywomen Press, 1980).

Wilson, Anna, 'The Reach', in *The Reach and Other Stories: lesbian feminist fiction*, ed. Lilian Mohin and Sheila Shulman (London, Onlywomen Press, 1984), pp. 9-12.

Wilson, Barbara Ellen, *Ambitious Women* (New York, Spinsters Ink, 1982; London, Women's Press, 1983).

Wilson, Elizabeth, *Prisons of Glass* (London, Methuen, 1986).

Wittig, Monique, *Les Guérillères*, Trans. David le Vay (Paris, Minuit, 1969; London, Peter Owen, 1971).

Theoretical and critical works

Abel, Elizabeth, '(E)Merging identities: the dynamics of female friendship in contemporary fiction by women', *Signs*, 6, no. 3 (Spring 1981), pp. 413-35.

Allison, Dorothy, 'Public silence, private terror', *Pleasure and Danger: exploring female sexuality*, ed. Carole S. Vance (Boston, Mass.; Routledge and Kegan Paul, 1984), pp. 103-14.

Arcana, Judith, *Our Mothers' Daughters* (Berkeley, CA, Shameless Hussy Press, 1979; London, Women's Press, 1981).

Ardill, Susan, and O'Sullivan, Sue, 'Upsetting an applecart: difference, desire and lesbian sadomasochism', *Feminist Review*, 23 (Summer 1986), pp. 31-57.

Auerbach, Nina, *Communities of Women: an idea in fiction* (Cambridge, Mass., Harvard University Press, 1978).

Barrett, Michèle, *Women's Oppression Today* (London, Verso, 1980).

Bart, Pauline, 'Review of Chodorow's *The Reproduction of Mothering*', *Mothering: essays in feminist theory*, ed. Joyce Treblicot (New York, Rowman and Allenheld, 1984), pp. 147-52.

Batsleer, Janet, Davies, Tony, O'Rourke, Rebecca, and Weedon, Chris, *Rewriting English: cultural politics of gender and class* (London, Methuen, 1985).

Beauvoir, Simone de, *The Second Sex*, trans. H.M. Parshley (New York, Alfred A. Knopf, 1953; *Le Deuxième Sexe*, Paris, Gallimard, 1949).

Beechey, Veronica, 'On patriarchy', *Feminist Review*, 3 (1979), pp. 66-82.

Belsey, Catherine, *Critical Practice* (London, Methuen, 1980).

Bickerton, Tricia, 'Women alone', *Sex and Love: new thoughts on old contradictions*, ed. Sue Cartledge and Joanna Ryan (London, Women's Press, 1983), pp. 157-66.

Brighton LTP Group, 'Problems of the progressive text: *The Color Purple* by Alice Walker', *Literature Teaching Politics, 6: Conference Papers 1985*, ed. Helen Taylor, pp. 117-46.

Brown, Jill, and Chambers, Jo, 'Two personal experiences', *Sex and Love: new thoughts on old contradictions*, ed. Sue Cartledge and Joanna Ryan (London: Women's Press, 1983), pp. 67-88.

Brownmiller, Susan, *Against Our Will: men, women and rape* (New York, Simon and Schuster, 1985; Harmondsworth, Penguin, 1976).

Bruch, Hilde, *The Golden Cage: the enigma of anorexia nervosa* (London, Open Books, 1978).

Brunt, Rosalind, '"An immense verbosity": permissive sexual advice in the 1970s', *Feminism, Culture and Politics*, ed. Rosalind Brunt and Caroline Rowan (London, Lawrence and Wishart, 1982), pp. 143-70.

Brunt, Rosalind, and Rowan, Caroline (eds), *Feminism, Culture and Politics* (London, Lawrence and Wishart, 1982).

Bunch, Charlotte, 'Not for lesbians only', *Building Feminist Theory*, ed. Charlotte Bunch et al. (New York: Longman, 1981), pp. 67-73.

Bunch, Charlotte, Flax, Jane, Freeman, Alexa, Hartsock, Nancy, and Manther, Mary-Helen (eds), *Building Feminist Theory: essays from Quest, a feminist quarterly* (New York, Longman, 1981).

Burris, Barbara, 'The fourth world manifesto', *Radical Feminism*, ed. Anne Koedt et al. (New York, Quadrangle, 1973), pp. 322-57.

Campbell, Beatrix, 'A feminist sexual politics: now you see it, now you don't', *Feminist Review*, 5 (1980), pp. 1-18.

Carter, Angela, 'Notes from the front line', *On Gender and Writing*, ed. Michelene Wandor (London, Pandora, 1983), pp. 69-77.

Carter, Angela, *Nothing Sacred* (London, Virago, 1982).

Carter, Angela, *The Sadeian Woman: an exercise in cultural history* (London, Virago, 1979).

Cartledge, Sue, and Ryan, Joanna, *Sex and Love: new thoughts on old contradictions* (London, Women's Press, 1983).

Chasseguet-Smirgel, Janine, *Female Sexuality: new psychoanalytic views* (London, Virago, 1981).

Chernin, Kim, *Womansize: the tyranny of slenderness* (London, Women's Press, 1983). First published as *The Obsession: reflections on the tyranny of slenderness* (New York, Harper and Row, 1981).

Chesler, Phyllis, *Women and Madness* (New York, Doubleday, 1972).

Chester, Gail, 'I call myself a radical feminist', *No Turning Back: writings from the Women's Liberation Movement 1975–80*, ed. Feminist Anthology Collective (London, Women's Press, 1981), pp. 67-71.

Christian, Barbara, 'Alice Walker: the black woman artist as wayward', *Black Women Writers: arguments and interviews*, ed. Mari Evans (New York, Anchor Press, 1984; London, Pluto, 1985), pp. 457-77.

Cixous, Hélène, 'Sorties', *New French Feminisms*, ed. Marks and de Courtivron (Brighton, Harvester Press, 1981), pp. 90-8.

Cixous, Hélène, 'The character of "character"', trans. Keith Cohen, *New Literary History*, 5, no. 2 (Winter 1974), pp. 383-402.

Coote, Anna, and Campbell, Beatrix, *Sweet Freedom: the struggle for women's liberation* (London, Pan, 1982).

Coward, Rosalind, 'Are women's novels feminist novels?', *Feminist Review*, 5 (1980), pp. 53-64. Reprinted in *The New Feminist Criticism: essays on women, literature and theory*, ed. Elaine Showalter (London, Virago, 1986).

Coward, Rosalind, *Female Desire: women's sexuality today* (London, Paladin, 1984).

Coward, Rosalind, *Patriarchal Precedents: sexuality and social relations* (London, Routledge and Kegan Paul, 1983).

Coward, Rosalind, 'Sexual politics and psychoanalysis: some notes on their relation', *Feminism, Culture and Politics*, ed. Rosalind Brunt and Caroline Rowan (London: Lawrence and Wishart, 1982), pp. 171-87.

Craig, Patricia, 'Review of Weldon's *The Life and Loves of a She-Devil*', *Times Literary Supplement*, 4,216 (20 January 1984), p. 70.

Dalla Costa, Maria, and James, Selma, *The Power of Women and the Subversion of the Community* (Bristol, Falling Wall Press, 1973).

Daly, Mary, *Gyn/Ecology: the metaethics of radical feminism* (Boston, Mass., Beacon Press, 1978; London, Women's Press, 1979).

Deckard, Barbara Sinclair, *The Women's Movement: political, socioeconomic, and psychological issues* (New York, Harper and Row, 1985).

Delmar, Rosalind, 'Broken agenda', *New Statesman*, 112, no. 2887 (25 July 1986), pp. 20-2.

Dinnerstein, Dorothy, *The Mermaid and the Minotaur: Sexual Arrangements and Human Malaise* (New York, Harper and Row, 1976; London, Souvenir Press, 1978; alternatively entitled *The Rocking of the Cradle, and the Ruling of the World*).

Duchêne, Anne, 'Review of French's *The Women's Room*', *Times Literary Supplement*, 3,968 (21 April 1978), p. 433.

Duncker, Patricia, 'Writing and roaring: In search of the truly political feminist novel', *Trouble and Strife*, 6 (Summer 1985), pp. 41-6.

Dworkin, Andrea, *Our Blood: prophecies and discourses on sexual politics* (New York, Harper and Row, 1976; London, Women's Press, 1982).

Dworkin, Andrea, *Pornography: men possessing women* (New York, Perigee, 1981; London, Women's Press, 1981).

Eisenstein, Hester, *Contemporary Feminist Thought* (London, Unwin, 1984).

Eisenstein, Hester, and Jardine, Alice (eds), *The Future of Difference* (Boston, Mass., G.K. Hall, 1980).

Ernst, Sheila, and Goodison, Lucy, *In Our Own Hands: a book of self-help therapy* (London, Women's Press, 1981).

Faderman, Lillian, *Surpassing the Love of Men: romantic friendship and love between women from the Renaissance to the present* (London, Junction Books, 1981; Women's Press, 1985).

Ferguson, Ann, 'Patriarchy, sexual identity, and the sexual revolution', *Feminist theory: a critique of ideology*, ed. Nannerl O. Keohane, Michelle Z. Rosaldo and Barbara C. Gelpi (Chicago, University of Chicago Press, 1981; Brighton, Harvester Press, 1982, pp. 147-61).

Firestone, Shulamith, *The Dialectic of Sex: the case for feminist revolution* (New York, Morrow, 1970; London, Women's Press, 1979).

Flax, Jane, 'The conflict between nurturance and autonomy in mother-daughter relationships and within feminism', *Feminist Studies*, 4, no. 2 (June 1978), pp. 171-99.

Forster, Jackie, and Hanscombe, Gillian, *Rocking the Cradle - Lesbian Mothers: a challenge in family living* (London, Peter Owen, 1981).

Freely, Maureen, 'Review of Atwood's *The Handmaid's Tale*', *Observer*, 10,145 (16 March 1986), p. 25.

Freeman, Alexa, and MacMillan, Jacie, 'Building feminist organizations', *Building Feminist Theory*, ed. Charlotte Bunch et al. (New York, Longman, 1981), pp. 260-7.

Freeman, Jo, *The Politics of Women's Liberation: a case study of an emerging social movement and its relations to the policy process* (London, Longman, 1975).

Friedan, Betty, *The Feminine Mystique* (New York, W.W. Norton, 1963; rev. edn., Harmondsworth, Penguin, 1968).

Gallop, Jane, *Feminism and Psychoanalysis: the daughter's seduction* (London, Macmillan, 1982).

Gardiner, Judith Kegan, 'Mind mother: psychoanalysis and feminism', *Making a Difference*, ed. Gayle Greene and Coppélia Kahn (London, Methuen, 1985), pp. 113-45.

Gauthier, Xavière, 'Existe-t-il une écriture de femme?', trans. in *New French Feminisms*, ed. Elaine Marks and Isabelle de Courtivron (Brighton, Harvester Press, 1981), pp. 161-4.

Gilbert, Sandra H., and Gubar, Susan, *The Madwoman in the Attic: the woman writer and the nineteenth-century literary imagination* (Newhaven, Conn., Yale University Press, 1979).

Greene, Gayle, and Kahn, Coppélia (eds), *Making a Difference: feminist literary criticism* (London, Methuen, 1985).

Gregory, Deborah, 'From where I stand: a case for feminist bisexuality', *Sex and Love: new thoughts on old contradictions*, ed. Sue Cartledge and Joanna Ryan (London, Women's Press, 1983), pp. 141-56.

Griffin, Susan, 'Rape: the all-American crime', *Women: a feminist perspective*, ed. Jo Freeman (Alto, Calif., Mayfield Publishing, 1975), pp. 24-39.

Griffin, Susan, *Pornography and Silence: culture's revenge against nature* (New York, Harper and Row, 1981; London, Women's Press, 1981).

Haber, Barbara, 'Is personal life still a political issue?', *Feminist Studies*, 5, no. 3 (Fall 1979), pp. 417-30.

Haffenden, John, 'Interview with Emma Tennant', *The Literary Review*, 66 (December 1983), pp. 37-41.

Hamblin, Angela, 'Is a feminist heterosexuality possible?', *Sex and Love: new thoughts on old contradictions*, ed. Sue Cartledge and Joanna Ryan (London, Women's Press, 1983), pp. 105-23.

Harford, Barbara and Hopkins, Sarah, *Greenham Common: women at the wire* (London, Women's Press, 1984).

Hartmann, Heidi, 'The unhappy marriage of Marxism and Feminism: towards a more progressive union', *Women and Revolution: a discussion of 'The unhappy marriage of Marxism and Feminism'*, ed.. Lydia Sargent (London: Pluto, 1981), pp. 1-41.

Hartsock, Nancy, 'Political Change: two perspectives on power', *Building Feminist Theory*, ed. Charlotte Bunch et al. (New York, Longman, 1981), pp. 3-19.

Hartsock, Nancy, 'Fundamental feminism: process and perspective', *Building Feminist Theory*, ed. Charlotte Bunch et al. (New York, Longman, 1981), pp. 32-43.

Heath, Stephen, 'Joan Riviere and the masquerade', *Formations of Fantasy*, ed. Victor Burgin, James Donald and Cora Kaplan (London, Methuen, 1986), pp. 45-61.

Huf, Linda, *A Portrait of the Artist as a Young Woman: the writer as heroine in American literature* (New York: Ungar, 1983).

Irigaray, Luce, 'And the one doesn't stir without the other', trans. Helene Vivienne Wenzel, *Signs*, 7, no. 1 (1981), pp. 56-67. (*Et l'une ne bouge pas sans l'autre* [Paris, Minuit, 1979].)

Irigaray, Luce, *Speculum of the Other Woman*, trans. Gillian C. Gill (New York, Cornell University Press, 1985, (*Speculum de l'autre femme* [Paris, Minuit, 1974].)

Irigaray, Luce, *This Sex Which is Not One*, trans. Catherine Porter with Carolyn Burke (New York, Cornell University Press, 1985). (*Ce Sexe qui n'en est pas un* [Paris, Minuit, 1977].)

Jackson, Rosemary, *Fantasy: the literature of subversion* (London, Methuen, 1981).

Jeffreys, Sheila, 'Prostitution', *Women Against Violence Against Women*, ed. dusty rhodes and Sandra McNeill (London, Onlywomen Press, 1985), pp. 59-70.

Jeffreys, Sheila, *The Spinster and her Enemies: feminism and sexuality 1880-1930* (London, Pandora, 1985).

Johnston, Jill, 'Return of the Amazon mother', *A Lesbian Feminist Anthology: Amazon expedition*, ed. Phyllis Birkby, Bertha Harris and Jill Johnston (USA, Times Change Press, 1973), pp. 66-76.

Jones, Ann Rosalind, 'Mills and Boon meets feminism', *The Progress of Romance: the politics of popular fiction*, ed. Jean Radford (London, Routledge & Kegan Paul, 1986), pp. 195-218.

Joreen, 'The bitch manifesto', *Radical Feminism*, ed. Anne Koedt et al. (New York, Quadrangle , 1973), pp. 50-9.

Joreen, 'The tyranny of structurelessness', *Radical Feminism*, ed. Anne

Koedt et al. (New York, Quadrangle, 1973), pp. 285-99.

Kaplan, Cora, 'Pandora's box: subjectivity, class and sexuality in socialist feminist criticism', *Sea Changes: culture and feminism* (London, Verso, 1986), pp. 147-76.

Kaplan, E. Ann. 'Is the gaze male?', *Desire: the politics of sexuality*, ed. Ann Snitow et al. (London, Virago, 1984), pp. 321-38.

Kaplan, Sydney Janet, 'Varieties of feminist criticism', *Making a Difference*, ed. Gayle Greene and Coppélia Kahn (London, Methuen, 1985), pp. 37-58.

Kelly, Liz, 'The new defeatism', *Trouble and Strife*, 11 (Summer 1987), pp. 23-8.

Klaus, H. Kustav (ed.), *The Socialist Novel in Britain: towards the recovery of a tradition* (Brighton, Harvester Press, 1982).

Koedt, Anne, 'The myth of the vaginal orgasm', *Radical Feminism*, ed. Anne Koedt et al. (New York, Quadrangle, 1973), pp. 198-207.

Koedt, Anne, Levine, Ellen, and Rapone, Anita (eds), *Radical Feminism* (New York, Quadrangle, 1973).

Kollias, Karen, 'Class realities: create a new power base', *Building Feminist Theory*, ed. Charlotte Bunch et al. (New York, Longman, 1981), pp. 125-38.

Kolodny, Annette, 'Some notes on defining a "feminist literary criticism"', *Critical Inquiry*, vol. 2 (Autumn 1975), pp. 75-92.

Kristeva, Julia, *About Chinese Women*, trans. Anita Barrows (London, Marion Boyars, 1977). (*Des Chinoises* [Paris: Editions des Femmes, 1974].)

Kristeva, Julia, *Desire in Language: a semiotic approach to literature and art*, ed. Leon S. Roudiez, trans. Thomas Gora, Alice Jardine and Leon S. Roudiez (Oxford, Basil Blackwell, 1981). (*Polylogue* [Paris: Editions du Seuil, 1977].)

Kristeva, Julia, 'Oscillation between power and denial', trans. in *New French Feminisms*, ed. Elaine Marks and Isabelle de Courtivron (Brighton, Harvester Press, 1981), pp. 165-7.

Lewis, Charlie, and O'Brien, Margaret, *Reassessing Fatherhood: observations on fathers and the modern family* (London, Sage Publications, 1987).

Light, Alison, Brighton L T P Group, 'Problems of the Progressive Text: *The Color Purple* by Alice Walker', *Literature Teaching Politics, 6: Conference Papers 1985*, ed. Helen Taylor, pp. 127-42.

Light, Alison, 'Review of Fairbairns's *Benefits*', *Spare Rib*, 91 (February 1980), p. 46.

Lorde, Audre, *Sister Outsider* (Trumansberg, NY, Crossing Press, 1984).

Lovibond, Sabina, Letter in *The New Statesman*, 112, no. 2888 (1 August 1986), p. 19.

MacLeod, Sheila, 'The way of all flesh', *The Guardian* (21 June 1983).

Marcus, Piri, 'Motherhood: a letter', *Sweeping Statements: writings from the Women's Movement 1981–1983*, ed. Hannah Kanter, Sarah Lefanu, Shaila Shah and Carole Spedding (London, Women's Press, 1984), pp. 196-298.

Marks, Elaine and Courtivron, Isabelle de (eds), *New French Feminisms* (Brighton, Harvester Press, 1981).

Miles, Rosalind, *The Fiction of Sex: themes and functions of sex difference in the modern novel* (London, Vision Press, 1974).

Miller, Jean Baker, *Toward a New Psychology of Women* (Boston, Mass.,

Beacon Press, 1976; Harmondsworth, Penguin, 1978).
Miller, Nancy A., 'The text's heroine: a feminist critic and her fiction', *Diacritics*, 12 (Summer 1982), pp. 48-53.
Millett, Kate, *Sexual Politics* (1970) (New York, Avon, 1971; London, Abacus, 1972).
Mitchell, Juliet, *Woman's Estate* (Harmondsworth, Penguin, 1971).
Mitchell, Juliet, and Oakley, Ann (eds), *The Rights and Wrongs of Women* (Harmondsworth, Penguin, 1976).
Modleski, Tania, *Loving with a Vengeance: mass-produced fantasies for women* (London, Methuen, 1984).
Moi, Toril, *Sexual/Textual Politics: feminist literary theory* (London, Methuen, 1985).
Monteith, Moira (ed.) *Women's Writing: a challenge to theory* (Brighton, Harvester Press, 1986).
Mulvey, Laura, 'Visual pleasure and narrative cinema', *Screen*, 16, no. 3 (1975), pp. 6-18.
Mulvey, Laura, 'Feminism, film and the avant-garde', *Framework*, 10 (1979), pp. 3-10.
Nava, Mica, 'From utopian to scientific feminism? Early feminist critiques of the family', *What is to be done about the Family?*, ed. Lynne Segal (London, Virago, 1987), pp. 65-105.
Oakley, Ann, *Subject Women* (Oxford, Martin Robertson, 1981).
O'Hara, Maureen, 'Prostitution - towards a feminist analysis and strategy', *Women Against Violence Against Women*, ed. dusty rhodes and Sandra McNeill (London, Onlywomen Press, 1985), pp. 70-9.
Onlywomen Press, *Breaching the Peace: a collection of radical feminist papers* (London, Onlywomen, 1983).
Onlywomen Press, *Love your Enemy? The debate between heterosexual feminism and political lesbianism* (London, Onlywomen, 1981).
Orbach, Susie, *Fat is a Feminist Issue* (London, Hamlyn, 1984).
Ortner, Sherry, 'Is female to male as nature is to culture?', *Women, Culture and Society*, ed. Michelle Zimbalist Rosaldo and Louise Lamphere (Stanford, Calif., Stanford University Press, 1974), pp. 67-87.
Palmer, Paulina, 'From "coded mannequin" to bird woman: Angela Carter's Magic Flight', *Women Reading Women's Writing*, ed. Sue Roe (Brighton, Harvester Press, 1987), pp. 179-205.
Pearson, Carol, and Pope, Katherine, *The Female Hero in American and British Literature* (New York, R.R. Bowker, 1981).
Perry, Ruth, *Women, Letters, and the Novel* (New York, AMS Press, 1980).
Piercy, Marge, 'The city as battleground: the novelist as combatant', *American Urban Experience: essays on the city and literature*, ed. Michael C. Jaye and Ann Chalmers Watts (Manchester, Manchester University Press, 1981), pp. 209-17.
Plaza, Monique, '"Phallomorphic power" and the psychology of "woman"', *Ideology and Consciousness*, 4 (1978), pp. 4-36.
Polatnick, M. Rivka, 'Why men don't rear children: a power analysis', *Mothering: essays in feminist theory*, ed. Joyce Treblicot (New York, Rowman and Allenheld, 1984), pp. 21-40.
Pratt, Annis, *Archetypal Patterns in Women's Fiction* (Brighton, Harvester Press, 1982).
Radford, Jean, *The Progress of Romance: the politics of popular fiction* (London,

Routledge & Kegan Paul, 1986).

Radicalesbians, 'The women identified woman', *Radical Feminism*, ed. Anne Koedt et al. (New York, Quadrangle, 1973), pp. 240-5.

Radway, Janice A., *Reading the Romance: women, patriarchy and popular literature* (Chapel Hill, University of North Carolina Press, 1984).

Raymond, Janice G., *A Passion for Friends: toward a philosophy of female affection* (Boston, Mass., Beacon Press, 1986; London, Women's Press, 1986).

Raymond, Janice G., *The Transsexual Empire* (Boston, Mass., Beacon Press, 1979; London, Women's Press, 1980).

The Red Collective, *The Politics of Sexuality in Capitalism* (London, Blackrose, 1973).

rhodes, dusty, and McNeill, Sandra (eds), *Women Against Violence Against Women* (London, Onlywomen Press, 1985).

Rich, Adrienne, 'Compulsory heterosexuality and lesbian existence', *Signs*, 5, no. 4 (Summer 1980), 631-60; London, Onlywomen Press, 1981.

Rich, Adrienne, *Of Woman Born: motherhood as experience and institution* (New York, W.W. Norton, 1976; London, Virago, 1977).

Rich, Adrienne, *On Lies, Secrets, and Silence: selected prose 1966–1978* (New York, W.W. Norton, 1979; London, Virago, 1980).

Rickford, Frankie, 'No more sleeping beauties and frozen boys', *The Left and the Erotic*, ed. Eileen Phillips (London: Lawrence and Wishart, 1983), pp. 139-47.

Rights of Women Lesbian Custody Group, *Lesbian Mothers' Legal Handbook* (London, Women's Press, 1986).

Riley, Denise, 'Does sex have a history? "women" and feminism', *new formations*, 1 (Spring 1987), pp. 35-45.

Roberts, Michèle, 'Questions and answers', *On Gender and Writing*, ed. Michelene Wandor (London, Pandora, 1983), pp. 62-8.

Robertson, Mary F., 'Anne Tyler: Medusa points and contact points', *Contemporary American Women Writers: narrative strategies*, ed. Catherine Rainwater and William J. Scheick (Kentucky, University Press of Kentucky, 1985), pp. 120-42.

Rose, Jacqueline, *Sexuality in the Field of Vision* (London, Verso, 1986).

Rowbotham, Sheila, 'The trouble with "patriarchy"', *No Turning Back: Writings from the Women's Liberation Movement 1975–80*, ed. Feminist Anthology Collective (London, Women's Press, 1984), pp. 72-8.

Rubin, Gayle, 'The traffic in women. Notes on the "political economy" of sex', *Toward an Anthropology of Women*, ed. Rayna R. Reiter (New York, Monthly Review Press, 1975), pp. 157-210.

Rule, Jane, *Lesbian Images* (Trumansberg, NY, Doubleday, 1975; Crossing Press, 1982).

Russ, Joanna, *How to Suppress Women's Writing* (Austin, University of Texas Press, 1983; London, Women's Press, 1984).

Scharfman, Ronnie, 'Mirroring and mothering in Simone Schwarz-Bart's *Pluie et vent sur Télumée Miracle* and Jean Rhys' '*Wide Sargasso Sea*', *Yale French Studies*, 62 (1981), pp. 88-106.

Scott, Sara, and Payne, Tracey, 'Underneath we're all lovable; therapy and feminism', *Trouble and Strife*, 3 (Summer 1984), pp. 21-4.

Segal, Lynne, *Is the Future Female? Troubled thoughts on contemporary feminism*

(London, Virago, 1987).

Segal, Lynne, '"Smash the family?" Recalling the 1960s', *What is to be Done about the Family?* ed. Lynne Segal (Harmondsworth, Penguin, 1983), pp. 25-64.

Segal, Lynne, ed. *What is to be done about the Family?* (Harmondsworth, Penguin, 1983).

Segal, Lynne, 'Women's retreat into motherhood: back to the nursery', *New Statesman*, 113, no. 2910 (2 January 1987), pp. 16-18.

Sevenhuijsen, Selma, and de Vries, Petra, 'The Women's Movement and motherhood', *A Creative Tension: explorations in socialist feminism*, ed. Anja Meulenbelt, Joyce Outshoorn, Selma Sevenhuijsen, and Petra de Vries, trans. Della Couling (London, Pluto, 1984), pp. 9-25.

Snitow, Ann Barr, 'Mass market romance: pornography for women is different', *Desire: the politics of sexuality*, ed. Snitow et al. (London, Virago, 1984), pp. 258-75.

Snitow, Ann Barr, 'The Front Line: notes on sex in novels by women, 1969-1979', *Women: sex and sexuality*, ed. Catherine R. Stimpson and Ethel Spector Person (Chicago, University of Chicago Press, 1980), pp. 158-74.

Snitow, Ann Barr, Stansell, Christine, and Thompson, Sharon (eds), *Desire: the politics of sexuality* (London, Virago, 1984). First published as *Powers of Desire: the politics of sexuality* (USA, Monthly Review press, 1983).

Spender, Dale (ed.), *Feminist Theorists: three centuries of women's intellectual traditions* (London, Women's Press, 1983).

Spivak, Gayatri Chakravorty, 'Displacement and the discourse of woman', *Displacement: Derrida and after*, ed. Mark Krupnick (Bloomington, Indiana University Press, 1983), pp. 169-95.

Spivak, Gayatri Chakravorty, 'French feminism in an international frame', *Yale French Studies*, 62 (1981), pp. 154-84.

Stephens, Eleanor, 'Out of the closet into the courts', *Spare Rib*, 50 (September 1976), pp. 6-8.

Stubbs, Patricia, *Women and Fiction: feminism and the novel 1880-1920* (Brighton, Harvester Press, 1979; London, Methuen, 1981).

Todd, Janet, *Women's Friendship in Literature* (New York, Columbia University Press, 1980).

Treblicot, Joyce (ed.) *Mothering: essays in feminist theory* (New York, Rowman and Allanheld, 1984).

Tuttle Hansen, Elaine, 'Marge Piercy: the double narrative structure of *Small Changes*', *Contemporary American Women Writers: Narrative Strategies*, ed. Catherine Rainwater and Willian J. Scheick, (Kentucky, University Press of Kentucky, 1985), pp. 209-23.

Wallsgrove, Ruth, 'Greenham Common Women's Peace Camp - so why am I still ambivalent?' *Trouble and Strife*, 1 (Winter 1983), pp. 4-6.

Ward Jouve, Nicole, *The Streetcleaner: the Yorkshire Ripper case on trial* (London, Marion Boyars, 1986).

Weldon, Fay, 'How to be Feminist', *New Society*, 68, no. 1123 (31 May 1984), p. 354.

Williams, Linda, 'When the Woman Looks', *Re-vision: essays in feminist film criticism*, ed. Mary Ann Doane, Patricia Mellencamp and Linda Williams (Los Angeles, Calif., American Film Institute, 1984), pp. 83-99.

Wilson, Elizabeth, *Adorned in Dreams: fashion and modernity* (London, Virago, 1985).

Wilson, Elizabeth, 'I'll Climb the Stairway to Heaven: lesbianism in the seventies', *Sex and Love: new thoughts on old contradictions*, ed. Sue Cartledge and Joanna Ryan (London, Women's Press, 1983), pp. 180-5.

Wilson, Elizabeth, 'The Context of "Between Pleasure and Danger": the Barnard Conference on sexuality', *Feminist Review*, 13 (Spring, 1983), pp. 35-41.

Wilson, Elizabeth, with Angela Weir, *Hidden Agendas: theory, politics and experience in the Women's Movement* (London, Tavistock, 1986).

Wyland, Francie, *Motherhood, Lesbianism and Child Custody* (Bristol, Wages Due Lesbians; Toronto, Falling Wall Press, 1977).

Zimmerman, Bonnie, 'What has never been: An overview of lesbian feminist criticism', *Making a Difference*, ed. Gayle Greene and Coppélia Khan (London, Methuen, 1985), pp. 177-210.

Zita, Jacquelyn N. 'Historical Amnesia and the Lesbian Continuum', *Feminist Theory: a critique of ideology*, ed. Nannerl O. Keohane, Michelle Z. Rosaldo and Barbara C. Gelpi (Chicago, University of Chicago Press, 1981; Brighton, Harvester Press, 1982, pp. 161-76).

Index

masculinity (cont)
and intellect, 20, 27
and militarism, 75
and parasitical attributes, 20, 143
reconstitution of, 21, 44, 50 54
see also men
masochism, 16, 19, 37, 61, 140, 143, 150–1
masquerade, 16, 22, 36
maternal jouissance, 97
maternal sickbed and deathbed, 115–17
maternity grant, 164
men
as allies of women, 68
and control of knowledge, 47–52
and economic privilege, 37, 141
and love of ritual, 75
and power, 36–7, 42–55, 69–77, 91, 119, 149–51
as victims of gender roles, 26, 37, 70
women's images of, 36–7
see also masculinity
Miles, Rosalind, 42
Miller, Jean Baker, 20, 25, 96, 151
Miller, Nancy A., 10, 12 n 20
Millett, Kate, 14, 43, 45, 48, 68, 71–3
Sita, 138–40
Miner, Valerie
Blood Sisters, 9, 61–2, 153
Movement, 60–1
mirror, 36, 105, 115, 119, 125, 138, 141
stage, 105
Mitchell, Juliet, 62, 69–70, 96, 128–9
Modleski, 11 n 2
Moi, Toril, 11 ns 1 and 5, 39 n 13, 122 n 6, 161
Monteith, Moira, 11 n 15
mother
as apparently all-powerful, 99–100, 139
death of, 115–16
as feeder and food of the child, 114–15, 118
as monster, 19, 101, 112–13
as socializer of the daughter into the feminine position, 96, 113
negative view of, 96–7, 112–13
positive view of, 96, 101–5
see also phallic mother
mother–daughter relations, 3, 9, 80, 105–6, 109–11, 112–22, 160
divisions and breakdown of communication, 115–21

and emotional paralysis and suffocation, 114, 115, 118–19, 139
and female friendships, 141–2
and guilt, 100–1, 116, 118–19
and language, 97, 118, 140
and lesbian relations, 107–12, 117–18, 137–41
as 'living mirrors', 115, 119, 125, 141
symbiotic bond, 114–21, 139
mother–son relations, 73–4, 111–12
motherhood, 3, 9, 164–5
and childbirth, 102–4, 110, 121, 124 ns 55 and 56, 164–5
contradictions and confusions of the feminist approach to, 95–8, 164–5,
contradictions of power/vulnerability, 74, 96, 99–103
lesbian, 107–12
nonbiological, 110–11
and self-sacrifice, 100–1, 115, 116, 118
and sexual politics, 74–5, 95–112
as site of political struggle, 99–112
as source of fulfilment, 95–7, 101–7
as source of oppression, 95–7, 100–1, 105–7
strategies for resisting and challenging the maternal role, 99, 101, 115–17
and women's writing, 97, 118, 140
see also maternal jouissance, maternity grant
Mulvey, Laura, 34
myth, 17, 32, 56, 75, 102, 139

narrative strategies
accumulation and repetition, 72–3
authorial address, 149–51
centring the narrative on two female figures, 50, 52, 61–2
dialogic interplay of voices (collectivity), 149–51
discontinuous narrative, 37, 56, 105
endings of novels, 160–1
framing device, 48–9
historical comparison, 62–4
internalized dialogue, 29
interplay of different narrative lines, 105–6, 115, 118
intrigue plot, 73–5
merging of different identities, 115, 118–20

Learning Resources